Around the World in 80 Dates

Head of PR and Spokesperson for Lonely Planet Publications for a decade, Jennifer Cox is one of Britain's leading travel experts. A presenter for BBC Holidays and co-presenter of BBC1's *Perfect Holiday*, Jennifer is also regularly interviewed on programmes such as *PM* and *GMTV*. She presented her own weekly travel show on BBC Radio 1 for three years, has a weekly slot on Sky News and has written for all the national papers as well as *Marie Claire*, *Esquire* and *Cosmo*. This is her first book.

Find out more about Jennifer Cox's quest by visiting www.aroundtheworldin80dates.co.uk

Around the World in 80 Dates

Jennifer Cox

WILLIAM HEINEMANN : LONDON

Published in the United Kingdom in 2005 by William Heinemann

1 3 5 7 9 10 8 6 4 2

STAND BY YOUR MAN
Words and music by Tammy Wynette and Billy Sherrill © 1968 Gallico Al Music Corp
and EMI Music Publishing Ltd, USA
Print rights controlled by Warner Bros. Publications Inc/IMC Ltd.
Reproduced by permission of International Music Publications Ltd.
All rights reserved.

Maps by ML Design, London
mldesign@btclick.com

William Heinemann
The Random House Group Limited
20 Vauxhall Bridge Road, London, SW1V 2SA

Random House Australia (Pty) Limited
20 Alfred Street, Milsons Point, Sydney, New South Wales 2061, Australia

Random House New Zealand Limited
18 Poland Road, Glenfield
Auckland 10, New Zealand

Random House (Pty) Limited
Endulini, 5a Jubilee Road, Parktown, 2193, South Africa

The Random House Group Limited Reg. No. 954009
www.randomhouse.co.uk

A CIP catalogue record for this book is available from the British Library

Papers used by Random House are natural, recyclable products made from wood
grown in sustainable forests. The manufacturing processes conform to the
environmental regulations of the country of origin

Typeset by SX Composing DTP, Rayleigh, Essex
Printed and bound in the United Kingdom by
Clays Ltd, St Ives Plc

0 4340 1335 8

To my parents Brenda and John Cox
with love and thanks for putting up with years of my nonsense.

And to G. who has all that to come.

Preface

So that's me packed and ready to go: passport; touche éclat; little black dress and the names of 80 men I'm going to date in 17 countries over the next six months. I'm off to find my Soul Mate, and I'm not coming back to Yonkers till I do.

CHAPTER ONE

This Time Last Year

Settling into a steady rhythm of drinking, crying, drinking, crying, I became aware of the music for the first time: '*Stand by your man, give him two arms to cling to* . . .' I glared at the radio: I've always hated that song. My feeling was that if the only way a man can remain standing upright is by leaning heavily on you, surely it's best just to let him fall right on over. But since today was the day I'd discovered Kelly had been cheating on me for pretty much the five years we'd been together, I let out a long, ragged sigh: too exhausted to cry any more. It was also the day I had to accept that maybe there's a little bit of Tammy in us all? I really loved Kelly. Which was surprising because he actually wasn't that loveable. He was very sexy – one of those dark, brooding types, with piercing green eyes and a tangle of curly black hair. He was tall and strong, with a gentle mouth and a chest broad enough to do a week's ironing on. But he was also self-centred, secretive and moody. The kind of guy who sits in the corner of a bar, smouldering over a beer and a shot. For some reason I was drawn to 'the difficult ones', and Kelly was as difficult as they came. A man who would sooner eat broken glass than tell you where he'd been, what his plans were or if he loved you. I have no idea why I kept trying: when he'd wanted to go to parties on his own; stayed out late; kept a phone number with just an initial next to it . . . In fact, for some reason it made me try harder. Over our five years together, as Kelly morphed into Clint Eastwood, I increasingly turned into Coco the Clown, pulling out all the stops to entertain him, make him feel involved, get his attention. I did the emotional equivalent of driving a small red pedal car around the ring of our relationship, frantically parping on my little horn as bunches of flowers popped out my shirt and small men in orange wigs, emptied buckets of custard down my trousers and twanged my big red nose. It was not dignified. And, ultimately, it was pointless. I knew in my heart we would only ever share a 'now'. Never a future. Then I rang the number with the initial next to it, and our 'now' was over.

As soon as I split up with Kelly I went straight to the airport and got on a plane to New York City. The experience of being in New York is like stroking a man-eating tiger: as much as it scares the bejesus out of you, for those moments it allows you to touch it, you know you are blessed and immortal.

And on this occasion, like every other I'd been there, New York uplifted me. I lost myself in the markets, boutiques and coffee shops around Greenwich Village and Harlem, whacked softballs in the batting cages over on Coney Island until my arms sang. Being in the city didn't cure my heartache but it distracted me and stopped it getting worse, and for that I was grateful.

I actually had to be in New York for work, so in a way it was good timing (if such a thing exists when you're talking about splitting up with your boyfriend). But then again, I worked in the travel industry so it wasn't that unusual for me to be heading off somewhere. I loved travelling and had been determined to get a job in the industry from the moment I discovered its unerring ability to make me feel really good.

This was especially true after an ugly break-up. Some say that time is a great healer, but I discovered years ago that it's actually travel that quite literally moves you on. Staying on the crime scene of an awful break-up is the worst thing you can do: too many painful memories and reminders. I subscribe to the 'pack up your troubles' school of relationship recovery, and let me tell you, it works. It had been almost by accident that I'd learnt travel mends a broken heart. I was 18 and William was the first big love of my life. We were at school together and shared the kind of pure and trusting love only possible when you have yet to experience that first deep cut. When William dumped me out of the blue for Melanie (a girl who shopped at Miss Selfridge, who had never even been to Glastonbury), I was completely unprepared for the shock. I spent that whole summer after my A levels moping around: crying on my best friend Belinda's shoulder, making her come for long walks so I could tell her (again) how awful it was and how I was never going to get over it. But when, at the end of summer, I left home for Leeds University, I was really surprised to discover that out of sight really was out of mind. Here I was in a whole new place, with no painful memories. There was no danger of bumping into Will and Mel in Leeds, I didn't have to go to *our* places on my own or have people drop into conversation that they'd all been out together the night before. So, free from constant reminders of my old Will and his new girlfriend, I got over him and on with my life.

All thanks to the M1 and National Express coaches. But my

lesson in the healing power of travel didn't end there. It was my next boyfriend who taught me that travel makes things easier for the dumper (as opposed to the dumpee) too. Peter was the guitarist in a band I sang with in Leeds, and we lived together for most of my time at university. He was gentle, kind and very cute. But sadly, as time went on, it became increasingly clear that 'gentle and kind' weren't enough. I really didn't want to hurt him – Peter didn't deserve that, plus I remembered how bad it felt – but as much as I loved him, I felt restless and the need to move on. But I couldn't end it. I really tried: I'd psych myself up, telling myself I was going through with it this time, but at the last minute I'd think about how upset Peter would be and I'd lose my nerve. Actually, a couple of times I did end it, but Peter persuaded me to give us another chance. I was hopeless: I just couldn't face his heartache and make a clean break. Until I went to Australia.

It was one of those whimsical decisions that only makes sense after you've done it. I'd just graduated from university and had no idea what I wanted to do next. Going to Australia on my own for three months suddenly seemed the perfect solution: it would be both an adventurous challenge and the chance to think everything through.

So I flew into Perth, Western Australia. And virtually the first thing I did when I arrived was to call Peter and split up with him. As crazy as it sounds, I needed to go to the other side of the world to do it: I wasn't there to watch him fall apart, knowing it was my fault and still caring about him. And because I didn't feel wracked with the guilt I would have felt at home, I got over it far more quickly (as did he). I was free to fall madly in love with Australia and I stayed, travelling all over Australasia for the next six years.

• • •

I think I have to be honest at this point and confess it wasn't only Australia I fell madly in love with. I might have been Peter's girlfriend when I flew into Australia, but six months after arriving I was Philip's wife.

I'd been in Australia for two weeks when I met Philip. He worked at a theatre company where I'd landed a job, and it was love at first sight. A spellbinding, charismatic, risk-all Outback Romeo, I immediately recognised Philip as one of my Soul Mates. (Well, cats have nine lives, who's to say we are limited to a single, solitary Soul Mate?) He wasn't afraid of anything and when I was with him, life was exciting and full of possibilities. We fell deeply and passionately in love. Although we got married very quickly, we *clicked* so powerfully together it felt the natural and right thing to do. Neither of us had really done much travelling, so we set off to explore, experience and discover together. We spent six months driving through the hot, red Outback in an old Holden panel van, living on wild fruit, swimming with dolphins, wrestling with spiders. We trekked through craggy outposts of India and Nepal, spent weekends snorkelling in the coral-studded waters around Vanuatu and the Solomons, took crazy surf-trips to Bali and sailed boats down the muddy Mekong in Vietnam. It was amazing. And in the end, maybe that was the problem: man cannot live on thrill alone. After six years of wonder and discovery I was all amazed out. I'd had one brief visit home in all that time. I missed my family and friends; I missed normal old England. I missed Marks & Spencer's crisps; I longed to sit in a pub on a damp autumn day (Australia doesn't do seasons) and pretend I cared about football; I was desperate for a colourful argument about politics and the chance to browse

through some decent weekend papers ('MAN LEAVES CHANGE
ON MILK-BAR COUNTER' was about the level of reporting in
Australia). It was time to come home, and as much as I loved
Philip, he was a creature of the Outback. Beautiful, passionate
and wild, he had – and wanted – no place in Britain, with its
crowds, traffic, litter and drizzle. I went to Australia alone. Six
years later, I returned home the same way.

It's been a year now since Kelly and I split up, and thankfully
I'm past the I'll Never Fall in Love Again stage. I spent a lot of
time thinking about why we stayed together for as long as we
did: also trying to work out how I could avoid making the same
mistakes again. And after that year going over past choices and
future options, I learnt two things. Firstly, anyone who wants
to know anything about Cher or Def Leppard should tune into
VH1 at 3 a.m. Secondly, trying to find even a halfway decent
boyfriend in London is a total nightmare. If you knew the
latter, chances are you've already discovered the former?
Londoners have the longest working hours in Europe, and the
highest number of stress-related diseases to prove it. It's hardly
the setting for a romantic Barry White-type encounter – *You're
my First, You're my Last, You're my Intray?* – yet precisely
because we spend the majority of our time in the office,
inevitably this is where we're hoping to meet Mr Right. And
failing to find him. Manners may maketh the man, but work
unmaketh him pretty damn quick. It used to be exciting
meeting someone in the office, but nowadays it means sifting
through a pack of lifeless men so stressed and depressed the
only relationships they have the energy or confidence for are
with their laptops and their lads mags. And we SIWWIDs

(Single Income Women, Working Instead of Dating) have bought into the whole 'mustn't try harder' myth: that being successful at work and having fun with our friends makes us independent and therefore unattractive to men. This really isn't the case: it's simply that the office – all floppy discs and soft launches – is not the place to find a satisfying relationship. Ten years ago when I moved from Australia back to England, I had to accept the sad truth that my marriage wasn't moving back with me. But I knew my love affair with travel was a relationship that would flourish wherever I went, so I lost no time getting a job in the travel industry. I became Spokesperson and Head of PR for guidebook company Lonely Planet Publications, as well as a travel writer and presenter for the BBC.

And as I travelled to and from my office in London, and to and from my work overseas, I was struck by how much more interested in women foreign men are, compared with British men. At times it felt as if you couldn't find a decent date in London to save your life, the bar being so low now that I mean any man who knows how to use a fork and possesses a matching pair of shoes, but you virtually have to fight them off with a stick in every other capital city around the world. I don't want to sound like an international slapper here, and I'm not even vaguely god's gift – I don't have Kylie's bum or Melanie Griffiths' lips . . . though to be fair, neither does she. But it is so much easier to meet men when you're abroad. Walk down the street in any other country and there'll always be men checking you out, coming over, chatting you up. In London, the only guys that make eye contact with you are the inmates on the Northern Line. I'm not saying British men are totally to blame: we women have to take some of the responsibility too. There are only so many hours in the day, and chances are that if you have a successful career it's your job that takes up most of them. As the economy flourishes are we in the grip of an emotional recession? Have we made our jobs the primary relationships in our lives, settling for a so-so boyfriend because that's all we have the time to either find or maintain?

I say *we*, but of course I mean *me*. Had I loved my job more than I loved my boyfriend? By putting in and getting back so much from my career, how much did I have left to give Kelly? And how much did I really need from him in return? If I had needed Kelly more, would I have been forced to accept that the relationship sucked sooner and saved myself from going through 'Jen and Kel – The Crap Years'? I know this sounds terrible, but is it really possible to have a great relationship and a great job? And if not, which would you choose?

And to get back to talking about me again (oh, go on), if I was right and all the *great relationships* were wandering down high streets in every country other than the one in which I lived, what was I going to do about it?

Before we go any further, I think we need to take a moment to discuss terms. It's important to clarify exactly what I mean by *great relationships*. What I'm not talking about is a shag. One-night stands are the emotional kebabs of the relationship world: easy to get after the pubs close, leaving you feeling rubbish for the next three days. No, I'm talking about meeting someone I actually like and want to get to know. Someone who makes me laugh, reads me bits out the newspaper, will nip out for tampons, lets me cut his hair (badly, once), has a bath while I sit on the loo seat cutting my/his toenails. Someone I'm willing to introduce my friends to. I'm talking about a Soul

Mate. And I'm completely serious when I say I don't believe he exists here in London.

If you think I'm being harsh and haven't given locals enough of a chance, or perhaps you're new to London and are considering the perilous climb up Mount True Love yourself, I'll outline the options. There are a number of well and wearily trodden paths to a new man. Your friends unconsciously reveal what they really think of you by the kind of *'someone I thought you'd like to meet'* man brought to dinner parties. Rather than catching up on your paperwork, you could squeeze in some *'best of a bad lot'* power-flirting on the commute to work (and be gutted when, even though you didn't fancy them to begin with, your *focus* knocks you back). Maybe you're considering signing up for online dating or going to places where you should, but absolutely never will, meet someone suitable? Since over the last year I've tried them all, I'll share what I've learnt with you. I've sat chatting to Belgian lawyers in Starbucks (willing them to be even a little more interesting); I've dabbled with online dating (where all the guys have done the *Nick Hornby's Guide to Women* course and are single parents with angelic but troubled kids, or run small, quirky yet failing businesses). I don't even want to think about going to another cultural event (to meet graduates of the *Tony Parsons' Guide to Women* course: bitterness over ex-wife, partially concealed by exterior of witty self-loathing, which in turn is momentarily obscured by an encyclopaedic knowledge of early punk bands). Maybe you can tell me about evening classes? I can't work out whether eligible guys need to do *Woodwork 101* or if the classes will just be full of women like me. Likewise, I haven't signed up for a 14-week religious or spiritual workshop and I won't go near any therapy that involves garden hoses, buckets or splash mats. I'm not looking to discover the meaning of life. Get karmic social services on to me, because I'm really not interested in my inner child. I just want a decent boyfriend. And by all means share your experiences with your girlfriends, but I am completely serious when I say that the actual task of searching for your Soul Mate, like getting your bikini line waxed, is strictly a one-woman job. It's a selfish, solo occupation that can't involve all your other single female friends. When too many of us in relationship recovery get together, new boyfriends are the last things on our minds. Instead we perpetuate and mythologise our misery, building a shrine to our exes out of empty wine bottles and Kettle Chip packets. I don't want to talk about old relationships. I don't want to spend months trying to understand what went wrong. If your car plunged through the central reservation of the motorway, you wouldn't spend a year showing your friends photos of the happy days when it was safely parked outside your house. You'd just go out and buy another one. Get right back into the fast lane. Move on.

But we're so busy working, we don't have the time to find the person we want to *move on* with. So we turn to the *labour-saving devices* on the market, designed to lead us to Mr Right in the small amount of time we have allocated to the task. A perfect example of this is online dating. Online dating seems convenient because you can do it surreptitiously from your desk, during meetings at work or with flirtatious, drunken abandon when you get home in the early hours of Saturday morning. That's pretty much where the convenience ends, though, because no matter how good the profile and nice the picture, you need to know more about them before deciding if they're worth meeting. So, you chat back and forth via email, maybe send a text message or two, then you're ready to talk on the phone. The first physical contact (i.e. ear-to-ear) is crunch-time since you can generally tell from their voice and conversation if you want to meet them or not. Unfortunately, it's generally 'not', but by this point you're involved with them and finding a reason to end that involvement – even though you don't know them – is cringingly hard (tip: keep a fictitious 'unresolved ex' up your sleeve for these occasions). Hope turns to guilt as you become locked into a continuous and exhausting process of assessing candidates, like interviewing people for a job you know they'll never get. And in the meantime, that's another two hours a day spent in front of your computer. Something has to change. Enough of these *relationship patches*, which, like nicotine patches, stave off the need without satisfying any of the desire. I wanted a fantastic, glorious, wonderful relationship. Otherwise, what's the point?

But for this to happen, I knew I needed to make a better job of meeting Mr Right. I felt I'd tried everything in London. Maybe it was time for a more radical and far-reaching solution?

Rather than travelling to recover from Mr Wrong, what if I went travelling to find Mr Right? I mean, I was sure Fate had him out there waiting for me, so why was I wasting time in London moaning when I could be out in the world searching? I'd put my heart and soul into my job: maybe it was time I put the same amount of effort into my love life.

So, after some soul-searching I quit my job at Lonely Planet. I had a new job now: finding my Soul Mate.

The business and management skills I'd developed over the years would most likely come in handy. Making programmes for the BBC has honed my research and interviewing skills. Setting up and running Lonely Planet's European publicity and promotional operations meant devising campaigns whilst jumping on and off planes to oversee launches, train staff, plus doing a ton of interviews and public speaking stints. Like anybody with a big, fat job, to do this well I'd had to be able to network, research, talk people into doing things they weren't that keen on, time-manage, meet deadlines, budget and plan.

So, travelling would be the answer to London's dearth of suitable men, and my professional skills would hopefully lead me to possible candidates, eliminating the unsuitable, undesirable and unstable from amongst them. But where should I start looking? I couldn't just get off a plane in another country shouting: '*Soul Mate, I'm here. Come and get me.*' I was confident Fate had a number of them out there for me to meet (as I've already said, I believe we have more than one), but where, and who could they be?

I decided that the first step to answering this question was to work out who they *had* been. If finding my Soul Mate was now my job, like any other job I'd need to put together an up-to-date résumé. A Relationship Résumé: a document that set out my romance history, giving me an insight into the kind of person I'd gone for in the past. In short, who I dated and when; the role I undertook in the relationship and the reasons for leaving it. Based on that, I then needed to write a Soul Mate Job Description, outlining the position I was looking to fill. The task was too big for me alone but I was hoping that my global network of friends would help. If I emailed them the Soul Mate Job Description, they could act as Date Wranglers, sending it out to *their* global network of friends and corralling suitable dates for me around the world.

The more I thought about it, the more I wondered why I hadn't done this sooner?

Okay, the Relationship Résumé:

DATE: 1984–5
TITLE: First Love
COMPANY: William
MAJOR RESPONSIBILITIES: Going to festivals; riding around on the back of a motorbike; protesting at Greenham Common; finding politics; losing virginity.
REASONS FOR LEAVING: Made redundant; replaced by someone who drank Bacardi Breezers.

DATE: 1985–9
TITLE: First Live-in Relationship
COMPANY: Peter
MAJOR RESPONSIBILITIES: Learning to cook; having lots of dinner parties; buying things for the flat; having Sunday lunch with his family; getting engaged.
REASONS FOR LEAVING: Applied for a position overseas.

DATE: 1989–95
TITLE: Wife
COMPANY: Philip
MAJOR RESPONSIBILITIES: Being spontaneous and not worrying too much about tomorrow; sharing adventures; being supportive of each other's dreams; saying 'No, Philip, that's too crazy'.
REASONS FOR LEAVING: Was relocated back to the UK.

DATE: January 1996
TITLE: Transition Relationship
COMPANY: Dan
MAJOR RESPONSIBILITIES: Drinking Jack Daniels and

staying up very late; watching a lot of Tarantino films; listening to heavy-metal music; bursting into tears.
REASONS FOR LEAVING: Short-term contract.

DATE: February – June 1996
TITLE: Career Advisor
COMPANY: Edmund
MAJOR RESPONSIBILITIES: Edmund was writing a book. My role was to go over to his house or sit on the phone every night and listen to what he had written that day. Criticism was not welcome: only attention and praise.
REASONS FOR LEAVING: Communication breakdown.

DATE: August 1996
TITLE: Fellow Adventurer
COMPANY: Jason
MAJOR RESPONSIBILITIES: To swap travel stories and talk about all the crazy places we had been/both wanted to go to.
REASONS FOR LEAVING: I met Jason a week before he was due to set off to *Pedal the Planet* for four years. NB: Carried out some freelance work for this company over Xmas.

DATE: 1997–8
TITLE: Company Trustee
COMPANY: Grant
MAJOR RESPONSIBILITIES: To listen to Grant complain about his ex-wife and how glad he was they had split up.
REASONS FOR LEAVING: They hadn't split up.

DATE: 1999–2004
TITLE: Coco the Clown
COMPANY: Kelly
MAJOR RESPONSIBILITIES: Feeling everything was my fault and that I was too demanding/needy/neurotic/successful. Believing things would get better if I could only understand what the problem was.
REASONS FOR LEAVING: I was unwilling to job-share.

Hmmm. Writing the Relationship Résumé had been an illuminating but not terribly uplifting experience: it looked like I hadn't been in a good relationship for ages. For a moment I wondered if I was better off forgetting about romantic relationships and sticking to having fun with my millions of other single female friends.

But that was silly. My single friends wanted to be in a relationship as much as I did: even if *I* bottled out and stayed single there was no guarantee *they'd* stay that way (and I hoped for all their sakes they wouldn't – I wanted them to meet their Mr Rights too).

No, I wanted to be in a good relationship. I missed having that close connection with one person, feeling that I was at the centre of something rather than bobbing around the edges. But I wanted one of the early happy-style relationships, not one of the hard, rubbish ones I seemed to have specialised in in recent years. Clearly the Soul Mate Job Description needed serious consideration if I was to avoid disappointment and disaster.

First I needed to decide on the kind of person I wanted to meet. Well, since I was 5 ft 11, height was very important: I need the chemistry when someone's tall enough to put their arm around my shoulders – I absolutely could not date someone shorter than me. I'd like someone who was affectionate without being overbearing – such a hard one to get right. Someone who was smart, funny, adventurous and had his own friends. Since divorced men have a 'marriage-shaped' hole in their lives that they are looking to quickly fill, and single women have a 'disaster-shaped' hole in their lives they want to keep empty for as long as possible, I didn't want someone who was going to take me over completely.

What else? An interest in music was good, too much interest in TV was bad. I am a vegetarian and although I don't mind meat-eaters, anyone with a love of offal should probably not apply. I don't like smokers (goodbye, Jean Pierre) but distrust anyone who doesn't drink. They don't have to have their own library card but a few books on the shelf would be good (Science Fiction and Self Help don't count). I don't mind guys who are slightly overweight but 'man breasts' are a complete no-no. Skinny guys are out: if their waists are smaller than my thighs, it's not going to work. I quite like laid-back guys but absolutely no slackers, potheads or wannabe poets (if I want to see the 'beauty' in anything, I'll go to the Mac counter, thank you very much). Sporty is good, but don't expect me to come watch if it's raining.

Having said all of that, I *was* open-minded and probably needed to challenge what I thought my type of man really was – with the exception of man breasts and offal: they were non-negotiable.

The next step was to assemble my network of Date Wranglers (DWs), including: Belinda, Charlotte, Simon, Cath, Ian, Eleanor, Sara-Jane, Hector, Jeannette, Jo, Posh PR Emma, Paula, Sophie, Madhav, Jill, Matt, Lizzy, Grainne . . . All old friends, either in the travel industry or journalists who have worked overseas for years. These First Generation Date Wranglers all had an extensive network of contacts and friends around the world, who would either be Dates or Second or Third Generation Date Wranglers in their own right. I'd already talked to everyone about my plans, but it was now time to send out a briefing email and get the team to work.

Dear Date Wranglers

A few of you have asked what kind of person I'm looking to meet and what I want to do on the date (thank you, Sophie — Jose the Chilean sheep farmer sounds lovely. And Jo, yes Jason the Buddhist lawyer in Nova Scotia might be perfect). I've pasted a Soul Mate Job Description below. Please read it carefully. If it sounds like a single someone you know anywhere in the world, and they'd be willing to date me, please let me know. I'll then sit down with a list of potential dates and pick the ones that look most promising and fall relatively easily into a route around the world. Dinner at my house on the 12th for questions/brainstorming/reality check.

Lots of love, Jxx

Soul Mate Job Description

I am a 38-year-old writer living in London. I've done a bit of travelling over the years and am planning another big trip soon. When not schlepping my backpack on and off Indian trains, maxing my card at Macy's or eating gelati in Italy, I love London Life. Sunday papers and coffee with my friends, plus shows, gigs and

movies. I'm a bit sporty, especially running
(though not very far or fast) and cycling (see
'running'). I'm bad at spelling but good at
cooking. I sing along to music and always seem to
forget Xmas cards till the last minute. I'm fairly
laid-back about most things, though get
pathetically competitive playing poker.

And what am I looking for in a man?

I'm pretty tall at 5 ft 11 but old-fashioned
enough to want to feel 'ladylike', so looking for
someone over 6 foot. What else? Well, I'd like to
meet someone who makes me smile, lets me read them
bits out the newspaper, has beliefs they're
willing to arm wrestle for and tells me
interesting things I didn't know. Like me, you'll
believe that life is short and you should make the
most of it; unlike me, you'll probably realise
that TV isn't real and remain calm when Lassie
doesn't come home. An interest in music and books
is good, a sense of fun and adventure essential.

The response was instant, overwhelming and very reassuring:
everyone was fired up with suggestions and ideas. Maybe all my
competitive friends just wanted to prove they each had the best
contacts, but I actually think everyone genuinely wanted to
help and believed that they had just the person for me.

Queries started flooding in. Sophie bluntly asked:

Do you want to sleep with them all or just
dinner/chat about life etc . . . ? Lemme know,
it'll influence who I put you onto. Love S

• • •

I have to be honest, this panicked me a bit. My journey had already been dubbed 'Around the World in 80 Lays' by most of my friends. I automatically replied with a '*It's not about sex, it's about romance*' mantra but was secretly worrying whether every date was going to end in a wrestling match.

Posh PR Emma rang and asked in cut-glass tones if I wanted to date a Count? Her impeccable accent made the 'o' completely silent. Realising how it sounded, she kept repeating the question, which drew attention to the mispronunciation, making it worse. I felt like replying: 'Ems, I've already dated so many.'

As my DWs went to work and word of what I was doing began buzzing around, potential dates started pouring in. Every morning I would log on to find up to a hundred emails from people looking to get involved.

First-generation DWs introducing me to second-generation DWs:

Jennifer, meet Abigail, she is the most high-flying woman in New York — head honcho, inspired party gal, groovy travelling companion of many years and dear, dear friend . . . AND I think she has the perfect date for you . . . she will tell you more . . . I can't wait to hear the outcome . . . SJ xxxxxx

Third-generation DWs signing up and asking for basic clarification:

Does he need to speak English? Would you be willing to go on a *ménage a trois* with a translator? Hannah, emailing from Budapest

Giving me a 'wake up and smell the fertility' reality check:

PS. You say you don't want to date men younger
than 30. I have two words for you: sperm
motility. If you're still in the race to have a
child before, say, 45, you'll need energetic
critters rather than those about to retire.
Leslie, emailing from Moscow

And forcing me to face the facts:

These are the details of the English lady I was
telling you about: I hope she sounds interesting
to you. She's a very nice lady, aged 38 (but this
is quite normal in the UK, to be old and still
single) . . . read the email trail between Alex
and his friend Beaver in Lithuania.

At the same time that I was being contacted by DWs and their
Dates, I was also out looking for myself, spending hours on the
Internet researching places or events that might yield my Soul
Mate. Anything to do with Love or a love of mine should have
potential, I reasoned. I scoured the search engines like an
intrepid love detective sleuthing for clues that would help me
identify and locate my missing man. In some instances this
threw up dreadful red herrings. I am a huge devotee of Marmite,
for example, and thought this might make me compatible with
the man who ran a Marmite appreciation website in America:

I started the Marmite site because I take Marmite
into work with me on a Friday (the company I work

```
for supplies breakfast, mainly bagels though we
do have toast as well and sometimes yogurt,
though I don't have Marmite with the yogurt. Just
the bagels. And the toast, if they've run out of
bagels). Other than eating Marmite, I write
information management and delivery software for
the Internet . . .
```

Thankfully, other leads proved to be more fruitful, such as The Costco Soul Mate Trading Outlet, one of the theme camps at the annual Burning Man Festival, held in the Nevada desert. I didn't totally understand what they were about, but I did manage to establish that Costco was a kind of anarchic dating agency at the festival. The CEO, Rico Thunder, agreed that I could be part of their camp and work on their 'front desk' in exchange for some light flirting duties. I felt I'd have some useful expertise to contribute by the time I'd made it through Europe and the West Coast of America on to Nevada, plus I fully intended to skim off any suitable Soul Mates for myself. Rico also put me in touch with a Seattle-based audio engineer in TV sports who was one of the Costco crew. He matched my Soul Mate Job Description perfectly and emailed:

```
The things you write in your description could
have been written by me! What is up with that?
   Love: Cooking, building/restoring cars (just
finished an Alfa), music, road trips
   Hate: Working out (still do it), rigid people,
being cold for long periods of time, speed bumps
```

Finally, the tsunami that was my Date Cultivate Timetable swept over me. The only way I could cope with the huge volume of correspondence was to ruthlessly compartmentalise. In the process of establishing a tentative rapport with the desirables and gently filtering out the inadvisables, Europe was given priority over America, which in turn took precedence over Australasia.

Big picture, that was how I saw my route working: Europe, US, Australasia. It wasn't logical from a geographical point of view, but it made it possible to attend specific events at certain times, plus – as importantly – ensured that I'd always be travelling with the sun. This meant I could stay warm, pack light and see people at their/my most foxy. There are valid reasons that all the feel-good songs – 'Summer Breeze', 'Summer Lovin'', 'Summer of '69' – are written about the summer rather than the miserable winter months. Who looks good with chapped lips and a scarf?

Communication all had to be via email: it was the only way I could keep track of what I'd said to whom, and reply to people in my own time rather than real time. Most people were fine with this but occasionally someone insisted that we had to speak on the phone:

```
I don't want to rush you but I much prefer
speaking as opposed to typing. Feel free to call
me on 877-722-****. Toll-free USA. In Canada or
elsewhere 561-178-****. Christopher, Florida
```

This always put me in a spin. I didn't really have the time for more than a single conversation with any one person and there was no way they'd just want to talk once: inevitably they'd want to know all about me as well as when I was coming over, how long I was staying for and all the other details of my trip. But I didn't have answers to these questions yet and the stress of organising this mammoth undertaking was taking its toll as I comfort-ate, putting the 'ate' in 'date' just at the time I really needed to look my best.

I was tentatively working towards a route that would start in the Netherlands, head up through Scandinavia, then down through Mediterranean Europe, central Europe and on to the States. This was just guesswork, though, because – for example – until Henk in Amsterdam got back from his skiing trip, I had no way of knowing if he was free on the 27th? If he was, that would mean I'd be able to make it down to see Frank on the Belgian border, thereby arriving in Barcelona in time to meet Carlos before he set off for his conference in Russia:

. . . though I am in with my good friends in St Petersburg and maybe it would be that you like to join us there if you are in a visit to this place?

I just needed everyone to stay still long enough to give me an answer that would allow me to include or eliminate them from my itinerary. Then – knowing they were locked in – I could work out who, logically, I should see next. And that was just the dating side of it. My friend Karin, who worked at the Netherlands tourist board, was hugely helpful in trying to work out how I would get between three dates spread over 250 miles:

I've been looking for public transport facilities from Schiphol to the Efteling and from the Efteling to the Keukenhof and I must say it's not good news . . . It will take you 2.5 hours to get

from Schiphol to the Efteling and 3 hours to get
from the Efteling to the Keukenhof. I knew it
would be bad as you have to use both trains and
buses, but I didn't know it would be this lousy.
A taxi is not really an alternative, that will be
really expensive, but I was thinking you could
maybe rent a car for two or three days? Do you
have your driver's licence and would it be a good
idea? I've attached an information sheet with car
rental companies at Schiphol and in Amsterdam. If
you like the idea, you could phone them and ask
for prices. If you do prefer to use public
transport I can tell you exactly which trains and
buses you have to take, so just let me know.

I felt guilty as she clearly wanted me to make a decision and all
I could do was be vague and noncommittal. The problem was
that she was asking about the minutiae of one aspect of three
dates while I was in a totally different place, struggling to get
the big picture straight on *all* aspects of *all* 80 dates. It felt akin
to being dragged from a burning building by the emergency
services, only to have them demand back an overdue library
book.

With so many options and nothing actually nailed down, I
started feeling the enormity of what I was attempting. I was
getting a tad tense trying to stay focused whilst having to
remain upbeat and chatty corresponding with the avalanche of
potential dates. I knew I wouldn't get much in the way of
sympathy (*'Help, I am being hounded by an endless supply of
eligible, international bachelors, all wanting to date me . . .'*) but
even if I'd been foolish enough to ask, I wouldn't have got

anyone's attention at this point. Brimming with enthusiasm and support, the DWs had gone off on a mission of their own.

I had clearly said I wanted to date my Soul Mate and explained in detail who that person was. But suddenly, girlfriends were less interested in helping me find *my* ideal man and more interested in helping themselves live out a cherished fantasy. They had found a way to date The One Who Could Have Been.

Could Haves are those intense, poignant relationships that, for some reason, never get actioned. But despite this, or maybe because of it, these people become imbued with an aura of exquisite perfection that only increases as the years go by. A pocket of my (mostly married) DWs had just realised that I could go on the date they had always longed for. No guilt on their part, plus I would be able to tell them afterwards if the date was as blissful as they had always imagined.

Jen, I have always, always had a huge crush on Paul but we were never single at the same time. You lucky girl, he's free now — I want to know EVERYTHING. Lucinda xxx

PS. Get him to take you to The Dove — we always used to go there together for drinks after work: it's really romantic. Sit at the table by the window. The Chardonnay's great. Order the fish.

Or they'd become distracted by their own idea of what the optimum Soul Mate was like, rather than working to mine: 'Oh, you should date a circus performer,' Dea said with great conviction, no explanation and a faraway look in her eye. 'Ohmigod, you could date a tramp,' Jo exploded, then gazed off in a similarly mute manner, lost in her own thoughts.

Clearly, I needed to get them to refocus and I knew the only way this would happen would be if I made them competitive about coming up with the best dates. I sent another email to the group:

I am so grateful to you all for coming up with such great contacts and the current joint favourites for the (Little Black) Booker Prize are Paul Mansfield and Belinda Rhodes. Eleanor Garland pulled away from the pack towards the end of last week, though, and is now gaining fast.

I am now fully dated up for N. America and Australia. Holland is looking good too. Can anyone help with France, Germany, Spain and Italy? How about Asia — HK, Thailand and Singapore?

Thankfully, this led to a fresh deluge of dates but also to a new phenomenon: Date Wrangler Anxiety. Hector, a journalist friend at *China Daily*, emailed from Beijing, frustrated that he didn't seem to be able to come up with any good dates. He felt he was letting me down and not being a good friend. 'Write an article about it,' I suggested. 'Interview me about why I'm doing it, include my Soul Mate Job Description and then anyone who thinks they're "it" can email me at a special email address I'll create.' Overwhelmed by the greater task in hand and consigning it to the *I'll worry about it when I'm on to Australasia* pile, I promptly forgot all about the conversation. Until two weeks later, when Hector sheepishly sent me a link for that day's paper. On the cover was a huge picture of me, smiling vacantly. Underneath, the caption read: 'IS THERE A MAN IN CHINA TO SATISFY THIS WOMAN?'

Most of the time that I was working on setting up this International Tour of Shame, as I'd affectionately come to think of it, I was too engrossed and in the zone to think about anything else. But occasionally there were stone-cold moments of sober clarity, when it really hit me how it must have looked to other people.

The *China Daily* cover was one of them. I sat in front of my computer, shocked and rather ashamed, wondering why I had started this crazy adventure in the first place. But then, as the responses to the article started pouring in, I was once again too frantic keeping up with the task at hand to have any more perspective or qualms.

Replies ranged from Tom in HK:

I am currently seeing someone but we don't really get on that well and on the off-chance I've split up with her by the time you get here, can we please stay in touch?

And Larry, the pilot:

I've seen your picture. You're not that good-looking and you make no effort with your hair: I like that kind of confidence in a woman and I'll definitely date you. But don't expect to go to expensive restaurants or be a nosy parker and talk about me to my friends.

To Tan the businessman:

I look forward to meeting a western woman, so

different from Asian women: you with your
'fuller' body and more voluptuous breasts. In a
country of billions, you will certainly stand
out.

Well, my comfort eating *was* getting out of hand now, and I
was putting on so much weight I'd started wondering if I
should just cut out the middleman and staple the biscuits
directly onto my thighs. Despite the weight gain, however, I
felt sure I lacked the prized voluptuousness that would make
me a worthy ambassador for Breast Western. And the idea that
a billion people were going to be disappointed with my
cleavage was frankly too much pressure to be dealing with right
now.

Fortunately I was saved from dwelling on this thought
because a combination of brute force and plaintive begging had
finally pulled my European schedule loosely together. There
was still a huge amount to be done: I knew who I was meeting
and where, but still had no idea where I was staying when I
arrived, or, indeed, in most cases how I would arrive at all? I
accepted I would have to work this out along the way.

It was time to start dating.

CHAPTER TWO

The Netherlands

He ordered for both of them: 'Two toast with butter and . . .
d'you want a coffee, Debs?' She nodded without looking up
from her handbag-rummaging. 'And two coffees: a latte coffee
and an ordinary one.'

The North Terminal of Gatwick Airport didn't exactly
smack of romance but it positively reverberated with relationships and everyday intimacies. It was awash with people who
had shared many breakfasts and went on holiday together
without giving it a second thought. Booked on to the 7.30 a.m.
to Amsterdam, I was sitting on my own, ordering my own
breakfast and feeling a touch out of sorts. I hadn't started out
on my Dating Odyssey yet, but I couldn't quite suppress the
small voice in my head that whispered: *It's not too late – you
don't have to go through with this.*

Like getting a tattoo or becoming a morris dancer, I sensed
that once I began this journey there would be no turning back.
I would be changed forever. The problem was that I had no
idea of whether the change was going to be good or bad, and
that uncertainty was unnerving.

Debs and 'ordinary coffee' husband were on my left. On my right, a guy my age was sitting on his own, reading *Q*, my favourite music magazine. I glanced at the remains on his plate: it looked like he was a vegetarian too. Did I really need to travel around the world to meet somebody? Wasn't it just possible that this man right next to me could turn out to be my Soul Mate? I sighed impatiently, disgusted with myself as I pulled on my jacket and signalled the waitress for the bill. I loathed people who relied on palmists or tea-leaf readers to 'learn' what was wedged up the sleeve of Fate for them. Yet here I was, divining my future amongst the smears of ketchup and greasy remains of a Linda McCartney vegetarian sausage. Exactly how desperate had I become?

Desperate enough to go around the world in 80 dates, I told myself matter-of-factly as I pushed a tip under the plate, picked up my bags and started the long walk to flight BA8111 and Date #1.

Date #1: Henk – Amsterdam, Holland

I was staying at Amsterdam House, a comfortably quirky hotel on a quiet part of the Amstel river, in the old diamond district. You could sit in the lounge flicking through piles of magazines, drink great coffee and watch the world go by. Well, *you* could, *I* couldn't: I was up in my tiny attic room, waiting to get the call from reception that would announce the arrival of Henk, my first date.

I met Henk through Sandrine, a third-generation DW that I'd initially acquired through Belinda. Henk and I had emailed back and forth a couple of times, but all I really knew about him was that he was balding, sporty and confident.

I started up my laptop to look at the photo he'd emailed, saved into a regional file along with all the others I was dating in that location. He looked quite cute. I wondered why he was single? And if he worried about it; he didn't look the neurotic type. I also wondered – and I know this sounds terrible – if I could I go out with a bald man?

Wondered was about my level of interest and anxiety over what I was shortly to do. I didn't feel at all nervous, more detached with a sense of curiosity, an eagerness to get on with it and a wish that I'd had time to go round the shops I'd passed on the way to the hotel.

In short, I was in denial.

Although, the knowledge that I had a date with Prince Charming tomorrow, with Willem the next day, and so on, took a lot of pressure off: if the date didn't go well, there'd be another along soon enough. What I was doing was a form of speed dating but more far-reaching: '*Today's Monday and Rome, you must be Date Number 12.*'

I had no idea what we were going to do on this date and, security aside – one of the reasons I set up dates through friends and carried a cell phone with me at all times – that was fine by me. I'd served my time planning thoughtful, lovely treats for boyfriends, I was really happy to have someone else in charge – and to learn to be okay with the results.

Thirty minutes had passed and Henk was late. I still wasn't nervous but I did wish he'd hurry up and get here. It was now 11.50 a.m. and I had perfected my '*Henk . . . it is so great to finally meet you*' smile; I was done with all the clothing crises my limited wardrobe allowed. I'd hidden my new duty-free Mac lipgloss in the bottom of my bag: I'd been applying it for over an hour to pass the time. If he tried to kiss me now, his face would skid off mine so fast, he'd get whiplash.

Peering out the window, no sign of anyone who looked like Henk. Time to go to the loo one more time? I was hungry but didn't know whether to eat or not? This was a drawback of not knowing what we were doing: if I didn't eat, guaranteed we'd go for a ten-mile hike; if I did, he'd immediately take me for a meal. Mulling it over, I unwrapped yet another gorgeous little spice biscuit and found myself hoping we'd go for a beer.

Ummmm, yes, a beer. Suddenly I really wanted a drink. God, if I was like this watching out for all the Dates, I'd be a 24-stone alcoholic by the end of the trip: from Date Watcher to Weight Watchers in 80 easy lessons.

The phone rang. Reception. Henk was here.

I was determined not to get tongue-tied and nervous, so before I had the chance I grabbed my bag and a jacket and, slamming my room door shut, ran down three flights of stairs to the lobby.

Henk was waiting for me, looking a little nervous himself. 'Don't think about it, don't think about it,' I was chanting in my head as, ignoring the amused look on the receptionist's face, I walked over to shake Henk's outstretched hand and thereby officially commit to my dating fate.

Henk was about 6 ft 3, with an athletic build, blond hair, blue eyes and a nice smile. My very first thought was: not as bald as I imagined, nice-looking, tall and rangy, a bit preppy, sensitive. 'I have a boat with me,' he said, smiling shyly. Beaming appreciatively in response, inwardly I was groaning: even looking at a boat makes me want to throw up. As Henk helped me onto the 35-foot barge, he added: 'I thought I'd take you on a bit of a spin around the canals and we'd have something to eat along the way?'

Out of the hamper by his feet, he pulled sashimi, strawberries and champagne. The date had begun.

I was touched. He had obviously put a lot of effort into making the date as romantic as possible. Unfortunately – and I didn't say this to him – it was more someone else's idea of romantic. I've always wanted to be one of those women sophisticated enough to function on a diet of protein and alcohol, but as a lactose-intolerant, lapsed Catholic vegetarian, I'm sadly more of a potato-and-bread girl, with a limited capacity for raw fish. But that was the old me. So, sailing up Prinsengraacht, I settled back in the sunshine and smiled at Henk as he passed me a glass of champagne as chilled as the Ministry of Sound music on the boat's MP3 player. We toasted each other's health and I silently toasted the elegant new me: Watery Hepburn.

Floating past the flower market full of roses and sunflowers, the queues outside Anne Frank's house, the red-light district packed with drunk British men (T-shirts declaring they were on 'Steve's Stag Weekend'), I asked Henk about his relationship history. People on bridges smiled down indulgently, thinking us the perfect couple, whilst Henk described how he had been happy with his first long relationship at university but wasn't ready to settle down. His next relationship was a bit of a disaster: the girl had been intense and spiritual and it hadn't worked out but he stayed in touch with her. His next girlfriend had treated him badly but he was crazy about her. ('She was very passionate,' he said helplessly, then added rather alarmingly, 'You remind me of her a lot.')

As Henk expertly navigated the waterways, I thought of the

last time I'd been to Amsterdam. It had been with Kelly: we'd argued fiercely about who knows what and I'd stormed off in the pouring rain. Why had Kelly never done anything like this? And, having to ask that, why then did I still miss him?

Meanwhile Henk sailed on, turning us into endless canals, reliving endless romances. It was cold and dark now, we'd been on the water for about seven hours. Although I hadn't felt quite as sick as I'd first anticipated, an unhappy blend of sashimi and champagne swirled ominously in the pit of my stomach as I listened with a growing sense of impatience when Henk talked. It dawned on me that other people's love lives are like other people's dreams: only interesting if you're in them, and then only if they're good. I started feeling a bit disheartened: *Another 79 of these conversations to go . . .*

I didn't want to be mean. I had actually really enjoyed being on the water with Henk. But I didn't fancy him, it was getting cold and I had to be up early to drive to Date #2 tomorrow morning. Fortunately, at this point Henk told me he'd booked a sofa at The Supper Club, which gave me the excuse to say, 'I've had a great time but I have to say goodnight.' I could tell he was disappointed but he was a good guy and turned the boat around obediently to start sailing back to the hotel.

We got back just before 9 p.m. and Henk helped me (as I shook uncontrollably from the cold) onto the towpath. Thanking him – with an effusion born of guilt – for a wonderful day, I suddenly realised we had entered 'The Long Goodbye', that awkward time at the end of a date when they want to kiss you, but you don't want to kiss them. I have always been completely hopeless at getting this right and, as someone about to date 80 men, it was a skill I needed to fast-track. I always opted for the Quick Peck and Hug (QPH) manoeuvre, the one where you say '*Okay, thanks for a lovely evening*', give them a quick kiss on the cheek then dodge into a hug before they can lock their mouth onto yours. This was an utterly rubbish technique that could go on for days, as the man let you hug him but then kept talking to you, so you had to endlessly start over.

Henk deftly neutralised my QPH. I admitted defeat and agreed to another date with him two days later, knowing I'd be on a plane when the time came. I felt bad but was too cold to come up with a better plan.

Date #2: Frank - Efteling, Holland

Horribly early the next morning, I picked up a hire car from Schiphol airport and drove south towards the Belgian border for Date #2.

I'd heard about a place called Efteling: an amusement theme park and hotel designed around classic national and international fairytales. I'd arranged to spend the night in the Sleeping Beauty suite and my patient friend Karin had set me up to date the guy who played Prince Charming at the park.

I felt a little uneasy about Henk (I should have just said no, rather than copping out and making him think we'd have another date – note to self: be firmer) but it was a gorgeous spring morning and soon I was enjoying the uncomplicated feeling of being '*on the road again*'.

That feeling lasted about ten minutes.

My pastoral appreciation of fields, churches and cows was soon completely overshadowed by the discovery that the Dutch, mostly a calm, liberal, egalitarian nation, evidently treated motorways as the place to exercise their Id and drive like complete maniacs. Cars shot across lanes into tiny spaces between the speeding vehicles without any warning or regard for safety. Convoys of huge trucks randomly (or so it seemed to me) honked their horns, making me increasingly paranoid that either the boot was open and my luggage was spilling out or I was breaking some vital Dutch driving law. Or maybe they were just being friendly? I had no idea and it was very disconcerting. I arrived at Efteling late, harassed and somewhat distracted.

As ever, I overcompensated by being very businesslike. I swept into the lobby of the Golden Tulip Hotel and up to the front desk. 'My name is Jennifer Cox,' I told the neat-looking receptionist briskly, 'I'm here to date Prince Charming.'

I knew how ridiculous it sounded, but it had been a testing morning and I gave her a look that stated very clearly: '*Say "Ooooh, aren't we all" and I will disembowel you where you stand.*'

But she didn't. Instead she smiled sympathetically and said: 'Ah yes, we've been expecting you, Ms Cox. I'm sorry but I have some bad news: Prince Charming has unexpectedly been taken ill. But please don't worry, he has arranged for his friend Frank, who runs the local bike shop, to date you instead. He's waiting for you over there.'

As she pointed somewhere over my shoulder, I sagged against the counter and squinted at her in uncomprehending astonishment. This was not good. Really not good at all. I'm not a hippy but I do believe in karma: when Prince Charming can't be bothered to show up and is replaced last minute by the local bike mechanic, romance is not writ large in the stars.

'*Be calm,*' I told myself evenly and unconvincingly. 'Fate is just testing you to make sure you're serious.' I took a deep breath and turned to Frank, who was sitting patiently waiting to introduce himself. I forced a weak, wobbly smile onto my face as I walked over to meet him. My first impression was that he was nervous (who can blame him) and a bit thin. He looked good when he stood up, though: about 6 ft 2, slightly curly, reddish hair and very blue eyes. He looked shy but not wimpy (I hate wimpy) and surprised me by taking my hand and saying firmly: 'Come with me, Jennifer, I'm going to date you.'

And that's exactly what he did.

Efteling theme park dated back to 1952 and was full of your regular fairies and Red Riding Hoods but also weird, freakish gargoyles called Laafs, who were a sort of cherished national goblin. The park had the air and appearance of a 1970s Disney Does Bruegel fantasy – rather dated and a bit disturbing – but in a nice way with lots of bright flowers and excited school kids running around.

Frank walked me round the gargoyles and daffodils with a sense of purpose. He had planned where we should go and was quietly in charge (which I liked). But I'd been up for five hours, had eaten nothing all day (the whole pre-date 'To eat or not to eat' question again) and was really starting to feel the effects. Noticing I was getting a little vague, Frank took me to a cafeteria by a huge aviary.

Food is always a nightmare for me in Europe: there's either too much dairy (France), too much meat (Germany) or too much lard (pretty much anywhere east of Zurich). There was nothing I really wanted but I'd left it too late to be fussy so bought us both smoked-salmon open sandwiches. Feeling a little faint as I went to take my first bite, the sandwich slipped out of my hand. Lightning reflexes honed by seven years in the school rounders team kicked in as I caught the sandwich in its upward trajectory, snatching it out of the air. The salmon, however, continued to fly pancake-esque upwards. It flipped over lazily before plummeting back down and slapping wetly onto the back of my hand, covering it completely like some vile-smelling glove. I stared at it helplessly. You don't eat food that's been on the floor, but what's the protocol for food that's been worn? Frank, who had stood quietly watching my freakish display, reached over, unpeeled the fish from my hand and folded it back onto the top of the sandwich.

'Shall we walk as we eat?' he asked politely. I nodded meekly and we set off to explore.

Once I'd eaten, I started to relax and enjoy myself. The park was great: Dream Ride was a Fairy Kingdom full of scary porn fairies with open mouths; Panda Dream was a highly inventive 3D film, in which Martin Luther King was reincarnated as a panda concerned about the environment. My favourite ride was the 'Arabic' boat trip along an indoor river that sailed past scenes from *Tales of 1001 Nights*.

We cruised around blind corners scented with apple incense, into market scenes where cheesy shop-window dummies with rolling eyes jerked stiffly on magic carpets. We sailed out of one dark, smoky tunnel between the legs of a huge genie, whose vast jowls hung down over us, disconcerting, like giant testicles.

The ride reduced us to helpless, conspiratorial giggles. Suddenly, I didn't resent that I'd been stood up by Prince Charming, as Frank was turning out to be the male equivalent of Cinderella: a slow burner full of fun. Earlier in the day he'd touched my shoulder a few times to make a point, and at the time the intimacy had made me feel uncomfortable. Now when he did it I felt relaxed and fond of him.

Despite the fact that I was having a good time, by 6 p.m. the spring air had grown cold and we were flagging, so Frank suggested we return to the hotel bar for a drink. Finding a table by the window and ordering wine, we were chatting and laughing easily by now. Sitting with our heads close together, Frank said something I didn't catch. I turned and leant closer to hear him better. Without warning he took my face in his hands and kissed me full on the mouth. I genuinely wasn't expecting this at all and I gasped out loud in shock (though not unpleasantly so).

'You can't kiss me in the bar,' I spluttered, pulling away and laughing.

'Where would you like me to kiss you?' Frank replied with a challenging smile.

I know this is going to sound completely naïve but I hadn't even thought about what I'd do if someone kissed me. It wasn't that I didn't like Frank – I did – but I had another date in 12 hours. I had already started to emotionally detach and was really looking forward to the peace and quiet of my room. I needed some time out to curl up in bed with a beer, crisps and a movie, not talking to anyone at all.

Although I knew I was staying in the Sleeping Beauty suite (cute and silly, with a spinning wheel in one corner and a life-size snoring knight in another) there hadn't been time to check in yet. While Frank and I were in Kiss Negotiations, the hotel manager chose this moment to walk over with my stowed luggage and introduce himself.

'Good evening, Ms Cox,' he said cheerfully. 'We hope you are enjoying yourself?' I blushed guiltily as he continued, 'I just wanted to let you know, we have moved you from the Sleeping Beauty Suite to the Bridal Suite. We are sure you will enjoy the room.' And, with a smile, he walked away.

The Bridal Suite was the one with the huge rotating bed and the Jacuzzi in the middle of the room. I didn't even have a chance to react – Frank was on his feet. 'Let's go,' he urged.

Suddenly it felt as if the date had accelerated past me and I was having trouble keeping up. 'Frank, you are NOT coming to my room,' I told him firmly, though feeling extremely flustered.

Frank acted as if he hadn't heard me. 'Come on,' he said. 'I want to kiss you.'

That he was so confident and focused, disorientated me completely. 'Frank,' I squeaked, struggling to stay calm and sound like I meant what I said. 'There is no way I'm going to sleep with you.'

And I meant it: Frank was cute and he was fun, but he wasn't The One. But even as I said it, I was aware that Frank was compellingly sexy. God, I really hadn't thought through the whole attraction thing.

'Why not?' he asked, sensing my confusion and smiling lazily, like a cat not so much with the cream but the entire cow. At gunpoint.

I breathed hard, gripping the edge of the table to steady myself: 'Because I dated a guy yesterday, I'm dating another guy tomorrow and I'm dating another seventy-seven after that. I can't sleep with all the Dates: what would that make me?' I beseeched indignantly.

But Frank had no pity. 'I'm not asking you to sleep with all the Dates,' he replied reasonably, stroking my hand almost sympathetically, 'just this one.'

God, he was good. This was like being back at a school disco with the cute bad boy trying to charm you out of your knickers with the selfish logic of, *'Well you'll be taking them off later anyway . . .'*

I had to act fast. I jumped to my feet, grabbed my suitcase and ran to the lift. Frank got there first. We were both laughing and flushed now. There was dangerous electricity that crackled between us, growing by the second.

'Frank, you are not getting in the lift with me,' I said firmly as the lift doors opened. Frank and I got in. The doors closed. Frank didn't say a word, he just turned, pushed his weight against me and started kissing me with a slow, hard certainty that made my head spin.

As the lift ascended, Frank and I staggered from wall to wall, locked in a deep, wet passion that lasted eight floors.

I fell out the doors as they opened on my floor, face red from Frank's stubble and eyes wild from the excitement. I was having trouble focusing. I had a teaspoon of self-control left, though, and I knew I had to exert it. 'Frank, stay in the lift,' I commanded hoarsely, swallowing hard. He looked at me steadily, his hair messed, his mouth wet, and his foot jammed in the lift door.

Then, coolly maintaining eye-contact, Frank stepped out of the lift. The doors closed behind him and he started walking towards me. I was lost: there was no way I was going to be able to keep resisting him. And, if I'm honest, I was starting to wonder why I was even trying?

I was transfixed and helpless as he moved towards me.

But suddenly, the mood was broken by the noisy chatter of a Dutch family rounding the corner, a nice-looking young couple with two kids under ten. They stopped their animated conversation abruptly and looked at us uncertainly. They must have sensed the tension in the air and hesitated in front of the lift next to us. They asked Frank something in Dutch which could well have been: 'Did you just snog the face off that woman?' but was probably just 'Are you getting in or out of the lift?'

The lift doors opened, and Frank stepped away from them, taking my arm as the family got in. I knew we were at the point of no return: with my last shred of willpower, I shoved Frank hard, making him stumble back into the lift. As the doors slid shut, Frank and the family all stood staring at me in astonishment. I grabbed my bags, ran to my room and locked the door behind me.

I sat on the bed panting, then, catching sight of myself in the mirror, burst out laughing: I looked like I was on the school playground, resting in the middle of a game of kiss-chase. And kissing was good. But on a first date anything more than kissing seemed a bit much. It wasn't that *anything more* was completely out of the question, it was more that I imagined it would be tender and romantic and with The One. I was two dates in and so far both had ended in a tussle, with the Dates wanting to go further and me just wanting to go. Maybe my friends were right to call my journey 'Around the World in 80 Lays'? But it was no big deal: I'd just forgotten what it was like to date; in future I'd be more prepared. Actually, in many ways it was quite reassuring – the world might have changed a lot since I was a teenager, but dating didn't seem to have changed at all.

The next day, before I left, I checked my emails. There was a lovely one from Frank telling me in broken English how much he had enjoyed our date and how he hoped:

>   . . . to meat you again.

I believed him.

Date # 3: Willem – Keukenhof, Holland

Another early start heading northwest to Keukenhof, the famous tulip fields that have graced a thousand postcards. There had been a silly misunderstanding with my Dutch friend Birgit. I'd told her briefly over the phone what I was doing and she thought I'd said I was looking for my Soil Mate. She knows I love my teeny backyard and just assumed it was a gardening thing and had set me up to date Willem, a gardener at Keukenhof.

Once I got past my eye-rolling about the date and started thinking about what Willem might be like, I was actually pretty excited. I imagined a sun-beaten, Lawrencian anti-hero: dirt under his nails; shirt pulled back roughly over his strong forearms; and the little eye-contact that was made would be both mocking and smouldering.

Still dizzy from nearly being *Franked*, I happily day-dreamed as I drove, cramming sweet almond-studded rolls filled with cinnamon cream into my mouth. I was not going to start this date digestively vulnerable. I was going to be prepared and ready.

It was another beautiful day and – like a plague of locusts off buzzing another field – the crazy drivers and hooting truckers had vanished. Sunny fields of cows and windmills, gorgeous churches with proudly domed roofs and canals bobbing with pretty barges, all hinted at a life lived less hectically.

I was in a great mood but a bit tired, mainly from the effort of emoting and drawing the Dates out of themselves. And the dates had been long too, both lasting most of the day and well into the evening. That's not a date, that's a DAY.

I had to find a different way to run the dates, I thought: One, limit the amount of time we had together, and Two, not let them talk about their old girlfriends too much. It would end up being exhausting otherwise and not much fun for either of us. Being able to talk through their Relationship Résumé was probably quite therapeutic for the Dates, though. Being a dumpee is the very definition of self absorption and here I was, some stranger parachuted in for a day, encouraging them to open up about things their friends were probably sick to death of hearing about.

But it would be a big disappointment if that's all I did over the 80 dates though: got frocked and Mac'd up just to listen to other people's problems. You know, it's funny, I'd focused on how much effort it had been setting up the dates, but it was only just dawning on me how much work going around the world in 80 dates could actually turn out to be. I really hoped it was going to be more fun than having 80 'trapped in the kitchen at a party' conversations. I almost wanted to speed date all 80 for ten minutes, then just have a proper date with the top ten. But I'd be cheating Fate and short-changing myself that way: I'd only meet my Soul Mate if I entered fully into the spirit of my Dating Odyssey, no holds barred.

Meanwhile, all this pondering had distracted me from reading the map properly and, as a result, I got lost on the ring road round Rotterdam and arrived in Keukenhof an hour late for meeting Willem.

I screeched to a halt in the car park and raced through the front gate, barely taking the time to check my hair and make-up. A sweet old man, unsteady on his walking stick, chatted about the seven million bulbs that had been planted at Keukenhof that spring, as he led me to the walled garden where Willem was waiting for me.

Willem was not what I expected.

Less Lawrence, more landed gentry, Willem had reddish hair, green eyes and pale skin. He was wearing a tweed jacket over a crisp, white shirt and pressed trousers. He also wore an expression that said he would rather be absolutely anywhere but here.

He rose formally from the wooden bench as I approached, and stiffly held out his right hand to shake mine. In his left he held a beautiful tulip. Long-stemmed and luxurious, its feathery yellow head pouted engorged lips like clams. I smiled, thinking how beautiful it was, and he caught me admiring it. 'This is what we Dutch men traditionally give on blind dates,' he said self-consciously in a voice that was deep and educated. I had no idea if he was serious or not, but noting his discomfort and sympathising (let's face it, it was a bizarre situation), I smiled encouragingly and waited for him to give me the flower.

But he didn't give me the flower. Instead, he sat back down on the bench, smoothing out the creases in his impeccable trousers and straightening his cuffs. Feeling more than a little disconcerted, I followed his lead and sat down next to him. Together we surveyed the rippling rows of nodding tulips stretching up to meet the weak spring sunshine. Row upon row of frilled heads: lilac, black, yellow, white shot with scarlet, some feathery, some furled, puckered tight, some blown and fading, all colour and life spent. It was magnificent, and, in a way, an intimate and emotional sight to share.

The atmosphere between Willem and me, however, was anything but intimate. It was completely silent and increasingly awkward. I was waiting for him to take the lead, but not only did he show no indication he would, he showed no indication that he even knew I was there.

'Do you know why I'm here?' I asked brightly, trying to hide the hurt I felt at his distant attitude and determined to break the mood.

'Not really,' he replied stiffly with the dignified resignation of a highly decorated military man, who for circumstances beyond his control or understanding now finds himself selling sex toys in a shop in Soho.

'Well,' I said brightly, taking a deep breath and launching into an explanation that was meant to be both reassuring and intriguing. 'It's just we all work so hard,' I trilled. 'We have no time for love, so I'm travelling the world dating people to see if I can find my Soul Mate.'

I finished with a flourish and turned, expecting to see Willem smiling, relaxed and ready to talk. Clearly I had fallen short of the tone I was striving for: Willem was still surveying the flowerbed, staring ahead stonily but now with a grim expression that unflatteringly hovered somewhere between disgust and disbelief. It was as if I'd suggested we both take off our underpants and look at each other's bottoms. A moment passed. Then another. Not a word was said. I sat rigid with rising panic, feeling a wave of hot shame wash over me, completely and horribly mortified. And this was only Date #3.

Willem, maybe sensing my distress, maybe just wanting to end his own, got to his feet.

'Shall we have some lunch?' he asked politely. I nodded gratefully, misery robbing me of the ability to speak. As we walked past the raspberry posies that peppered the rhododendron and the soft papery apricot of the azaleas, I watched Willem take the tulip he had picked for but not actually given to me. As he walked, he neatly and methodically folded the flower over and over and over on itself until its broken stem and crushed head was no more than a ruined, sap-bleeding ball. I pretended not to notice when he silently dropped it into a bin at the side of the path and continued marching without breaking his stride.

Willem relaxed a little over lunch and actually turned out to be quite amiable, with a dry sense of humour. But after a gentle walk around the beautiful gardens and a look at the gorgeous displays of scented lilies, I was grateful to be back in my car and heading for Schiphol airport, alone with my thoughts about the journey ahead. What if my Dating Odyssey failed to find me a boyfriend and just succeeded in making me feel freaky and bad about myself?

As I took endless wrong turns and dodged through rush-hour traffic, trying to make it in time for my connection, the phone started ringing on the seat next to me. An Amsterdam number. It would be Henk ringing to collect on the promised second date. I frowned and gripped the steering wheel harder, ignoring the phone: I just didn't have the emotional energy to deal with Henk now. Also, I don't mean this horribly, but I didn't want to go back over old dates; I wanted to look forward and get on to the new ones. I was flying to Sweden in the hope that my next date would give me some much-needed insight and perspective on the journey I had undertaken. Professor Lars-Görsta Dahlöf at Gothenburg University was one of the world's leading authorities on Psychology and Sexology – the science of love and attraction.

This was one Date I'd happily devote a day to.

CHAPTER THREE

Gothenburg, Sweden

Gothenburg does itself no favours having a Volvo museum. Drawing attention to the fact that it's the birthplace of arguably the dullest, least-adventurous car in the world is not a PR coup for a city that's easily as hip as Stockholm and just as much the party town as Malmo.

But Sweden generally seems to suffer from a bit of a personality crisis, and I don't think I'm going to win any awards for insight by suggesting it's probably down to the weather. Nearly a sixth of Sweden is north of the Arctic Circle and winter nights last anything up to 18 '*stay indoors, stare at the walls for four months*' hours. From May to August, however, the height of the sun and the tilt of the earth's axis goes to the other extreme, creating the 'Midnight Sun' and up to 23 hours of sunshine a day.

And when the Midnight Sun shines, so do the Swedes. Everyone seems to spin and show, like over-wound ballerinas in a musical box, making the most of every bright second before the lid slams shut for another winter of introspective darkness.

But maybe the city does its thinking in the dark because over the last 40 years, Gothenburg has been at the forefront of pioneering research into Sexology: the science of human sexuality and how it affects us chemically, socially and physically. And I had an appointment at the university to meet one of the world's leading sexologists; I had come to date the Love Professor.

Date #4: Professor Lars-Görsta Dahlöf – Gothenburg, Sweden

I'd come across Professor Lars-Görsta Dahlöf in an online article, reporting on a conference he'd held on The Science of Love and Passion. At the time it was casual curiosity; I thought it would be fascinating to learn more about his theories and ideas. But now that I was here I realised my questions were less theoretical and more personal. I was slightly unsettled by how my journey was turning out and hoped he'd have some theories that would help me establish if I stood any chance of success, or could, at the very least, emerge with a shred of dignity? The memory of Willem's blatant disapproval still stung . . .

The plan was that we'd meet at the reception of my downtown hotel and then drive out to the Japanese Gardens past the university for a walk and a chat. Now it was 11.30 a.m. and I had literally just checked into my room when reception rang to say the Love Professor was downstairs waiting for me. Damn, he was 40 minutes early. I'd hoped to have a quick shower and a moment to gather my thoughts before I met him.

I flipped my bag onto the bed. I'd packed my waterproof jacket and sweater on top – even without his early arrival I'd known it would be a tight turnaround. As I pulled the jacket out I noticed a puddle of sticky white fluid over the sleeve. I stopped dead and looked at it, mystified. Gingerly checking my bag, nothing was broken. I really didn't want to smell it, but – and I had no good feelings about this – what the hell was it?

I was tired and feared I was going crazy but . . . was it possible a baggage handler had opened my bag and . . . ?

NO, it was too much to even think about. Why would they do that? Holding my breath and grimacing, I plucked the coat carefully out of my bag and took it into the bathroom to sponge the fluid off, all the while painfully aware that the Love Professor was downstairs waiting to meet me. At arm's length, I dropped the sleeve into the sink and, stepping back, turned the tap on full. As soon as the water hit the sticky mess, it started frothing and foaming. Foam? I hadn't expected foam. I looked at the sleeve in confusion, turned the water off, put the wet coat down on the edge of the sink and walked back into the bedroom. Minus my coat, there was now more room in my case to investigate. I gingerly lifted out the rolled clothes and peered cautiously underneath them.

A bottle of shampoo I had missed earlier was lodged in the corner of the case, its lid unscrewed and white soap oozing out the unsecured top.

I closed my eyes and groaned in exasperation. Apparently, it wasn't just the lid that was coming unscrewed. Was the fact that I was meeting the Love Professor making me see sex everywhere or was I doing this to myself by undertaking this journey? Just imagine what kind of interpretation he would put on this: 'Ahh, so, Jennifer, you imagine your travelling persona to be the focus of unsolicited sexual attention, and yet it is a journey you have chosen to make. Is it not possible that you are filled with a desire to have your "baggage handled" by strangers and you are seeking to make this fantasy a reality?'

The Love Professor was looking out of the window into the Nordstan shopping centre outside when I finally made it down to reception. He was a kind-looking man, about 50, a 'Woody Allen Does Academic' appearance, with a lived-in tweed jacket and sparse brown hair framing a thin, contemplative face. My entrance felt a bit scattered, in utter contrast to his quiet, serene pose at the window, and on seeing him I became gripped with the urge to fling myself down onto the reception sofa and blurt out everything that had happened to me so far. With steely resolve I resisted the impulse. Instead, waiting for the Love Professor to transfer a huge armful of papers from right to left, I smiled warmly, shook his outstretched hand and answered: 'Yes, I had a lovely journey here, thank you, no problems at all. Quite uneventful. I'm sorry if I kept you waiting, shall we go?'

He drove me out to the Japanese Gardens, a tranquil refuge at the top of a steep trail in the public gardens beyond the university where he worked. As we settled in a wooden arboretum, off the path overlooking a bamboo garden, I explained my theory and mission to the Love Professor. I asked him, if I did meet my Soul Mate, how would I know he was The One? Were there any signs or signals I should be looking for?

'Well, we have a physical response which we define as sexual . . . ,' he began cautiously, as if realising for the first time that I had a vested interest in his answers. 'Also understanding that although we all fall in love, few of us know anything more about it than how we feel.' Like technology: I can send you an email without either of us having the faintest clue how it got from my computer to yours. The Love Professor was about to explain the Love Equivalent of firewalls, IPs, wireless applications and the daisy-wheel printer.

'. . . but it starts in the earliest relationship: the one between the mother and the child. It is an intense experience of trust and well-being: feeling everything is as good as it could be. To fall in love and to be close to another human being at any age in your life . . .' Uh oh, not the whole Oedipal thing.

'So when you fall in love,' I interrupted impatiently, 'you're looking to relive those bonds of comfort and security?'

'Yes, you are seeking to relive something you don't consciously remember but your body does,' he replied.

I knew this must be relevant somewhere, but time was short and I wasn't looking to date either of my parents on this trip, so I moved it along.

'So apart from my historical needs, what about the physical side? How will I know if I'm attracted to somebody?' An obvious question, with an even more obvious answer, but the Love Professor didn't seem to think me odd for wanting to know. Apparently you fall in love in three stages: lust, attraction and attachment. Each stage has distinct characteristics, accompanied by set behavioural patterns and a variety of hormones. Evidently it was more complex than just thinking someone looked good in a leather jacket.

The Love Professor gave me an example: 'There are a number of factors working beneath your consciousness, and one of them is smell. Not only does smell influence you, your smell also carries information about your genetic make-up.'

This was intriguing. 'So am I wasting my time kissing when I should be sniffing?' I demanded.

The Love Professor looked momentarily confused and then

replied: 'No, because kissing is a good opportunity to take a good sniff.'

We both laughed. 'I'm intrigued and a little concerned for your kissing technique,' I teased. Funnily enough, I found the fact that we were compelled to do romantic things for practical reasons really reassuring: almost as if it wasn't totally my fault if I made a mess of it, nature had to take a share of the blame too. 'Okay, that's a fantastic piece of information.' I beamed; we were getting somewhere now. 'Are there any other things that will help me work out if my Dates are compatible or not with me when I first meet them? I only have one date with each of these people, so I have to take in a lot of information and make a lot of decisions very quickly.'

The Love Professor warmed to the subject. 'When two people are attracted, we send messages that we are interested and want to become better acquainted, often by mimicking each other's actions. If a woman strokes her hair, the man will make the same movement a second later. After a while, if everything works and there is a mutual interest, there will be a perfect synchronicity. We tend to like a partner who is a reflection of ourselves: finding a person who mirrors you in such a positive way is very easy to fall in love with.'

Presumably the same was true from a negative perspective too: if you felt rubbish, you were more likely to pick a partner who made you feel you were rubbish?

Again, the Love Professor concurred. 'If you have a secure and positive image of yourself – being nice, liking yourself – you will be more likely to pick someone who sees and affirms that in you. However, if your self-esteem is absent or very low, you find it harder to believe there is someone else out there like you or who will like you.'

I could see how that would be true. 'So you're saying: work at making yourself feel good before you get involved with anyone else, because they'll only be good for you if you're good to yourself?' But what did this mean for me? I was a pretty positive person – generally cheerful and comfortable with myself – yet I had chosen relationships that had not been in my best interest. Wasn't it possible there were other important factors that played a role in who you chose as your partner? I had my own theory on the subject and wanted to ask the Love Professor what he thought of it?

'So, to go back to the idea of selection. I have a theory – which I'm hoping is wrong – about work and relationships. Basically, work is where we meet our partners, but work is more demanding than ever, and men are coping less well with the pressure than women. As a result, working women find their jobs the most emotionally satisfying relationship in their lives, so they either settle for so-so romances or end up chronically single. Could there be any truth in this?'

The Love Professor thought for a moment. 'Traditionally the most important reason for being in a relationship was to reproduce: couples married and had children. The man supported the family, the woman stayed at home and looked after it. Most women these days are not looking for partners in order to have babies, or at least not right away. A change has taken place in a very short period of time; men and women have become more equal. Although we have acknowledged the change, we have yet to address how the needs and expectations of relationships have changed as a result.'

I genuinely found this sad and disturbing: was the implication that men were only attracted to women who wanted to have children? I tried to get it straight in my head:

'You talk about how we telegraph information in non-verbal ways, through smell etcetera . . . If women want careers, could we be unconsciously transmitting a desire not to have children and be less desirable or attractive to potential partners as a result?'

The Love Professor considered what I was asking. 'I don't know about that, but body odours are certainly affected by high levels of stress. Working too much; too many problems; no time for leisure, etcetera, can – on a subconscious level – be recognised in the way you smell.'

So maybe the issue wasn't about wanting or not wanting kids, it was that career women literally smelt like hard work? I felt the need to bring the conversation back around to me. 'But I've quit my job, I'm not stressed and I've nurtured a positive self-image. I should be smelling relaxed, right?'

The Love Professor nodded noncommittally, not sure where this was going but willing to let me carry on until I got there. I got there: 'Do you think I'm going to meet Mr Right?'

Faced with such an emotionally charged question, the Love Professor retreated to the safety of science: 'Our research has shown that when you are waiting or starving for a relationship, you will be very open to all types of stimuli that will tell you this is the right person. That means you will probably be quite uncritical . . .'

The scientific way of saying 'desperate' . . .

'Looking at it from a scientific view,' the Love Professor said evenly, 'when two people meet and get involved, they each bring their own history with them. How you bring these histories together provides the condition for the future of your relationship. A person who gives you too much of their "history" shows an inability to choose or prioritise their relationships.'

This reminded me of a guy I dated, Grant – 'I'm separated,

I just forgot to tell my wife.' He seemed incapable of going anywhere without at least two of his friends, and his mobile never stopped ringing when we were out. It baffled him that I thought this was a problem.

'And also, from the opposite perspective, it can be quite disappointing, when the one you want to share your life with will not share very much of his or her own life with you. The person who will not share their past is unlikely to see you in their future.'

This was Kelly: Captain Compartmentalise, never wanting me to meet his family or friends.

Interesting stuff, but, looking at my watch, I was running out of time. I was meeting my friend Ann-Charlotte for a drink at 6 p.m. to hear about tomorrow's date with her foxy-sounding friend Anders.

I wondered if, after all his measuring and dissecting, the Love Professor believed in the existence of Love?

He answered immediately, with total conviction and heartfelt certainty: 'Yes, yes, I think it exists. And there is so much data supporting this. Being touched and caressed by your partner will stimulate the brain to release the chemicals oxytocin and vasopressin – both have been linked to our ability to forge strong and lasting emotional bonds. When you meet someone you're attracted to, within two seconds your heart rate will increase dramatically; your blood pressure goes up; muscle tension increases and your intestines shut off, giving you that "butterflies in stomach" sensation.

'Your brain should interpret this as enjoyable,' he added helpfully.

'But I always get really anxious and start babbling,' I confessed. 'I talk far too much and make far too many hand gestures. And in my head I'm going *"shut up, shut up, you're being weird"*, but I find it really hard to stop.' I said all this in a small, pained voice, before asking equally pathetically: 'I mean, do guys find that attractive?'

The Love Professor looked at me sympathetically, clearly thinking *'this woman will have died of anxiety-induced exhaustion by the end of eight dates, let alone eighty'*. He took a deep breath, paused a moment to find the right words, then said: 'I think this is a way of handling a fear of losing control. One way – which is perhaps not the best way – to try and regain control is to talk, talk, talk.'

He said this very gently as I hid my face and squirmed on the park bench. Bemused parents out walking with their kids – memories of the horrors of dating long erased – looked over quizzically. I caught sight of my watch; it really was time to go. I had a lot of information, but did the Love Professor have just one tip for my date tomorrow? Was there one thing above all others that I should do?

He looked at me with the kindly expression of someone who knows no amount of advice will help. 'I think you should not plan too much,' he said simply. 'Just let it happen. Use all your senses and take in whatever comes. You should not watch too much what kind of message you are sending. Afterwards you can analyse, but not at the time. What is attractive to the person you are dating is that you are present in all aspects: mind, body and soul. That is a very good start.'

We sat and looked at each other for a moment, both a bit drained from the intense conversation, and me from the recognition that I felt far more exposed and unsure about my journey than I had ever realised. I gave him a big hug and thanked him sincerely.

As we walked back through the park to his car, we chatted about 'normal' things: family, work, places we had visited. We strolled under the comfortable shade of linden and oak trees: it was a beautiful place and I hoped to come back one day when I was less preoccupied. The Love Professor had given me plenty to think about – not all of it easy to hear – but I'd have the chance to talk about it all tonight with Ann-Charlotte, over a large drink.

I knew Ann-Charlotte from when she'd worked for the Swedish tourist board in London. I'd been sad to see her move back to her home city of Gothenburg the year before, but was reaping the benefits now. Not only had she promised to take me to the 'only locals know' funky parts of town, she'd also done a great job as local Date Wrangler-in-chief.

Back at my hotel, getting ready to meet her, I felt happy and relaxed, looking forward to the uncomplicated evening I knew we'd spend together. I'd just started to realise how important it was to intersperse my 80 Dates with some normal socialising, preferably with female friends. Dating was really demanding: there was all the stress of preparation and anticipation. Then there was the date itself: fraught with revealing body-language and full of silent '*I can't believe he just said that*' moments.

We were obliged under the International Girlfriend Charter to re-enact dating highlights for each other's entertainment, but, just as importantly right now, I needed relaxed, 'no agenda' fun with girlfriends to help offset the pressure of dating and stop me obsessing about the '*I can't believe* I *just said that*' moments of my own.

Avoiding The Avenue (the main tourist drag), Ann-Charlotte

took me to a place in Linnégatan, a cosmopolitan area, awash with trendy bars and chi-chi restaurants. It was next to Slottskogen, another of Gothenburg's big parks, and close to Haga, the old town where tall 'Brothers Grimm' wooden houses lined the twisting cobbled streets.

After we caught up with old news, Ann-Charlotte sat rapt with fascination as I explained the Love Professor's scientific theories on love and compatibility. Wine flowed like wine, as we compared notes on how scarily accurate it all was: exes who had refused to be intimate; girlfriends with ready excuses about why their awful relationships really weren't that awful.

She asked if I was going to test what I had learnt from the Love Professor on Anders, the friend of hers I was dating tomorrow. But since Anders had insisted everything about him and the date remained a mystery until the date itself (I was starting to see this as one of the ways Dates felt they could retain a degree of control. Maybe it made them feel special and not just 'one of 80'?), it was impossible to know how I was going to be with him. But, in theory, 'of course', I told her. I would sniff him; mimic his movements; give him enough but not too much of my history; try not to talk too much and – most importantly – let it happen. BUT, I stressed to Ann-Charlotte, only if he was cute. The last thing I needed was more flirting flotsam: to attract another guy I wasn't seriously interested in, when I needed to concentrate my efforts on finding Mr Right.

As we stumbled back to our beds at 4.30 a.m., the streets were full of people; the people were full of alcohol. Ann-Charlotte and I were no exception. It was as bright as the afternoon and there was a friendly party atmosphere, the warm air heavy with possibilities. As the night porter of my hotel opened the taxi door for Ann-Charlotte to climb in, she gave me a big hug and wished me luck for the days ahead.

'I think maybe it is a crazy thing that you are doing, Jennifer,' she said intensely. 'But you are brave enough to do what the rest of us can only dream of. Go date the world for every woman,' she declared flamboyantly, collapsing into the back of the taxi and giving me a wobbly salute. I watched the taxi drive off. Just as it rounded the corner, I heard her shriek: 'And don't forget: for your date with Anders, you must take a bikini.'

Date #5: Anders – Gothenburg, Sweden

When I woke at 11 a.m. later that morning, I was immediately confronted by two facts: firstly, I had the kind of hangover that made my eyes look like a hamster's cheeks stuffed with peanuts, and secondly, in six hours I had to wear a bikini.

I'd brought one with me. Before I'd left London, Ann-Charlotte had repeatedly impressed upon me that it would be needed, but I'd managed to block it out until she'd reminded me last night that I was actually going to have to wear it.

All she'd told me about tonight was that her friend Anders would pick me up from my hotel at 5 p.m.; I should pack a bikini and be ready for a boat trip.

As I have already explained, I will never be ready for a boat trip.

My crushing hangover made it impossible to focus on anything, but – as much as I was capable – I was worried. People who don't suffer from seasickness refuse to accept that the condition is genuine. Instead, they see it as a kind of laziness that can be cured with a little effort and a better attitude. I was forever being told by sailing friends: '*Oh, if you sit up on deck/eat a biscuit/keep your eye on the horizon . . . you'll be fine.'* Did they not think I had tried all these things? I mean, it wasn't like I was some kind of aquatic bulimic and wanted to be sick.

Mariah and Whitney don't do stairs: I'd told everyone who had anything to do with my journey, I don't do boats. My Dates seemed to think they knew better, though, stubbornly championing the inherent romance of *man woos woman on the open seas*. Well, fair enough, maybe they'd see the inherent romance in *man watches woman throw up on the open seas*?

However, my concerns about being sick were nothing compared to my feelings about wearing a bikini in front of a complete stranger. I had great thighs, and I don't mean that in good way.

When I first heard about the whole bikini nightmare, I went straight to the gym and asked my Swedish trainer Emma for a high-impact, fast-result programme. As I sweated and shook through a series of lunges and lifts, I explained the reason for the emergency. Emma immediately wrinkled her perfect nose, pursed her pink, cupid-bow lips and declared: 'Oh, but Swedish men are so boring.'

'Really?' I gasped, turning to look at her, my lunge wobbling off to the side. 'I thought they were all tall and utterly gorgeous?'

'Exactly,' she replied with the judgement of Solomon. 'They have never needed to develop a personality. You should try Australians,' she added helpfully.

Could this be true? Had the Swedish gene pool developed a race so beautiful, evolution had deemed personalities as superfluous as the male nipple? Or did we all just have a 'familiarity breeds contempt' attitude towards our 'home boys'?

Pushing all futile thoughts to one side, I booted up my laptop: I had work to do. I needed at least three hours a day, every day, to keep on top of the practicalities and logistics of my trip, as well as taking care of the minutiae of 'normal life'. Although I had started my travelling and dating, there was still so much to be done.

Logging on, there was the usual deluge of dating detail emails. Italy was demanding decisions. I was meeting Umberto, a guy who ran a 'traffic dating' website (stuck in a traffic jam and fancy the driver two lanes over? Note down their numberplate, search for it on Umberto's website and send them an email suggesting a date). Umberto wanted to know were we meeting in Siena or Rome?

I was going to Verona to do the balcony scene with Romeo. The people who looked after Juliet's house wanted to know my medieval dress size?

Meanwhile, over in Paris, I was going on a Skate Date and the guy I was to skate with wanted to know my foot size.

There was also a two-day-old email from Anders:

```
I have heard the weather shell be sunny on friday
so you dont need any warm clothes, i will
recemend jeans, maby a windbreaker, and of course
bikini (leasure).
```

Hmmmmm.

I worked my way through the emails. I also surfed the Net trying to work out if it was feasible to get from Paris to Berlin by train, and if not and I needed to fly, could I go direct or did I need to backtrack via London? I'd forgotten to pay my credit-card bill and had left my online password in my palm pilot at home (in a misguided attempt to travel light), so needed to call the bank and sort that out. I also checked my answering machine in London. My sister Toz had called: what day was I arriving at her house for the bank holiday weekend? Gareth had rung from Wales to make sure I was still on for the hike over the bank holiday weekend? On my mobile, Cath had texted to see we were still on for Norfolk over the bank holiday weekend? Obviously, whilst I meticulously cross-checked my dating schedule, I'd forgotten to pay the same attention to my home life and had now triple-booked myself. I couldn't face hearing all those irritated voices now, so made a mental note to call them later.

I looked at my watch: 4 p.m. No time to catch a nap, I had to get ready. An hour later, hoping I didn't look as hungover and sleep-deprived as I felt, I grabbed my bag (including the dreaded bikini) and made my way down to reception.

I had no idea what Anders looked like, but felt sure I'd know when I saw him. As I looked discreetly around the lobby, the door crashed open and a large woman in a tailored black jacket stormed in. She pointed at me: 'You are Jennifer?' she boomed, as if daring me to disagree.

I nodded, hesitating in my confusion. Where was Anders?

'Then you come with me,' she commanded, turning on her heel and striding back outside without a backward glance.

It wasn't quite what I had expected. Unsure of exactly what was happening, I walked slowly out the open front door after her. Scanning the street, I spotted her waiting in the driving seat of a taxi, engine running. She motioned impatiently for me to get in. I knew Ann-Charlotte was in on this, plus I had done crazier things making travel programmes (on one national radio show, listeners were invited to show me unaccompanied around their home cities. As I climbed into a strange man's car in Istanbul, I remember wondering if we had really thought through the personal security implications of the programme and if I'd ever be seen alive again).

We drove south out of town through the busy port area. The shipyard was hard at work, huge cruise liners moored alongside fleets of fishing boats, proving that Gothenburg was wise or fortunate enough to have more than one industry paying the bills. The industrial warehouses looked successful enough, for now, to resist the yuppy developments claiming more vulnerable waterfronts around the world, from Auckland and Sydney to Vancouver and London.

My taxi driver chatted as she drove but I wasn't really listening. I was thinking about how I was being played. Anders was keeping me guessing: he obviously liked to be in charge, calling all the shots. 'Let him,' I said to myself, smiling. I had no problem with that. This was going to be fun.

After 15 minutes driving along the coast road, we came to a stop at a picturesque wharf. Although small sailing vessels tugged gently against their moorings, the air was still and, even this late in the day, the sun was hot on my skin.

The driver parked the car and together we walked the short distance to a wooden pier on which a cheery man in his sixties seemed to be waiting for us. He looked like an ad for *Crewing Monthly* with his turtleneck sweater and pipe, periwinkle eyes flashing mischievously in his tanned face. I had thought Anders would be younger, more edgy? Although he looked fun, I was a little disappointed. I shrugged it off, though; it was fine, at least the waiting was over, and I was sure there'd be more game players further down the line.

The driver introduced us: it wasn't Anders, it was one of the local captains. Another twist – Anders and I had yet to meet.

The driver made her excuses and disappeared for a moment, leaving the captain and me to chat. Was I going out on a boat, he asked? Memory of the date with Willem made me hesitate: was there a good way of explaining that not only did I have no idea what I was doing here, but I was doing this 80 times over with strange men around the world? It was a tricky thing to say nonchalantly to someone not in on my plan (and, as Willem had demonstrated, sometimes tricky to say to someone who was).

I was saved from having to explain my presence by the return of my driver. She was accompanied by a man in his mid-twenties, with classic Swedish looks: fine, clean features, white-blond hair, incredibly clear skin and blue, blue eyes. Was this Anders? Again, I felt a twinge of disappointment. Fresh-faced and sweet-looking, he was young and had the air of an earnest, uncomplicated boy, quite at odds with the foxy game-playing vibe Anders had been putting out.

He walked over, holding out his hand to shake mine. 'Hello,' he said. 'I'm Martin.'

Ahhhh, I thought to myself with a grin, the game is still on.

'If you will please come with me, I must take you on my boat. Anders is waiting for you.'

I laughed and picked up my bag, following Martin onto a small, incredibly sleek speedboat. I sat on the jockey seat next to him, strapped on the life jacket he handed over and braced myself as we gently accelerated out of the wharf and into the open water.

The water in question was part of the Scandinavian southern archipelago, where the North Sea forms Kattegat, a wide channel between Sweden and Denmark. Even while I was concentrating on my dulling mantra of *'don't be sick, don't be sick'*, I could appreciate it was intensely beautiful. We knifed through the clear water; the sharp-edged waves from our boat had turned to gentle ripples by the time they reached the shores of the tiny islands we passed. I could hear the local children chatter and laugh as they milled around in rock pools and dived off rafts into the cool water. Behind them, pine trees crowded down to the boulder-studded shoreline, like kids around an ice-cream van. The occasional tiny red stave house peeped shyly from between branches, pristine white roof bright against the deep green of the needles. We flew across the clear blue water; the air felt clean and fresh. I was both nervous and excited: I felt sure this was the final leg of the journey before Anders and I would meet.

Some of the tension must have shown on my face: Martin, sweetly misunderstanding, took one hand from deftly skimming the boat from tip to tip of the bouncing waves. 'Don't worry,' he shouted over the noise of the engine and crash of the water, touching my arm reassuringly and frowning with concern. 'We have all been told you get very, very sick on boats and I am to watch and see if you will vomit.'

I smiled weakly and wiped some of the salty spray from my face to hide my embarrassment, as we ploughed ever onwards into the surf.

Half an hour later, I was watching a cluster of tacking boats filled with orange-life-jacketed children learning to sail. I reflected on how wonderful it would be to grow up having sailed dinghies, ridden horses or hiked and biked mountains virtually from the age you could walk. In England, it seems everyone has watched TV or idled in traffic from the age we could sit. I snapped out of my ruminating: the roar of the engine had become a gentle purr. Martin had slowed the boat and was standing at the wheel, scanning the horizon.

'Are we lost?' I asked, suddenly really nervous about meeting mysterious Anders. Maybe going back to the hotel, having a big bath and catching up on sleep wouldn't be such a bad thing?

'No,' Martin replied politely but preoccupied as he eased the boat through a rocky channel, all the time scanning the horizon. 'They are here somewhere.'

Where the hell am I being taken?' I suddenly thought crossly. 'Why didn't Martin know where they (THEY?) were? What was next? To get into a submarine? Who was the goddamn date with – Captain Nemo?'

I was starting to get impatient. Enough was enough, let's get on with the date or take me back to the hotel so I can watch cable and be as one with the minibar.

But at that very moment, Martin pushed the throttle down on the boat and we sped forwards: he had spotted them.

I was about to meet Anders.

We were sailing towards a floating pontoon moored to a rocky outcrop in the middle of the sea. It was a big pontoon, about 18 feet by 30, a large cabin in the middle with a deck front and back. I could make out two men standing on the front deck, one pale, fiddling with ropes, one tall and dark, looking straight at me. He waved.

Oh my god, it was Anders. Finally.

Except, all of a sudden, 'finally' felt like it had arrived far too soon. I didn't feel ready. Clutching my bag protectively to my chest, I felt completely overwhelmed with nerves and I suddenly wished my date had been with lovely, sweet Martin after all.

I waved back to Anders with a confidence I didn't feel.

The sun was bright in my face. My hair had been whipped insensible and my eyes were stinging and weeping after an hour being buffeted by the salty wind and surf. As Martin sailed closer to the pontoon, Anders steadily came into focus. I groaned to myself wretchedly: he was absolutely gorgeous. Completely and ridiculously handsome. I was utterly out of my depth.

As Martin navigated the boat alongside the pontoon, Anders, who had been leaning against the railing watching our approach, stepped forward to help me aboard. My legs wobbling, my nose running, I pleaded with myself not to fall in or do or say anything stupid, as he reached down, took my hand in his and pulled me up towards him.

Now both on deck, we stood six inches apart and gave each other a long, appraising look.

Anders was about 6 ft 3 and in his early forties. His skin was tanned golden, his thick brown hair wavy and swept back from his face, which was lined in a manner that suggested he knew his own mind and was used to getting his own way. He was deeply handsome: his green eyes were offset by a strong jaw and full mouth. He was obviously very fit: dressed casually in a white vest, a khaki shirt loosely buttoned over it, strands of hair curled up from his chest.

He looked a lot like Mel Gibson.

What the hell was Ann-Charlotte doing with a friend like this? How was this possible? She was like me: we didn't know people like this. We knew normal people, people who played

table football and smacked into the full-length mirrors in the
Met Bar, thinking it was another room. We knew people who
looked like 'the boy next door', because in all probability they
lived next door. This man was in another league altogether.

'So, I shall go now, Jennifer. It was a pleasure meeting you.'
I stopped staring at Anders and spun around. Martin was
climbing back into the speedboat with pale, rope-fiddling guy,
and they were getting ready to sail back to the shore.

I would have paid any amount of money to go with Martin
rather than stay here with Anders, but I knew that wasn't going
to happen. Plus, I told myself sternly, attempting a degree of
control and to stop my thoughts free-falling, *This is what my
journey is all about: to challenge my 'type comfort zone' and be open
to the possibility that a 'new type', although unfamiliar territory,
might actually make me happier.*

And with a friendly wave, Martin motored off. This was it:
short of faking a burst appendix, I was committed to dating
Anders.

Maybe sensing my apprehension, Anders did the best
possible thing. Dipping into the cabin and emerging with a
bottle of chilled Moët and two glasses, he gestured that I
should sit on one of the chairs by a long, wooden bench.

'Jennifer,' he said in a deep voice, his Scandinavian accent
drawing out the syllables, 'it is a pleasure to finally meet you. I
think your story is a brave and fascinating one, and I am very
much looking forward to hearing more of it. But first, I hope
you are a little hungry as I have prepared some light food for
us? I must return to the kitchen for a few moments so why
don't you just sit and relax and enjoy the view.'

I remained standing: I was still keyed up and didn't feel
comfortable being waited on.

'Oh, Anders, please let me help,' I protested, but Anders just smiled warmly, handed me a glass glistening with bubbles and pulled out the chair for me to sit on. Realising Anders was being gracious – and knowing it would be undignified to argue – I settled into the seat. His hand lightly brushed my shoulder then I heard him turn and walk into the cabin – which I now knew to be a kitchen – behind me.

Moments later, the sound of strings, gliding like a shoal of fish around Frank Sinatra crooning 'Young at Heart', came from speakers mounted on the side of the cabin.

When I was a kid my parents used to play us 'Songs For Swinging Lovers'; I've always loved Frank. I immediately relaxed and smiled appreciatively. I was allowed to do this. I could let someone treat me really nicely without over-thinking or fighting it. I remembered the Love Professor and realised this was one of my tasks: to learn to surrender a little control and trust that my feelings would still be considered. Also that I wasn't the only person who could make events run smoothly.

It was about 7.30 p.m. by now and the sun was still hot and bright. The water seemed to have a soft haze over it, a gentle mist that floated above the protruding rocks making them appear like the head and shoulders of a small crowd dressed in cashmere sweaters.

I was enjoying both Frank and the Moët but I was also very curious about Anders. I didn't want to interfere with his preparations, but maybe he could cope with me chatting whilst he cooked (one of those comfortable relationship intimacies that I really missed).

I walked with my glass over to the cabin door: 'Room for a passenger with a lot of questions?' I asked.

Anders looked up from a chopping board full of smoked fish and lemons, a ramekin of what looked like dill mustard dressing in his hand. He smiled welcomingly. 'I would like that very much,' he replied. 'Please make yourself comfortable. Maybe you would like to look around too?'

The kitchen was surprisingly well equipped: a full-sized stove and fridge, plus, from what I could see, cupboards full of crystal glasses and fine china. The windows were fringed with blue and white gingham curtains, a stack of pressed white linen tablecloths and napkins on a counter. Agreeing that I would set the table outside, I busied myself with cutlery.

Stepping between the lovely kitchen and the picturesque deck looking out onto the water, I found it a little hard to get my head around how perfect this all was.

'Anders, you really do have the most incredible boat,' I told him. 'I'm so happy that you invited me out here, thank you.' Anders, who was ferrying trays of cheese, crudités and fish out to the table, laughed.

'I wish it was my boat,' he said sincerely, 'but I have just borrowed it for tonight. Besides,' he continued, returning to the kitchen and pausing to inspect the open fridge of wine before selecting a bottle, 'haven't you noticed, it's not a boat, it's a floating sauna.'

I laughed out loud, not particularly because I thought he was joking but more because it seemed too farfetched to be true.

He smiled back at me: 'No, I'm serious. Go and have a look.' He gently took my arm and turned me towards the back of the galley kitchen. Still laughing, I walked over, pulled aside the curtain and stepped through into a narrow corridor. To the left, another curtain screened off a little toilet and sink; at the end of the corridor was a glass door, the view beyond it obscured by the steam streaming in rivulets down the length of it. Gingerly turning the handle on the door, I was immediately hit by a blast of heat that made my eyes sting. Anders had been serious, it was a full-size sauna: two long, wooden benches, white towels and gowns folded on the end, a grate filled with glowing coals in the middle. At the end of the room, another glass door looked out onto the rocks on which we were moored. It was incredible: I'd never seen anything like it.

Anders, who was still busy with food, and, I suspect, keeping a respectful distance in the kitchen, looked up when I walked back in. 'Well?' he asked playfully. 'Did you find the sauna?' I rolled my eyes at – what seemed to me at least – the insane opulence of it.

'Anders, that's just crazy,' I stated with incredulity.

'Why crazy?' he asked with a grin.

For a moment, I was worried I would appear a bit of a country bumpkin. 'It just seems so extravagant,' I replied slowly, trying to put my culture shock into words. 'In England, to go to a sauna is a real treat, to go sailing is a bit of an event. To go sailing on a sauna seems the equivalent of bobbing for Ferrero Rochers in a barrel of Moët.'

He laughed at this, appearing as it must have to him like a scene out of *Pygmalion*. He reassured me by putting it into context: 'Don't forget in Sweden we think to take a sauna is very normal. And as for the floating part, this is a coastal city: water is a big part of our lives.'

He seemed gently charmed by my reaction and I in turn felt more relaxed that we had subtly acknowledged our differences but not found them too much of an obstacle. When I had arrived, Anders had scared me. He was too *everything*: handsome, rich, powerful . . . He was still all those things, but I was less fazed by them now that I was starting to get a sense of his personality.

I did still feel apprehensive about one thing, though. 'So, that was why I needed to bring the bikini then?' I asked, trying to keep the I-would-sooner-throw-myself-over-the-side-than-let-you-see-me-in-a-bikini note from my voice.

Suddenly Anders looked awkward too. 'Yes,' he replied. 'I thought it might be romantic, but . . .' my heart leapt at the 'but' '. . . maybe it is too much too soon? Perhaps it is good just to relax and enjoy each other's company?'

I could have kissed him.

And Anders, maybe sharing my performance anxiety, looked relieved too. Picking up the final tray of food and flipping a cloth over his arm, he bowed mockingly. 'If Madam is ready, dinner is served,' he announced with a flourish.

Sitting across from one another at the table on deck, Anders unveiled exquisite dish after dish: strawberries dusted with sugar and threaded onto skewers; hot, tender fish sandwiches dressed in a piquant sauce, each a single mouthful dripping warm olive oil down my forearm; baked cheese coated in crunchy herbs served with a tangy mustard dip. Crisp chunks of bread and brimming bowls of glossy salad acted to counterpoint the rich flavours and textures.

We ate with our fingers, after a while forgetting to wipe them clean on our napkins so that, unnoticed, our wine glasses became imprinted with buttery impressions of our lips and fingertips.

And all the while we talked. We talked about my journey; our friends; our lives and what we thought might be our futures.

Anders was a local events organiser and had just finished his two big shows for the year: a huge arts and music festival and the Gothenburg Grand Prix. He admitted he was exhausted and was looking forward to catching up with friends but mostly to spending time on his own in his very basic log cabin in a nearby forest.

'Really?' I asked in surprise. I must have said it with a little too much surprise, as Anders raised his eyebrows quizzically. 'Sorry,' I said quickly. 'I didn't mean that rudely, I just meant . . .' I groped for a tactful way to say he looked too urban and sophisticated to rough it . . . 'you look like someone with a taste for city life. I can't quite picture you drawing water from a well and combing your hair with twigs.'

He smiled, looking vaguely flattered. 'I need time in my cabin,' he explained. 'It is my retreat; the place I go to recharge my batteries and switch off from everything that pulls and makes demands of me.'

I could understand that. 'I get like that too,' I agreed, 'but I always feel guilty: I spend so much time travelling and away from my friends, I feel I have to put the time in with them when I get back or they get really shirty and difficult.' And, to be fair, I wanted to put the time in too: travelling for work might be wonderful but it was also pretty lonely.

Anders looked a little sad. 'Yes, it is hard with friends as they do not understand that yes, my work is fun, but it is also very demanding and with long hours. As I have become older, I am less troubled by the demands of others and enjoy my own company more and more.' He explained that it had caused his most recent relationship to break up, as they were both travelling extensively for work and spending long periods of time apart. Although he looked hurt by this, I also sensed that

Anders was someone happy to be on his own: reconciled to and actually enjoying his own company in a way I suspected I never could. He had a grown-up son from a marriage long over. When you're a guy and you've had children, maybe that particular need is sated and it's your own company you value for its peace and continuity?

We talked for hours. We talked through dinner; we talked through juicy spikes of chopped tropical fruit; we talked through rich, bitter chocolates; we talked through coffee; we talked through cognac. We talked through Frank Sinatra; U2; Bruce Springsteen; Matt Monro. And as we talked about Gothenburg and London, and relationships we'd loved and relationships that had broken our hearts, jobs we'd adored . . . I knew he was not my Soul Mate. I enjoyed being with Anders and found him very attractive, but ultimately we were looking for a different relationship. He was an educated, passionate man with a true appreciation of fine things. But he was a loner. Being on my own scared me to death: I wanted to meet someone who was open to the possibility of falling in love, running the risk of getting hurt along the way, but still believing there was someone wonderful out there for them. I didn't want to experience life solo, I wanted a Soul Mate to share it with, and was willing to travel the world to find them.

By now it was 3 a.m. There was still light in the sky, but it had a silvery luminosity about it, like it was the moon shining rather than the sun. We both had early starts the next day, Anders to help a friend move house, me to catch a train to Stockholm. He rang another of the ubiquitous captains to come and tow us back to land.

• • •

Back on dry land, a taxi was waiting. We sat very close on the back seat as we drove back to Gothenburg. I felt we had really shared something – I'm certain he did too – but I was unsure exactly what?

When we arrived at my hotel, Anders got out and walked me to the door. We stood looking at each other without speaking, just as we had done all those hours ago on the deck of the boat. But so much seemed to have happened since then. He held my hands in his and studied me, smiling enigmatically. He then took me in his arms and pulled me tightly against him.

'You are a very special woman, Jennifer, it has been an extraordinary evening,' he said in a low voice, tense with emotion. I felt the same way and got quite teary. 'Will you be okay to catch your train?' he asked softly. 'It's early, isn't it?'

I made a face. 'Eight thirty,' I told him. Loosening his hold on me a fraction, he looked at his watch. It was 4 a.m. 'It's fine, though, there are a ton of trains to Stockholm,' I said. 'I can easily get a later one if I'm too tired.' I sensed he knew that nothing was going to happen tonight and he wasn't going to make a move. I'd started thinking that breakfast together would be nice but didn't want to suggest it myself.

'Maybe you'd like breakfast then?' he suggested.

I beamed. 'That would be lovely,' I replied. 'But I know you have to help your friend move.'

A cloud flitted across his face and he frowned for a moment. 'Ah yes, my friend. I will have to call him and see what can be done. In the meantime, though,' and again he held me close, this time brushing his lips across my ear, 'I want to thank you for this evening. It has touched me greatly.'

And then, taking my face in his hands and tilting it up towards his, he looked into my eyes and kissed me very lightly on the lips, touching my mouth gently with his fingers. Complicated emotions played across his face: sadness, indecision, desire? I was unsure but he held my gaze intensely. Mesmerised, I held my breath. Tracing his fingers up my face and stroking my hair, he kissed me lightly once more, then turned and got back into the taxi. The door closed and it pulled away.

I have to admit, I was so tired by now that I was almost relieved to see him go. I desperately needed some sleep. But watching him gaze at me through the window of the taxi, I felt thrilled and tantalised. The whole exchange had been romantic, electric, complicated and unresolved. Would I hear from him tomorrow? Did I want to? Too tired to search for answers, I went up to my room, lay down fully clothed on the bed and fell into a deep sleep until the alarm went off three hours later.

By 9.30 a.m. the next morning, the train had already carried me an hour east of Gothenburg.

When the alarm had gone off, I'd taken a quick shower and packed, listening for the phone the whole time. It hadn't rung. Neither had it when I'd queued to buy the ticket to Stockholm. I'd boarded the train in a dream: it would make a mess of my schedule if he did call and I had to take a later train. But if I couldn't deal with a change in my plans, there was no point in me being on this journey in the first place.

But seriously, were we even compatible? He looked like someone used to women with drawers full of sheer lingerie, who wouldn't need to sit at weird angles to attain the illusion of a perfect fit. My underwear drawers were full of 'favourite' (i.e. unattractive but comfortable) bras, mismatched socks and bars of soap I kept meaning to use but constantly forgot I owned. Was I too old to change? Was I an old dog that could be taught new tricks? It was hard to know. I suspected that in order to meet my Soul Mate I needed to embrace new ideas, but if those ideas were too much of a stretch (or squeeze), I'd never really be happy.

Had Anders known all this? Or had I been putting out 'not interested' vibes? Or was it all part of him being a loner, that he didn't feel the need to follow up? Or maybe he had a whole basket of issues I knew nothing about?

It felt unresolved, but curiously I was fine with that. Although I wanted the satisfaction and closure of him calling, I wasn't troubled by the fact that he hadn't. My self-confidence wasn't freefalling and I didn't feel rejected.

Then my phone rang and I nearly fell off the seat. Was Anders opening it all back up, just as I was going through the rationalising ritual of closing it all down? No, it was Ann-Charlotte, incandescent with curiosity about how the evening had gone. She ooohed and ahhhed and ohmigoded through my account before exploding: 'And so, has he rung?'

'Of course not, you nit, or I wouldn't be on the train,' I retorted in exasperation.

'Well, for goodness' sake, Jennifer, call him. You must call him, what are you waiting for?'

But I wasn't going to call. I'd spent one magical evening with Anders and had enjoyed every moment of it. But I knew that that was it and – unlike the past – I was going to trust my instincts. We'd had fun but we weren't right for each other; more time together wouldn't change that.

Then it suddenly hit me with a jolt: Hey, *I don't get seasick on floating saunas*. Pleased with my new-found expensive tastes and certain it was only a matter of time before I'd be bobbing for Ferrero Rochers, I curled up on my seat and fell into a deep sleep that lasted until the train pulled into Stockholm five hours later.

CHAPTER FOUR

Stockholm, Sweden & Copenhagen, Denmark

You've got to admire the nerve of the Swedes. At a time when the rest of the world was denying it had ever even owned a tank top, let alone worn a pair of beige slacks that fitted snugly around the (pre-thong) bottom, Sweden – in particular Stockholm – was embracing and refining its entire 1970s back catalogue.

Manmade textiles were cherished not vilified, and everything from couture to cutlery came in a variety of bold designs, resplendent in the entire rich spectrum of the colour brown.

And then, as the rest of the world came back around to the idea that the Seventies' look wasn't gauche after all but actually knowing and cutting edge, Stockholm was crowned the most knowing of them all. If cities were people, Stockholm, absorbed in its own fashionable introspectiveness, was Andy Warhol.

I've always wondered if the whole thing was just a double bluff? Was Stockholm really that hip, or was it more a case of not knowing any better than to have a soft spot for flares and flammable fabrics? Isn't it possible it just got lucky that the rest of the world was too insecure to call them out and folded first?

The reason I'd been contemplating design issues was also the reason I'd been reluctant to get a later train: I had a Designer Date in Stockholm.

Date #6: Thomas Sandell, Designer – Stockholm, Sweden

Thomas Sandell was an über-award-winning Swedish designer whose interiors and furniture designs had earned him commissions from the Swedish government to Eriksson technologies. He was even represented in the stores of what was arguably Sweden's most effective Cultural Ambassador: Ikea.

I say the date was with Thomas but it was actually with one of his designs. Stay with me on this: I'll explain.

I was booked into the Hotel Birger Jarl, a hip, modern hotel in which all the rooms had been created by Sweden's top designers. I was staying in one of the two rooms created by Thomas.

I wanted to test my theory that if your job is your most important relationship, will it eventually start to resemble you? I mean, dogs famously take on the appearance of their owners, so is the same true of a job? How much of who you are can be seen in what you do?

Specifically, would I get a true sense of Thomas by staying in a room he'd designed? I'd check into his room, then meet up with him in a couple of days, tell him the impression I had of him from his work and see if I was right.

Feeling groggy from my weird new sleep patterns, and arms aching from dragging my case over cobbled streets (*'God, it can't be much further?'* being the misguided mantra of travellers everywhere), I arrived at the minimalist lobby of the Birger Jarl. As I checked in, the desk clerk, chic and understated in his black suit and 'Bond baddie' wire glasses, handed me a number of messages.

I immediately wondered if one was from Anders? I didn't think he knew where I was staying, so I doubted it, but that didn't stop a flame of hope flaring up. So much for my *trusting my instincts/he's not the one for me* moral high ground.

Scooping up the messages and the key to room 705, I went up in the tiny lift, en route to the first stage of my Designer Date.

A plaque outside my door told me my room was called 'Mr Glad'.

'Oh at last, an upbeat boyfriend,' I thought to myself as I slid my keycard into the lock and let myself in.

The first thing I did when I walked into the space was laugh. The room was long, bright and silly. The windows that ran down the far wall were fringed with white window-boxes of bright green Astroturf. It didn't even look vaguely natural or pastoral, instead it seemed like someone was growing green plastic broom-heads.

In the middle of the room, a white gauze curtain acted as a gossamer screen between the room and a larger-than-life bed, like something out of *Goldilocks and the Three Bears*. The white wall behind the pillow-laden bedhead was covered with black-painted dashes, reminiscent of a cow-print design. The chairs in front of the bed were equally 'who's been sitting in my chair'-esque.

Putting my bags down on the floor, I clambered up onto the bed. The whole room felt friendly and funny, generous and openly welcoming. 'Thank god,' I thought as I bedded down in a nest of pillows and fished the messages out of my coat pocket: I could so easily have ended up in the scary room with the black bed and claustrophobic black-and-white-checked walls.

Hotel rooms are like relationships: intimate and powerful. The good ones nurture, making you feel relaxed and happy. The bad ones get under your skin and fill you with impotent rage.

Well, I was Ms Glad: so far my Design Date was going very well indeed.

I opened the messages. The first one was from Lorna confirming my 10.30 at the Nobel Museum in a couple of days. Second message was from my sister Mandy, just calling to check I was doing okay. Third message was from Maria, my Designer Date Wrangler. 'Uh oh.' I sat up on the bed, sensing bad news.

'Hallo, Jennifer, I hope you have arrived safely and are enjoying the hotel? I wanted to let you know that unfortunately Thomas will be on business in Moscow for the next few days and may not be back in Sweden in time to meet you. He has left his number if you want to call him.'

Not wanting to think about how much it would cost on my mobile phone to bounce my voice via satellite from Sweden to England to Russia to England and back to Sweden, I decided to call tomorrow. It was a lovely evening: I was going to take a walk, find some food, then have an early night. I was dating a Viking tomorrow and needed to catch up with myself.

The hotel was a short walk from the funky Odengatan and grungy Kungsgatan areas, and I soon discovered that my trip to Stockholm coincided with a big Metallica concert and that the fans owned the city that night.

Heavy metal was king in Scandinavia, and Metallica was probably its oldest ruling dynasty. The streets were crammed with roving gangs of teenage boys looking strangely like baby hedgehogs, the backs of their denim jackets spiky with tiny metal studs. The bars spilled over with long-haired bikers – fuelled by excitement and Jack Daniels they roared across the street at each other like Norse warriors going into battle.

I have a bit of a heavy-metal soft spot and ordinarily would have enjoyed the display, even seen it as a warm-up act for the Viking tomorrow. But the atmosphere seemed tense and volatile rather than fun. I stopped at a supermarket for some crisps and biscuits (just because I was travelling was no reason to let my diet go) and settled in the hotel bar with a book and the ubiquitous ambience of Ministry of Sound.

Date #7: Ny Bjórn Gosterssen, Viking and Archaeologist – Birka, Sweden

At 10 a.m. the next morning, I boarded a ferry from the quay outside City Hall and set sail for Birka.

Birka was an island, situated one and a half hours west of Stockholm, along the inland archipelago of Lake Mälaren. Although there wasn't much to see now, this UNESCO site was an important part of the Viking heritage. Founded in the eighth century, Birka had been Sweden's first city and a busy trade centre between Northern Europe and the Baltic Sea. It also contained the largest Viking-age cemetery – over 3000 graves scattered throughout the island – and excavating archaeologists were still uncovering important finds.

It was actually one of the archaeologists I was on my way to date. Each summer a number of them, specialising in

Viking-age studies, stayed on the island as part of a living history display but also to learn more about the Vikings by emulating what is known of their living conditions and habits.

This was all good news for me, as I wanted to date a Viking.

I know this is going to sound terrible and wildly politically incorrect, but I've always thought the Viking image deeply sexy. Ruthless warriors conquering all in their path, Vikings always seemed to be depicted as having big hair, bad attitudes and hard, hot bodies. I realised as a peaceful vegetarian I should have found this image appalling rather than appealing, but there you go, that's hormones for you. Vikings were the stuff of daydreams as far as I was concerned, and this was my chance to find out if my fantasies survived scrutiny.

Stockholm had been really warm when I'd left, but as I walked from the ferry down the metal gangplank into the steady drizzle that enveloped Birka, I didn't need to be told I had got my outfit completely wrong. Although I'd thought to wear a waterproof coat, underneath I was freezing and being bitten to death in my open-toed sandals and capri pants. Rain and mosquitoes? I was failing Viking 101 from the outset.

I followed a gravel path towards a thin copse. The sound of wood being chopped rang energetically through the trees and echoed off the rocks, scaring dark clouds of guttural crows into the darker rain clouds that hung low above Birka. I knew that Ny Björn, archaeologist and part-time Viking, was re-creating a Viking-age kitchen with his fellow archaeologists. Unless Ikea dated back much further than I realised, I guessed that sound was them cutting up trees and building the kitchen from scratch?

As I came through a clearing, I saw a group of people surrounded by tree trunks stripped of their bark and piles of fresh shavings. The stakes were loosely laid out on the forest floor in the shape of a small one-room house. A cold-looking woman in a long woollen dress was crouched at the edge of the clearing, stirring a cauldron over an open fire. The rest of the group were men and stood in the centre of the clearing, blunt saws and axes at their feet. Two wore long, woollen, monk-like robes, cinched at the waist by a long twist of thin rope. The rest wore sturdy leather trousers and boots, topped with rough woollen shirts and tweed jerkins. They all stared at the arrangement of wood, hands on hips and nonplussed expressions on their faces. Maybe it was early Ikea after all?

Catching sight of me, they immediately busied themselves, moving around bits of wood and generally trying to give the impression that they were very busy and knew exactly what they were doing. I was touched that they were bothered about impressing a woman who was dressed as if going for coffee in the south of France, when actually on a rain-sodden island that clearly hadn't seen the sun in months. But I suppose none of us would have been on the island if we didn't have some issues to work through.

One of the group, in leather trousers and a crazy flat cap, smiled and strode towards me. 'Auch, hellooo Jennifer, welcome to Birka,' he called out in a broad Scottish accent. I was confused: I thought my Viking was Swedish – Ny Björn was surely never a Scottish name?

He got close enough to shake my hand, by now so cold it was shaking anyway.

'Hello,' I said. 'Are you Scottish?'

'Ooh, noo,' he replied with a grin. 'But I've done a fair bit of

excavating in the Scottish Highlands, so I've got a bit of a burr.'
He actually had so much of a 'burr' that just saying the word
took him about 15 minutes.

'But you are a Viking?' I asked, looking to establish some
facts, 'or at least you're dressed like one.'

'Yes,' Ny Björn replied, 'or as we assume they dressed, from
the remains we have found in Denmark, York and Northern
Germany.'

Rather than the ruthless warrior I had imagined, Ny Björn
actually looked more like a wandering minstrel. My first
impression was of a tall, thin and engaging man, clearly having
the time of his life on this cold, wet island. Long reddish-blond
hair tied back into a ponytail, Ny Björn had a mischievous-
looking face, punctuated by an energetic goatee that wagged up
and down like a happy dog's tail when he laughed. I knew
straight away that he wasn't my type: he looked like the smart
kid you enjoyed chatting with because you sat next to him in
chemistry but never fancied. I didn't mind, though, I was still
fascinated to learn more about him and what he was doing
here.

Ny Björn and I retreated to a large, cold rock to talk. He
explained that until they had finished building the cook house
in two weeks' time, they would be sleeping rough on rainy
Birka.

I had my first inkling that maybe Vikings were tough not
because it was cute and sexy but because they had to be. And I
– with my pathological hatred of the cold, not to mention
mosquitoes – might not find myself a natural fit into Viking
society. I asked Ny Björn to explain who the Vikings actually
were.

'The word "Viking" is used for all people in the North

cultural sphere, but Vikings were really just a tiny part of the community, mostly those who went raiding and taking things with force,' he replied.

'So they were like unionised burglars?' I asked.

'Exactly, that's the Viking part. They were seen as heroes by the local community who watched them come back loaded up with bounty, but by the end of the Viking age, to call someone "a Viking" was really seen as quite rude.'

'Umm, so as a Viking you could be fairly prosperous, by the sound of it.' I found this reassuring from a comfort point of view, but what about from a dating point of view? The key question (that I was too ashamed to ask outright) was exactly how hot were the Vikings?

I paraphrased: 'We have an image of Vikings as being rough, roguish types and you're sitting here in leather trousers, which have gone on to become the uniform of rock stars. Were Vikings seen to be the sexy rock-star gods of their age?'

That was me – a Pulitzer just waiting to happen.

Happily Ny Björn didn't seem to think the question too idiotic: 'The famous ones, absolutely. You just need to look at the Icelandic sagas to see that – Gretty the Strong . . .'

'Ohhh, I like the sound of Gretty the Strong,' I cooed, all pretence of dignity completely abandoned. 'It sounds like the lead singer in a heavy metal band.'

'Oh yes,' Ny Björn replied with equal enthusiasm, clearly warming to the subject. 'He lived in the early eleventh century and although he was finally killed, he was outlawed for eighteen years and seen as the superstar of his days.'

'Really?' I swooned, knowing absolutely nothing about him, but instantly having a huge crush on him anyway. 'What did he do that was so great?'

'Well,' said Ny Bjórn excitedly, suggesting that if he wasn't a man and a Viking and a thousand years too late, maybe he would have had a bit of a crush on Gretty too, 'he did a lot of things: he was a great warrior, he was really strong, and he was a good wrestler.'

The idea of wrestling cooled my ardour for a moment, conjuring up images of bouffanted fools basted in baby oil working the WWF circuit, but then I had a mental picture of huge leather jerkins being ripped off broad, sweaty chests, as muddy warriors grunted and rolled around on the ground for real. I could barely contain myself. This was great: Vikings were every bit as sexy as I imagined.

'He even killed a ghost once . . .' Ny Bjórn boasted, like a kid getting carried away in front of a playground audience and saying his Dad could beat up all of theirs.

'Huh?' Dragged from my daydreaming, I picked up on Ny Bjórn saying something about ghosts. Ghosts? I wasn't interested in 'ghosts'. Ghosts weren't sexy.

'Oh yes, he was the idol for people back then,' Ny Bjórn continued unabashed. He was on a roll, delighted to have an audience for a subject that he clearly lived and breathed. 'People who were "good at the trade" of being a Viking were pretty much the role model of what men should be back then. There was deep resentment about the Vikings who came to settle around York, or Yorvik, for example, because they took away all the women from the Englishmen there. And the reason was that the Vikings washed every Saturday and combed their hair, etcetera . . . They were really well-groomed by the standards of the times.'

Back on safer ground and feeling that we shared an appreciation, albeit for different reasons, I summed up: 'So can I just clarify, the Vikings wore leather and washed?'

'Yes, yes,' Ny Bjórn replied.

I gave a big happy sigh: 'This just gets better and better.'

We both laughed.

I knew why I was into Vikings, but what about Ny Bjórn? What was the appeal for him? The leather? The machismo? The beards?

'No, no . . .' he spluttered. 'It's . . .'

'Oh, come on, a bit . . .' I persisted, determined not to let him off the hook.

'Well, okay, yes,' he admitted sheepishly. 'But the real attraction is I'm totally into artefacts. I really like "things" and gizmos and how they were made. This is a great way for me to increase my understanding of things made by the Vikings.'

All my instincts went on 'geek alert' when Ny Bjórn said this, but I suppose you don't live on a cold, wet island for the summer unless you are seriously passionate about the place, and who was I to judge? I was passionate about Vikings; Ny Bjórn was passionate about Vikings' 'things', that's all.

'I mean, cooking fish over an open fire in an enamel pot,' he continued, now lost in a romantic revelry of his own, 'it worked back then. If we can make it work here, we can learn from it, that's one of the main reasons I do this.'

I was proving myself to be superficial and shallow: I wanted to go back to hearing about strong men wrestling, not how to cook fish over a fire. I guess that was the thing, though, the guys who were satisfied with leather and machismo were the ones who'd been gathering for the Metallica concert in Stockholm the night before. Here on the island, the fascination was with the life behind the myth. I'd arrived a thousand years too late.

Frozen to the core, I stood up and gently massaged some

blood back into my hands and feet. The ferry back to the mainland had just docked and it was time for me to go. I had loved meeting Ny Bjórn, even if he hadn't turned out to be the Viking of my dreams. I was interested to see how immersed he was in his work – even if my Designer Date didn't end up proving my '*you look like your job*' theory, Ny Bjórn certainly did.

I wished him luck building the cook house and for the summer ahead, then walked woodenly back to the warmth of the boat and the challenge of the next 73 dates.

Sailing back, it was so cold and wet I had to sit below deck. There was one spare seat at a coffee table, where two women leant towards one another, deep in conversation. They invited me to join them and I did, but although busying myself with my book I found it impossible to ignore their conversation.

Sarah was in her thirties, from London but working for the EU in Brussels. Katia was in her fifties, living and working in Stockholm. She was a part-time therapist who also made money selling dicts over the Internet. They were several hours into a conversation about their love lives.

Sarah was torn between a relationship with a cute commitment-phobe in Brussels and a safe-bet/dull-as-ditchwater back at home in London. The thing she was really struggling with, though, was, as she put it: 'We are all born alone and die alone.'

I could see how that would put a damper on the evening.

Katia only had the one relationship to contend with but it was more than enough by the sound of it. She was in love with an ex-Soviet General and was unresolved as to if and how she could accept or change his fierce anti-Semitic views.

The places, faces and details changed but I had had these conversations a million times on the road over the years. Wherever you travel, there will be women struggling to come to terms with the big, emotional issues in their lives. I'd like to think I was less desperate and better dressed about it, but I had been that woman over the years too. Who knows, maybe I was that woman now? As I watched Katia pick up her copy of *The Answer Within: Learning to Love Yourself* and disembark with Sarah, I knew I would never discover how their dilemmas worked out. But maybe that wasn't the point? Having the chance to think and talk about your issues was what was important. Perhaps that was where the idea for my Dating Odyssey had come from, except I didn't want to talk about my past, I wanted to be talked into my future.

When I got back to the hotel, I called Thomas in Russia. We agreed I would email him my impression of him and he would email me back with his response, so, in a way, our date would have taken place in spite of his absence. I got to work immediately:

Okay, so to my impression of you from your design:
   CARING – you wanted me to be happy, and it seemed important to you to try and make me so.
   CALM – the room, although bright, was very tranquil: soft colours and smooth edges; a feeling of space with wide, uncluttered surfaces.
   THOUGHTFUL – The room had 'breathing space', like you were encouraging me to take the time to think about things?

SMART – you knew how to control the mediums and get the effect you wanted. There was a challenge in your 'smartness' though – as if you were testing me to 'get it'.

FUN/SENSE OF HUMOUR – I loved the plastic grass, the black dashes on the wall and the larger-than-life bed – it made me think of *Goldilocks and the Three Bears*!

SENSITIVE – feeling for textures and subtle form.

FEELING THE NEED FOR BOUNDARIES/COMPARTMENTALISING – the curtain at the end of the bed; the divisions created by the juxtapositioning of bold colours in the bathroom.

In short, the sense of you that I got from your room is that you are a kind man and selfless friend. Someone who listens, returns calls no matter how late and puts others before himself. You are reliable and thoughtful: people know you will be the one to bring a lovely dessert to a party or stay sober to drive the car home.

There is a darker side that most don't see, though (the bathroom has an utterly different mood to the bedroom): you feel the need to keep that out of view and compartmentalised 'for yourself'. You see the challenge being from within yourself rather than from others.

You are also a passionate perfectionist, with a strong, restless vision. You cannot rest until a project has been completed to your high standards (this is something you hope for but don't necessarily expect in others).

Or I could be completely wrong!:-)
Thomas, I do hope I haven't said anything
insensitive or too personal here? You came across
as being utterly lovely from your room and I hope
that is clear in what I have just written? I'm
curious as to how right and wrong I am?
Take care, Jennifer

Date # 8: William – Nobel Museum, Stockholm, Sweden

The next morning I walked to Rådmansgatan Station and caught the Tunnelbana metro to Gamla Stan, Stockholm's medieval centre. It was built on an island and was good for lazy sightseers as the charismatic castle, cathedral, parliament buildings and museums were all within spitting distance of each other.

It also meant that it had the highest concentration of tourists, expensive ice-creams and 'customer only' toilets of anywhere in Sweden. I bypassed all of these and headed straight for the Nobel Museum and my 10.30 with William.

William was a student here. He was also the brother of my friend Lorna from Australia. I had more than enough Swedish dates already, but Lorna had begged me to meet up with him:

Think of this as a favour to me, Jen: he doesn't
know a lot of people there as he's pretty shy so
a bit slow making friends. I know he'd love to
have the chance to talk to someone. I'll owe you
big-time.

To be told someone will 'owe you big-time' means you're pretty much being told to expect the worst but for noble reasons. It wasn't the Nobel Date I wanted, but 'its just coffee,' I told myself firmly as I hiked up the steps outside the Nobel Museum. 'It's one morning out of my life.' Get in, date him, and boom – I could be heading out the country and on to the next date in under four hours.

It had just gone 10 a.m. as I walked into the entrance hall. I wanted the chance to have a look around before I met William. The Nobel Museum honoured the 743 Laureates who had tirelessly devoted themselves to the fields of physics, chemistry, medicine, literature, economics and, of course, peace.

The museum was wonderful: as you entered, a huge Orwellian track ran around the ceiling of the entire building, laminated A1 profiles of the Laureates rattling along it on hangers. At various points the track dipped down so you could read the profiles.

The museum was divided into sections by solid screens of what looked like chicken wire covered in Plexiglas, white fibre-optic lights glowing inside. I bumped into the publicist, Anna, who pointed me in the direction of the Nobel electronic Museum, where I wanted to surf the online database of the Laureates' acceptance speeches.

Martin Luther King, Marie Curie, Samuel Beckett, Kofi Annan, Mother Teresa . . . Reading them, I was struck by how much passion these people had poured into the ideals they championed. Out of curiosity, I entered the word 'Love' and searched for references to it amongst the speeches.

The screen filled and I scrolled down. The Laureates' love of ideas; their love of humanity; freedom; god; science and discovery; home, even their love of cars. It struck me very powerfully that this kind of love was a dedication: a devotional love, abstract, not interpersonal. There was no mention of romantic love; no real celebration of people other than as concepts or ideals.

Clearly the Laureates were accomplished, unique people. But was being accomplished and unique at the expense of something more everyday and vital to our happiness? In short, to be a great idealist did you need to be pretty self-centred and emotionally unavailable? Were they just a smarter, more noble version of me: choosing a job over a partner? But since they were making the world a better place rather than writing about where to go on holiday, did that make it okay?

Another thing that really struck me, was how few of the Laureates were women: only 31 out of a total of 743. What did that say about gender roles and the pursuit of ideals? Were women more interested in people, and men in ideas, or was the judging system just crap?

But it was time to meet William. As I walked back out to the lobby, I bumped into Anna again. I asked her if she thought it was true the Laureates didn't value romantic or personal love?

Anna smiled wryly: 'You know, when I started working at the Nobel Museum, I was told: "Here you are not loved for being witty or beautiful, you are loved for your ideas." Most of the people associated with the Nobel Prizes – winners and staff – give up their families and well-paid jobs so that they might explore and prove their ideas. It takes a certain type of selfishness to be so dedicated.'

So it was as true for Nobel Prize winners as it was for guidebook publicists: too much work wrecks your love life.

William and I had arranged to meet at the Kafé Satir. Modelled on Café Museum, the Viennese intellectuals' hang-out in the early 1900s, it was where the Nobel Museum encouraged you to debate and reflect. I figured if William didn't have much to say for himself, at least there'd be enough going on around to distract us. The café was small; I should have no problem spotting William: brown collar-length hair, bookish and 'normal' looking according to Lorna.

There was only one person in the café when I arrived. Sunk low in his chair, huge booted feet propped up on the table, a young man with long, greasy hair slouched with his eyes shut and his mouth open. The serving staff stood tensely behind the counter, watching him with open hostility, outraged at the bad manners, worse attitude and unforgivable hair.

This could not be William.

I don't know why I even bothered thinking that, because I instantly knew that it was. This heavy-metal dating disaster was 'shy', 'normal' William. And from the look and smell of his T-shirt, he hadn't been home since the Metallica concert the night before.

Rather than feeling worried or intimidated, I felt like someone's Mum arriving home unexpectedly to find her son bunking off school and reading Dad's hidden stash of porn.

Walking over to where William sat oblivious to my stern judgement, I gave the staff an '*I'll deal with this*' look. Putting my bag and coat on the table next to William's feet, I sharply rapped on the sole of one of his boots. His eyelids flickered, his brow creased, but he continued to sleep, the studs on his jacket rising and falling gently with each deep breath.

'William,' I said crisply. This time his eyes snapped open and he looked around in alarm, completely disorientated, clearly not recognising where he was. 'William,' I repeated, this time a little more gently but still with a '*wait till I get you home, young man*' tone to my voice. He blinked twice and blankly focused his gaze in my direction. Like being behind a learner driver waiting and waiting to pull out on a busy roundabout, sometimes you have to give them a nudge or you'll be there forever. 'William!' I shouted, knocking him hard on the shoulder.

Pausing as if manually connecting brain with body, William shambled into life. Crashing his legs off the table onto the floor, he stumbled to his feet. As the chair toppled over noisily behind him, the counter staff flinched collectively. The smell of cigarettes and alcohol was overwhelming. William looked at me uncertainly: he knew he was expected to speak but was obviously having difficulty knowing exactly where he was and what he was meant to say.

I revved my engine and shunted him into the oncoming traffic.

'William, I am Jennifer,' I said briskly, Mary Poppins suddenly my default personality.

'Yes?' he asked dully, something about this sounded familiar, he just needed more time to work out what?

'I am a friend of your sister Lorna's: she arranged for us to meet.'

William was suddenly completely in the moment, totally lucid and very much awake. 'Hey,' he said slowly, looking at me attentively as if seeing me for the first time. 'You're that chick going round the world banging all those guys,' he reported matter-of-factly. I sensed all movement behind the counter come to an abrupt halt; the kitchen staff stopped watching William and – like spectators at Wimbledon – collectively turned their attention to me, their faces alight with frank incredulity and wonder.

Although the café was designed to foster the lively exchange of ideas, I doubted very much that this was what they had in mind.

'William,' I said witheringly, summoning all the dignity I could manage. 'I am not – as you say – "banging guys around the world", I am on a quest, travelling the world in search of my Soul Mate.' I snorted at the ridiculousness of his statement, as much to convince the staff in the kitchen as William.

'But you bang some of the guys, right?' he asked hopefully.

I rolled my eyes. I didn't have the time or energy to explain the niceties of my Odyssey to some teenage boy optimistically and inappropriately awash with hormones. With a dignified sniff, I picked up my bag and coat. Casting a disdainful eye in the direction of the counter staff, who by now had given up all pretence of rearranging the chocolate biscuits and were openly following our conversation, I thanked William for meeting me.

'I'll tell Lorna you looked, ummm . . .' I struggled for a suitable description '. . . well.'

William just stared at me, his unwashed face puckering into folds of exasperation as he realised I was going, and he was not coming with me. 'Maaan,' he groaned in frustration, 'I only came here because I thought I was going to get laid. I'm telling you, there is no way I am ever doing my sister a favour again.'

Doing my sister a favour?

Whatever did he mean? I was the one on the mission of mercy here. Had Lorna given him the impression *I* was the one who needed help? Her desperate friend destined to end up Internationally Single, but if he could help make up the numbers, at least there'd be a shag in it for him? Could she really have said that?

I never got the chance to ask, because William, like a child who's been told 'no more *Robot Wars* until your room's tidy', had already stomped out the café and up the street, without so much as a backward glance.

I raised my eyebrows and let out a long, steadying breath. That – I said to myself – was what happened when you dated a Viking. Giving the kitchen staff an '*at least wait until I am out of earshot*' look, I left the museum for my hotel, where I packed and left for Denmark.

The man sitting in front of me on the plane to Copenhagen was easily the most nervous flyer I've ever seen in my life. He puffed and panted through gritted teeth like he was flying Air Lamaze. At one point I was woken by him shrieking 'Oh My God!' involuntarily, before returning to his steady panting again.

No one watched the film: we all watched him.

I shouldn't have taken this as a bad omen, but I did. I was in an ugly mood. I still felt irritated, less by how William had been and more by what Lorna might have said. Although I only had two dates in Copenhagen, I'm afraid to say I didn't feel in the mood for either of them.

Date #9: Lars – The Free State of Christiania, Copenhagen, Denmark

My mood was not improved by getting soaked on the way to Christiania. It was dead in the water by the time I'd finished dating Lars.

Christiania was on the site of a redundant military barracks on the edge of Copenhagen city centre. Taken over by squatters in 1971 and declared a 'free state', it was now home to around 800 people, with another 700-odd who worked within the community.

Christiania was a self-governing, car-free society that functioned as a collective. It ran its own school, recycling programmes and small businesses that catered to both residents and the tourists who flocked here (mainly to buy the pot openly sold on 'Pusher Street').

Its very existence was a challenging expression of civil liberties. I had loved the sense of community I got from living in a housing co-op in Leeds when I was a student. Could my Soul Mate be found in this community?

My date Lars had just split up with his girlfriend. His friend Vessie, who was a friend of my friend Kirk, thought it would cheer Lars up to meet me. I have no idea if it cheered Lars up, but it depressed the hell out of me. 'I'm only here so I don't have to be on my own at home,' he told me bluntly the second we met.

Our date consisted of three hours walking along Christiania's muddy paths in the pouring rain, as Lars poured his heart out. His girlfriend had left him for someone else; he was a good guy who couldn't catch a break; she'd never appreciated him, he was too good for her; what was so great about macho guys anyway . . . ?

Regardless of the fact that Lars had just been dumped, to me he seemed one of those people who had a horrible, negative attitude anyway. When we parted company, I felt like asking for his ex-girlfriend's phone number just so we could go out for a drink together and slag him off.

Date #10: Paul – Tivoli Gardens, Copenhagen, Denmark

I slept badly after my date with Lars. His negativity weighed down on me and made me feel despondent about my own chances of success – not because he had been unlucky in love but because I feared I might be unlucky enough to have another 71 dates just like him.

But my next date was with Paul, a chef who worked in one of the 'It' restaurants in Copenhagen. We'd both been too busy to talk or email, but my friend Georgia had arranged for us to meet on the Kissing Bench at Tivoli Gardens, the Victorian amusement park full of old-fashioned rides, busking orchestras and beautiful flower gardens. It was one of my favourite places and I knew it would cheer me up.

But four hours later, as I sat solo on the Kissing Bench in the pouring rain, I realised that rather than being cheered up, I was being stood up. Paul was a no-show. I shouldn't have been as upset about it as I was, but I took it really badly and very personally: not only did he not want to see me, he couldn't even be bothered to let me know he wasn't coming. Too embarrassed to get in contact with Georgia and too wretched to do anything else, I went back to the hotel, ran a hot bath and cried.

CHAPTER FIVE

France

I love Scandinavia: like the Dutch, its people seem liberal and smart without making a big deal about it. In complete contrast, the French national identity has an air of disdainful elegance, like old money at Ascot. But the back-to-back dating disaster in Copenhagen, preceded by William in Stockholm, made me sincerely glad I was heading for the complicated, cosmo-politanism of Paris. I felt like a complete change of scene and atmosphere.

The last time I had come to Paris was Kelly's and my four-year anniversary. After extensive nagging, he'd agreed to go to the Buddha Bar. Apparently, the beer was too expensive, the staff too fashionable: it hadn't been a great success.

If I hadn't been travelling for the purpose of dating, I think I may have resented that so many cities around the world seemed to contain little Kelly booby traps – painful or irritating memories that exploded out of nowhere. But I was determined not to be one of those people who stayed involved with the bitterness longer than they'd been with the person who'd actually caused it.

And if I step off my martyr's pedestal for a moment to be honest, Kelly wasn't the only man I thought of when I came to Paris. Wild, sexy and dead, I also had a thing going on with Doors' singer Jim Morrison. Over the last five years I must have visited his grave, just inside the eastern edge of the Périphérique, half a dozen times, either to make programmes or with friends.

I've always been fascinated that Jim Morrison – a parallel Elvis: sexy, iconoclast gone to seed – ended his days in Paris. Erotic and playful as he, Paris was also cultured and subtle. As the Lizard King became the Lard King and tired of himself, maybe that was what drew him here?

I suspect that as a boyfriend Jim Morrison would have been an absolute nightmare: unfaithful, self-indulgent and often cruel. But he was also a lithe sex god who created the sound-track to my teen years, and the affinity I felt with him ran deep. I decided to spend the day with him at his grave in the stately Père Lachaise cemetery, to try and pinpoint the attraction.

Date #11: Jim Morrison, The Doors – Cimetière du Père Lachaise, Paris, France

Père Lachaise was the most visited cemetery in the world and has been a fashionable address for the afterlife since its inception in 1804. It was Napoleon who converted what was originally a slum neighbourhood into a vast cemetery, arranging to have Molière reburied here at the 'launch party'. Its reputation as the 'in' place for the 'over' crowd thus established, its million residents now included Gertrude Stein, Edith Piaf, Oscar Wilde, Pisarro and Proust. But as you made your way up from the metro, the proliferation of signs, maps and memorabilia overwhelmingly pointed to Jim Morrison being the grave célèb here.

Finding Jim Morrison's grave was quite tricky: Père Lachaise still had all the winding avenues and tree-lined boulevards from the days when people lived (rather than died) here and it was easy to get lost. Getting lost wasn't such a hardship though, as the cemetery was a moving and beautiful site: tombs varied from Art Deco Egyptian pharaohs and larger-than-life muscular bronze angels to austere black granite obelisks, painstakingly scrubbed mirror-clean by stooped middle-aged women every single day.

Like Cemetery Number 1 in New Orleans, this was a place where the living had an ongoing relationship with their dead. And nowhere was this more true than at Jim Morrison's grave.

I was grateful for the short shadows cast by the broad trees as I walked through the cemetery looking for Jim Morrison. It was only 10 a.m. but the sun already probed like a dentist's drill, burrowing ruthlessly into the top of my head. The air was hot and still; a raven perched on the marble head of a weeping Madonna watched me balefully as I marched by full of purpose. My daypack was heavy with bottled water, the Doors biography my sister Mandy bought me when I was fifteen, sunblock and other bits to get me through the day. The bag bunched my cotton skirt up at the back but sweat glued it to my legs, preserving my modesty in this place of rest.

Turning the corner of a wide boulevard, hidden amongst the headstones and next to a large tree trunk, I found Jim. Or rather the crowd around Jim.

Three nineteen-year-old boys were camped on one of the tombs, the ubiquitous backpackers' banquet of plain French bread and Orangina spread before them, plus an assortment of boxed CDs and Walkmans. Two were baseball-capped, fresh-faced Americans, the other a baggy-jumpered, straggly haired Frenchman. They had one set of headphones between them and were taking turns, passing it around like a joint.

'"LA Woman" . . . that's my favourite song. Maaan this song is amazing,' said the first young American, transported by the music in his headset.

The second one nodded hard: 'Yeah, it's awesome. My brother's in a band and he can play that solo.'

'Maaan,' the first breathed hard, looking deeply impressed, 'he must be really good.'

The French guy – clearly a bit more of a technician – started banging on about recording techniques and living in a room lined with eggboxes. Sensing he was losing their attention, however, he asked: 'You know the Beatles?'

'Yeah, awesome,' the two Americans chorused in unison. Then, seeing the The Who badge on his bag: 'Have you got Tommy?' one asked.

'No, but I meant to watch the film,' the French boy replied slightly defensively.

All nodded sagely: so much music, so little time.

But their discussion was suddenly disrupted by a furious Frenchman bursting from between the trees and marching over: '*Ce que faites-vous ici?*' he bellowed. 'What is wrong with you that you are sitting on the burial place of the dead eating your lunch? Have you no respect?'

The boys quailed and looked uncomfortable. The Frenchman, too agitated to remain still, angrily paced on the path a few feet away. The two Americans turned frowning to the French boy: 'Man, was he talking to us? What did he say?'

The French boy shrugged sullenly, sharing their bewilderment but more affected having understood the diatribe: 'Oh,' he replied, feigning nonchalance, 'he said we were sitting on graves.'

The American boys looked shocked, as if it hadn't occurred to them: 'So should we, like, get off?'

'Umm, yes, I think so,' the French boy replied quietly, pulling a lock of long, brown hair from his eyes but making no attempt to move. The three of them looked at each other uncertainly, then all went back to studying the CDs laid before them.

Back on the path, the Frenchman became incandescent. 'Ah,' he snorted in disgusted English. 'Tourists! What do you know?' and he stormed off, leaving clouds of dust hanging over the gravel path in his wake. The teenage boys left maybe half an hour later.

In the five hours I stayed by or near the grave, around a hundred people visited. The Frenchman was right to say that the tourists were insensitive but he was wrong to say they lacked respect. It was the very reason they were here: out of love and respect.

Jim Morrison's grave was unimposing. A plain, squat headstone stated without fuss that James Douglas Morrison lived from 1943 to 1971. The grave itself was a shallow granite frame around a sandy pit, maybe 3 ft by 6 ft.

Every mourner stepped up to the grave with a sense of the theatrical, individual players each featuring in their own one-act drama. A group of Latino boys in gang insignia, silently regarding the grave, their heads bowed in fresh grief as if Jim Morrison had died yesterday, not 30 years ago. The tallest of the group took a bottle of bourbon from his bag. Passing it between them, they each took a swallow. Taking an extra swallow, the leader then poured a measure directly onto the grave before placing the bottle gently on the headstone. Standing straight, he touched two fingers to his heart, his lips, then onto the headstone. One by one each of the gang repeated the sequence. Ritual completed, without a word they turned and walked away.

A Midwestern couple in their forties pointed to the grave and poignantly told their three teenage children: 'When we were your age, he meant everything to us. We wanted you to meet him.'

A woman in her twenties, dreadlocked and comprehensively tattooed, stood in the shadows, looking angry and smoking a joint. With each deep inhalation she stared moodily at Jim's grave, her face a furious mask of intimate thoughts. Watching disdainfully as the latest group left, with an angry sigh she stalked over to the deserted grave. Standing before it thoughtfully, she took one last drag on the joint then flicked it burning into the grave. It landed on a single red rose and immediately melted through the plastic wrapping, coming to rest amongst the fragile petals. It glowed for a moment, one amongst the litter of cigarettes and half-smoked joints that already made the grave resemble a pub ashtray at closing time. She watched until it dimmed and died, then, muttering something inaudible, slunk off into the maze of graves.

Finding a lull in mourners, I put down my bag and walked over to the grave myself. It wasn't just bourbon bottles and cigarettes, the grave was full of poems and dedications, some written on purple metro tickets:

Thanks for all the hours of music and memories.
  Jenni, Cape Town xxx

Some on cigarette papers:

Jim, thanks for sharing your talent with the world!
   The Molina Family, San Antonio, Texas

Some short and sweet:

Jim, it's been a pleasure meeting you. Thanks for all the great times.
You've been an inspiration to my life.
   Rest in Peace, love Nicholas

Some so very long:

> *Amongst the Ants*
> *I sit my stand*
> *And spill the words*
> *Clean from my head*
> *Next to your grave*
> *I sit and write*
> *There is no rush*
> *I have the tree*
> *You rest in peace* [*pieces* crossed out]
> *And now so do I*
> *For both my eyes*
> *Have seen your reside*
>
> *Rest in Peace, Jon*

As I read the dedications, I wondered why I – and all these other people – nurtured such enduring love for Jim Morrison? The Love Professor had described successful, healthy relationships as ones in which our positive traits are reflected back by our chosen partner. By choosing Jim Morrison, were we claiming some part of his creative, sexual vitality as our own? By liking Jim were we saying we were like Jim?

Or could it simply be that we didn't want to forget how good it felt to be young, passionate, misunderstood and alive? Music is a powerful memory and mood trigger and Jim Morrison was a Door that took us back to that time and state.

There was also the fantasy element. The Love Professor said we all had to know and nurture *the real me* to be truly happy. But I loved fantasising about the *imaginary me*: the person I could but never will be. Apart from travelling, the best time for this was at the start of a relationship: unhindered by routine or too much information about the other person, you imagine both of you doing all the things you've always dreamt of. You see yourself as a person who goes horse riding every weekend (you've never been on a horse in your life); taking a Spanish evening class together (you miss enrolment); wearing trainers less and stockings more (ummmm). Fine, what does it hurt to savour the thought you'll get a chance to do all these things, whether you actually do them or not?

And if I was shacked up with someone as crazy and unstructured as Jim Morrison, surely the conversation would be elevated above whose turn it was to put the kettle on, or how bad Saturday night TV was these days? His energy would inspire and stretch me.

Yes, yes, I'm a feminist too: I know I shouldn't need to be in a relationship to do these things but it makes it easier.

So, how much of my love was about Jim Morrison and how much was about me? Did I imagine a relationship with Jim's juju would allow my – as yet untapped – potential to be the coolest, smartest, sexiest person on the earth to be realised? Was I interested in him as a person or just for what he could do for me?

But I was pulled from my introspection by two Australian women walking over to where I was sitting. 'Aww, I'm really sorry to disturb you,' one asked awkwardly, 'but would you mind taking our photo? We want to see what we look like Post-Jim.'

I smiled as I took the camera: whatever ego issues I was suffering from, I was clearly not suffering alone. The girls stood either side of the grave and smiled into the camera as I took their picture.

Amanda and Luciana were both in their late twenties and spending the summer visiting France and the UK. When I told them I was here to date Jim and why, they both squealed their approval. 'Oh I know why you would want to do that,' Amanda burst out, squeezing my arm in further emphasis, 'he was really gorgeous, really wild too. Sexy and crazy.' She ran her tongue over her lips as she said it, momentarily lost in thought.

Luciana sounded far more downbeat. 'Men aren't like that any more,' she observed ruefully.

They asked me some questions about my journey. Was I going to Sydney? I confirmed I had several dates lined up there. 'Oh, good luck,' Luciana said bitterly. 'And trust me you'll need it finding a man there.'

This shocked me a little as Luciana was gorgeous: a voluptuous, curvacious 'Italian' figure topped with a glossy cloud of curly brown hair and fantastically trashy earrings. She saw me noticing her figure and looking surprised. 'I dressed up for Jim,' she said with a sly smile. Amanda laughed, picking up on my 'you get more attention away from home' theory: 'You know you're so right,' she agreed. 'It is just incredible how much more the guys notice you here. And in a good, fun way, not sleazy.'

Luciana chipped in. 'Like those guys last night,' she said excitedly, nudging Amanda. Luciana turned back to me: 'We were walking past some steps and these guys were just hanging out. Anyway . . .' Luciana and Amanda were both in fits of giggles by now '. . . when they saw us, they called out, "You are beautiful, come and kiss us." It was so nice, so cheeky and flattering. It'd never be that way at home.'

We all sighed together, thinking about how much fun cheeky guys could be.

And that made me realise, as much as I enjoyed the fantasy of Jim and the life I'd have with him (if . . . you know . . . he wasn't dead), I actually liked the life I already had. I had fun being me; I didn't want to morph or be moulded into someone else. What I needed was to find someone else like me: a Soul Mate I could relate to.

And I wanted fun with cheeky guys. I wanted to laugh and feel sexy. It was time to bury my dead and make a date with the living.

Date #12: Olivier – Paris, France

I was booked into a hotel in the Marais, my favourite Parisian neighbourhood. Touristy in parts, the area was mostly elegant and couture but, thankfully, its relentless chicness softened by pockets of pretty squares fringed with pungent fromageries and cafés stocked with casually fantastic pastries.

I rushed back and changed in a hurry: I had an hour before my next date.

Showered and dressed in my new baby-blue linen top (I had

spotted a gorgeous boutique on the corner of my street and raced in on the way back from the metro), I took the short walk from my hotel to the Place des Vosges. This elegant square of houses dated back to 1612, and amongst its residents were Richelieu and Victor Hugo. The park at its centre was once used for duelling; tonight it would be used for dating: this was where I was to meet Olivier, Date # 12.

I was very curious about Olivier. He seemed extremely French: flawlessly educated and virulently contemptuous. He worked in the French film industry and would leave long gaps between emails as he (and he described it with 'pulling teeth' loathing) had to be at meetings everywhere from Brussels to Cannes. His emailed photos were taken from about 500 yards away, the only discernible features a crazy mop of dark hair and severe horn-rimmed glasses.

I was curious about him, but didn't feel I knew or had developed much of a rapport with him. He admitted in one email he could: *stay mute and prostrated for hours, not even noticing someone is sitting by my side . . . depends on my mood . . .*

This might have made me nervous but for the fact that the date had been set up by my friend Muriel, a smart, exuberant French woman living in London. I knew any friend of hers was going to be worth meeting.

It was a warm early summer's evening and the pavement cafés were already full of loquacious Parisians enjoying the sunshine and unhurriedly sipping glasses of red wine (the French were restrained enough to order wine by the glass – to the binge-drinking Brits this felt about as logical as buying a house by the room).

I spotted Olivier as soon as I walked into the park, but skirted around a statue so I could check him out before he saw me. First impression: tall, slim without being skinny, but glasses and hair – as in the photos – the dominant features. Was an evening with Olivier going to be hard work? I took a deep breath and stepped out from behind the statue to introduce myself.

As he turned to greet me, I was shocked by something I had not prepared myself for.

He was cute.

Under that mop of dark-brown curly hair and severe glasses, Olivier had gorgeous green eyes, clear, freckled skin and a fine nose. I smiled instinctively: I'd been prepared for an interesting, possibly argumentative date; I was quick to revise my opinion and put my 'flirt face' on.

'Hi, I'm Jennifer,' I said unnecessarily (we'd both seen each other's photos), holding my hand out to shake his. Olivier's hand was warm and firm in mine.

A middle-aged man a few feet away waited patiently for his dog to finish adding yet more crap to the park. He whiled away the time watching us with a neutral expression. We were clearly on a blind date; maybe he was glad he was beyond all that? Maybe he was sad that on such a beautiful evening his only companion was a crapping dog?

I tended not to get too nervous about the dates (apart from Anders, of course), as I knew it was actually harder on the Dates than it was on me. Up until they met me, the Dates treated the occasion as a sort of *community challenge*, as they, their Date Wrangler and gradually most of their friends became involved in designing The Perfect Date. My date-a-thon was like a street carnival where each Date and their group wanted to make and show off the best float.

My date-a-thon also revealed the competitiveness of men: they were so concerned with imagining what the other 79 might have arranged and whether they could do better, they quite forgot that when the time came they'd be on their own dating a real live woman (me). As a result, during the first 30 minutes of the date, the guys tended to suffer from DRI (Dating Reality Impact) and all my energies were focused on getting them safely through the transition period until they felt normal enough to *be* normal.

However, because I hadn't expected Olivier to be good-looking – plus he was French so didn't care what I thought anyway – I was caught off-guard and went straight into full-blown DRI myself. I launched into a manic account of how my mother and sister used to live in Paris and wasn't the weather great and wasn't Paris better than London because it was so much smaller and Oh I love the Marais, there are so many cute shops . . . I listened with horror as the anecdotes and opinions poured uncontrollably out of me at top speed. Olivier studied me with an amused expression, which was all he could do as my jabbering made it impossible for him to get a word in.

But suddenly, just as I'd launched into an excruciatingly superfluous story about bees, the wise words of the Love Professor floated – Obi-Wan Kenobi-esque – into my head: '*Jennifer . . . Jennifer . . . just let it happen. Use all your senses . . . take in whatever comes . . .*'

And I stopped talking.

Olivier waited to see if I would start again. I didn't. So he smiled and asked: 'Would you like a drink?'

I nodded gratefully, we left the park and began our date.

• • •

It was a wonderful evening. Olivier and I wandered along the banks of the Seine, stopping for glasses of wine, dinner in a little bistro, coffee in a café by now lit by moonlight, whisky in a crowded after-hours bar . . . We walked and talked through the romantic streets of the Marais; crossed the Seine to the touristy twists and turns of the Latin Quarter and back again through the crowded club-land of rue de Lappe and Bastille.

Olivier was every bit as challenging as I imagined and ten times as interesting. He had lived and studied all over Europe and was passionate about art and films. His personality was like a medieval city of switchback streets opening up into beautiful courtyards: impenetrable and magical in turns. And as he opened up, he became more tactile: touching my hand to make a point or standing close behind me and reaching over my shoulder to show me something fascinating and obscure about a building.

I had decided after Denmark that I was only going to stay out late or agree to see the Date again if I felt he was a genuine prospect. It was now after 3 a.m. and I still felt intrigued and utterly entertained by Olivier. I was also attracted to him and felt comfortable enough with the pace at which things were progressing to anticipate with pleasure the French Kiss that I was confident would come at the end of the date.

By 3.30 a.m., we were both completely talked out and I was glad when Olivier offered to walk me back to my hotel. I'd had a wonderful evening and felt really good about seeing him the next day if he asked. It was the perfect time to end the date.

Thirty minutes later, we stood together outside my hotel, our faces gently lit by the fading streetlights and the approaching dawn that now warmed the sky.

Olivier admitted, 'I really did not know what to expect from this evening, Jennifer, but it has been extremely enjoyable. It is unlike me to talk of myself so much; you are charming and very good company.' Studying me through his glasses, his eyes were dark and intent. He was about four inches taller than me, so when I told him how much I had enjoyed the evening too, I had to tilt my face up towards his to answer, smiling warmly into his eyes.

I watched his mouth as he talked: I was going to get kissed and I was feeling really good about it.

'If you have time, I would very much like to see you again tomorrow?' Olivier asked.

'I would like that too,' I replied simply.

Olivier smiled. 'It is agreed then.'

I relaxed. He smiled at me, I smiled at him. I waited happily, I was in no rush.

'Umm, okay, then I shall see you tomorrow,' Olivier suddenly blurted and with an awkward half-shrug he turned and walked off down the street.

Huh?

I watched in astonishment as my cheeky-guy fun vanished around the corner. What had just happened? Why hadn't he kissed me? I shook my head vigorously, as if trying to shake some sense into it. I didn't understand: why hadn't he kissed me? We'd liked each other. He'd asked me out again. Why didn't he want to kiss me? Why?

I suddenly felt furious with him: how could he do this? I'd stayed out most of the night with him and would now undoubtedly spend the rest of the night wide awake, agonising over why he hadn't wanted to kiss me. I mean, I know he didn't have to, but I was really sure he'd wanted to. What terrible thing had I said or done that had made him change his mind? Could I isolate the thing which had made me an Unkissable?

One thing was certain: I had no intention of ever seeing him again. I know that sounds harsh but I have absolutely served my time dating men who are hard work and take tons of understanding. I was here on my Soul Mate Mission and that did not include second dates with men who disturbed my self-confidence and peace of mind by treating me as an Unkissable.

I said all this over breakfast the next morning to my friends Jilly and Stevie who were over from London for the weekend.

'Oh, Jen, that's not fair,' Jilly remonstrated as we divided up the last buttery flakes of croissant, trying to catch the eye of the waitress so we could order some more. 'He sounds lovely, you must see him again.'

'Bugger that, why must I?' I protested indignantly. 'The whole point of what I'm doing is to find someone who'll make me happy and not invest time in guys who DON'T any more.'

'Maybe he's a slow starter?' Stevie observed reasonably, whilst continuing unsuccessfully to flag down the waitress.

They were being sweet and lovely. I knew they wanted the best for me: to see me happy and with a boyfriend again. But if I was going to ignore my instincts and make excuses for someone from the first date, I might as well have saved myself all this effort and settled for the first ('you've got') male that came along. I knew from personal experience that to give him another chance was just courting trouble and disappointment.

'Stevie,' I said firmly, licking the delicious pear confiture from my fingers and pouring out more coffee. 'I really appreciate you saying that and maybe you're right, but it's not like I'm upset because he didn't propose to me. It's a kiss we're talking about here. It was a date, we liked each other. It shouldn't have been that difficult.'

But none of us had had much sleep the night before and the task of getting the waitress to serve us turned into a major production. Soon the topic of whether I should see Olivier again or not was forgotten by everyone.

Except me. When my phone rang, I pushed it deeper into my handbag and nudged my bag under the table with my foot until the ringing stopped.

Date #13: Max – Paris, France

I would have dearly loved to have gone shopping that afternoon, or even to have popped back to the hotel for a quick nap, but I had a date in a few hours with Max, an old friend of Clare's, one of my neighbours from home.

Max was a lecturer in art history at one of our neighbourhood schools and Clare had been trying to orchestrate a meeting for months. He was spending half-term taking a school group around Paris and when Clare heard I would be over the same week she nearly broke her fingers trying to dial his number and lock us into a date before I could come up with a reason why it wasn't possible.

It wasn't that I hated the thought of meeting Max, he just didn't particularly sound my type: a little too earnest and proper. But Clare was determined we should meet and I had run out of energy to keep persuading her otherwise.

Max had an afternoon off from the kids, so we had arranged to meet outside Varenne metro station at 2.30 p.m. He was easy to spot: around 6 ft 5 ('You can't say he's too short for you,' Clare boasted triumphantly) and extremely thin with a long, pale but boyishly eager face, crowned with an explosion of curly red hair. There was a Cambridge University scarf wrapped tightly around Max's neck (even though the temperature must have been about 70°F) and he was sniffing vigorously.

He beamed as soon as he saw me and stalked straight over: 'Ah, Jennifer, what a pleasure, what an absolute pleasure to meet you.' He smiled and sniffed, nervous and excited in equal measures. Towering over me like a huge praying mantis, he bent his upper body down to kiss me 'hello'. I wasn't prepared, he misjudged my height, and at the last minute I over-compensated and stretched up to meet his kiss.

It was an awkward mess: I got a mouthful of shirt as I ended up kissing his collar; he missed my head altogether, his mouth sucking the air two inches right of my cheek. He sniffed and laughed in embarrassment, but as he pulled his head self-consciously away, he caught one of my big silver hoop earrings in his hair and ripped it clean out.

I let out a high-pitched yelp of pain and surprise. Max frowned in alarm: he had no idea why I was shrieking, he also had no idea that one of my earrings was dangling incongruously from his tight red curls.

Following my astonished stare, he gingerly reached into his hair and found my earring. He beamed in confusion, now sniffing furiously, like a beagle at customs angling for a promotion. 'Ah, well, yes,' he stammered, 'I, ermm, well, but . . . this must be yours . . .' Max pulled the earring from his hair and plummeted from his great height back down towards me. I realised with horror he intended to try and put it back in.

'No,' I shrieked automatically, taking a sharp step backwards, my hand clamped protectively over my throbbing ear. 'I
mean . . . please don't worry,' I managed to say, slightly less
dramatically. 'I'll take it, it's fine.' And I took the earring from
between his long, outstretched fingers and dropped it out of
sight into my handbag.

Words didn't exist to describe how much I was hating today.
I mean really, really, really hating it. It wasn't really poor Max's
fault and it was important that I didn't make him feel it was.
You can't blame someone for not being your type; it was myself
I blamed for giving in to Clare – she had the married person's
compulsion to match up singles, the way some tuck in a
stranger's sticking-out shirt label on buses: the desire for
neatness is greater than their sense of tact.

But this wasn't working. In fact, at that moment, it seemed
the whole premise my Odyssey was based on wasn't working.
Clearly, there were far more 'wrongs' than Mr Rights out there.
And I was wrong about the ones I thought were 'rights', as they
all turned out to have something wrong with them in the end.
Was I wasting my time? Should I be back in London either
trying harder or accepting my single life? Did this mission have
any chance of success at all?

At school when I was about five, I picked up someone else's
jumper by accident. One of the teachers noticed and asked me
to give it back. Perversely, I insisted it was mine, and before
anyone could take it away I tried to put it on. It belonged to a
girl half my size, though, and the jumper got stuck over my
head. Embarrassed at being caught out, enraged at not having
pulled off the bluff and very, very agitated at having my head
trapped in someone else's jumper, I had the kind of whirling
dervish, feet stamping, screaming-my-head-off meltdown that

on a slower day would have made it into every single textbook ever written on behavioural difficulties.

The same kind of impotent rage was rising up dangerously in me now. I was trying on and getting stuck in ill-fitting Soul Mates; I'd nearly lost an ear in this one. It was really starting to get on my nerves.

As I furiously debated these points in my head, outside in the real world I was still standing with one hand clamped to my ear, staring murderously at Max. His sniffing long stopped, he stood mute with anxiety and embarrassment. God, I was being a total bitch to poor Max.

'Max, I am being rude, I am so sorry,' I apologised gently. 'I'm just feeling a bit all over the place at the moment.' My heart went out to him as he gave a wobbly smile, like a little kid whose ice-cream just fell in the sand and was trying to be brave about it. He gave an exploratory sniff, as if testing the waters, then another. 'Ah, please don't . . . that's to say . . . umm, well, then I really do hope you like sculpture, Jennifer?' he said, gradually regaining confidence and enthusiasm. 'Because I am going to take you to see one of my absolute favourites. It's at the Musée Rodin. I'm sure you'll know it . . .' his face lit up happily '. . . it's called *The Kiss*.'

I could have killed him.

Actually, it turned out to be a fascinating visit. Rodin's impressive eighteenth-century house now houses his work and I enjoyed hearing Max talk about the artist as we walked around the museum and gorgeous landscaped grounds (where we bought equally gorgeous *glaces*).

Rodin sounded difficult as hell and his muse and lover

Camille Claudel spent the last 30 years of her life in an asylum as a result. There were too many tourists around *The Kiss* to get a good look at it, so instead Max and I inspected the clay 'working model' prototype next to it. Although the lovers were passionately entwined, their mouths were actually a good inch apart. The most famous kissers in the world did not actually kiss at all. Maybe Olivier wasn't the only faux French Kisser? And no wonder poor Camille ended up bonkers.

Date #14: Nick, Skate Date – Paris, France

It was raining when I said goodbye to Max back at the metro, which was a shame as I needed good weather for my next encounter: the Skate Date.

Every Friday night in Paris, anything up to 28,000 people took part in *Pari Roller*: three hours spent whizzing 25 kilometres round the closed-off streets on inline skates. I'd made a programme about it a couple of years earlier and thought the atmosphere was so incredible – pensioners blowing whistles, kids zipping in and out of their parents' legs – I wanted to take part myself. I also thought this would make a perfect date.

I'd spent six weeks wobbling round Fountains Leisure Centre in west London, being shown not so much the ropes as the wheels by Citiskate, the people who organise something similar to the Paris event in London.

My class were just the nicest bunch of people, and – all as terrible as each other – we quickly bonded as we encouraged each other to make it through the embarrassing, painful learning curve. A group of about twelve of us had vowed we'd all get good enough to do the Pari Roller together. And one of the group, Nick, had shyly asked if he could be my Skate Date even though our conversations had rarely consisted of more than 'oohh, that had to hurt' or 'waaaatch ooooout' as one of us smacked into a wall or body-checked an oncoming skater.

Well, tonight was the night. I ran through a curtain of rain back to my hotel. I needed to quickly check my emails, then change and pick up my skating gear (kindly delivered and being taken back by Jilly and Stevie). As I dumped my bags down on the bed, I noticed the voicemail light flashing. It was from Nick: '*Hey Jennifer, hope you're doing okay? How f***d is this rain? I just spoke to Marianne and she said it's probably off tonight. We're meeting at Bastille anyway, see you there – and hey, get your skates on or you'll be late!*'

He never tired of that joke.

If tonight was cancelled it would be disappointing though no great surprise. Actually, it was probably a good thing: my skating skills were a triumph of enthusiasm over ability. Speed skating the wet, cobbled, hilly streets would invariably result in me completing the rest of my dating tour on crutches.

I got stuck on the computer trying to finalise a football date in Barcelona and writing another pleading email to the Date Wranglers to help me out on the US leg, which was proving to be a nightmare. When I rushed out of the metro at Bastille, wearing an old pair of jeans and clutching a bag with my skates, helmet and padding, there were only a few of the skaters around. Clearly the efficient website had spread the word that the skate was off.

I couldn't see Nick but spotted Marianne from our class, with Anne, Russell, Lisa and about five others. They were huddled under a café awning looking very wet. Marianne waved happily as she saw me sprinting over: 'Jennifer, can you believe this bloody weather?' she shouted over the din of the

rain. 'All that work and now we won't get to skate.' I smiled
sympathetically: she was the best skater in the group and had
been itching to go do this since we started.

'So what's happening?' I asked, hugging her and the rest of
the group. 'Is Nick here yet?'

'Oh you just missed him,' she shrugged. 'He wasn't sure if
you were coming so he went off with some of the others to
some Irish pub.' We both rolled our eyes: Irish Pubs – the
McDonalds of the new millennium.

I shrugged too. It was fine: no skate, no date. There was
almost a logic to it. But just then, Nick and the rest of our
group careened around the corner, running from canopy to
canopy, yelling madly as they got increasingly drenched. Nick
saw me with Marianne and came straight over, giving me a big
hug: 'Hey Skater Dater, I thought you weren't coming?'

I laughed as he flicked his wet coat at me: 'Sorry, I got held
up. Hey, I thought you guys had gone Oirish?'

'That we did,' he replied. 'But we thought we'd better come
back for the rest of you Roller Rookies.'

We all laughed at this, then trooped into the café and found
tables at the back big enough to fit the whole group around and
dump our gear under. Nick sat next to me and for about 20
minutes we chatted about my date-a-thon and life in general.
But soon the rest of the group joined in and our gossiping,
teasing and storytelling was still going strong when closing
time came hours later.

And not only was that fine – it was wonderful. I realised
that in a way, my date was with the whole group. Together
we'd worked really hard to get to the point where we could
attempt the Pari Roller. And okay, after all that work, here we
were, unable to skate because of the weather but we'd all

made it this far, hadn't we? That was surely something worth celebrating.

Kicked out onto the street, we hugged and shouted our goodbyes. I felt comforted and rejuvenated by the camaraderie of the evening. Our joint failure had turned into something lovely and reassuring, that instinctively gave me courage and hope for my own journey. I realised I had to make the time to celebrate the little triumphs, taking pride in how far I had come, rather than getting bogged down in one or two bad days and dates, believing they set the tone for the rest of my life.

CHAPTER SIX

The Rest of Europe

Dates #15 –27: Barcelona, Lisbon, Athens, Verona, Siena, Berlin

When I say the next thirteen dates were whirlwind romances, I'm talking about the travelling rather than the quality of the dates. I hurtled in and out of capitals so fast, I barely had time to open my bags before I was off again.

Back when Phileas Fogg embraced the challenge of travelling *Around the World in 80 Days*, Heathrow meant *man bowling*. But now travelling is so cheap and easy (we ask when rather than how), I went online and booked the short flights between Paris, Barcelona, Lisbon, Athens, Verona and Berlin without giving it a second thought.

Maybe *thinking* was something I was trying to avoid?

Paris had taught me an important lesson: I needed to be less melodramatic. Date & Go, Date & Go; stick to the schedule, stay focused. If I was to survive all 80 of these dates without my self-esteem crashing and burning altogether, I had to establish some boundaries. I needed to find a cut-off point for the amount of time and energy I invested in each of the dates, so I wasn't continually churned up about something someone had/hadn't done/said. I couldn't take it all so personally.

I've never been the best at keeping things in perspective but it was imperative I learnt to do it now. I don't mean being cold and unfeeling (I really did want to find my Soul Mate on this journey, not just meet my quota of dates), I just needed to be more sensible. These were dates, social engagements; I had to stop being over-sensitive and stick to logistics.

It was only when I paid some long overdue attention to logistics, however, that I discovered logistics were having a few problems of their own.

I was so busy dating, travelling and – in any spare moments – arranging the next lot of dating and travelling, I'd forgotten to build in any downtime. I was becoming tired and disorientated. I'd wake up in the middle of the night needing to pee, but could only start looking for the bathroom once I'd remembered which date I'd just had/was about to have, therefore which country, city and then hotel I was in.

I was also having to buy knickers and T-shirts as all my clothes were dirty and there was no time to do laundry. I knew I should make the time but I also had to apply for my Chinese visa, check the trains between Verona and Florence, plus see if that cheap hotel in LA had any rooms available?

And every single day was a 'new day' for potential future dates, making initial chit-chat contact to test the dating waters. I wanted to email back *'for chrissakes you're one of eighty: date me or don't, I don't have the time to talk you into it'*, but I knew I couldn't.

It felt like there wasn't a minute to lose: taking time off to do laundry just seemed impossible.

And then there was the issue of personal grooming.

My decision to travel 'with the sun' made for a waxing dilemma. The hair on my legs was long enough to be noticeable but not really long enough to be waxed. Should I boil to death in trousers or stick to dinner dates so I could hide my legs under the table?

The same applied to my bikini line. Could I bear to leave it, as I normally did, until I got 'Koala Ears' – when it appears there's a koala down the front of your knickers with the ears sticking out the sides – but then risk literally being caught *out* on an unannounced 'bikini date'?

These might sound like small considerations, but it was what preoccupied my thoughts as I crashed into furniture looking for the bathroom in the wee small hours.

I raced from date to date, country to country.

Steve (Date #15) in Barcelona was a friend of Hillary's from university. We had a date to watch football in a bar: England versus one of the Spanish teams. I love watching the big championships and thought I knew enough about football to hold my own. Steve soon put me straight. 'Are England in the white strip?' I asked just after kick-off. Mortified, he spun around to see if anyone had heard, before hissing, 'Keep your voice down.'

I was just another girl who thought that because she could name three players from Man U, she knew football. England lost; the date didn't go into extra time.

Ray (Date #16) I vaguely knew through my friend Theresa. For years he'd been a dealer in the city before burning out and giving it all up to move to Barcelona. Like me, he'd invested all his energy in his job and taken radical steps to find a more healthy balance. I wondered if it had worked for him and if he felt he'd made the right decision?

Theresa had omitted to mention Ray now worked as a street mime on La Rambla. When he arrived at the tapas bar, he was still 'dressed for work': silver catsuit and body paint. Apparently he was in the middle of a turf war with his rival, the Clockwork Bronze Man, and couldn't stay long.

I don't think I'm exaggerating when I say we were the subject of a fair amount of attention. I was mortified. Ray was silent: an admirable quality in a mime, less so in a Date.

I caught the first flight to Lisbon the following morning.

Paolo (Date #17) and **Jose (Date #18)** were friends of Jane, a South African woman I'd met travelling through Europe years ago. I knew Paolo played flamenco guitar and was taking me to the famous Pastéis de Belém café for *pastéis de nata*.

We drank intense, bitter espressos to balance the rich pastéis, crisp buttery cups of flaky pastry filled with creamy custard, dusted with icing sugar, made to a closely guarded, secret recipe. Paolo was chatty and funny, but there was no spark.

It made me feel good to dance off some calories, clubbing with Jose in the trendy Bairro Alto district. He was extremely charming and his friends were lovely, but my 'dancing till dawn every weekend' days were behind me. Jose was fun but not The One.

I went straight from the club to the hotel, to pick up my bags, then on to the airport for Athens.

Drakoulis (Date #19) was the cousin of Effie, a Greek friend of mine from the gym. Maybe I could have coped with his heavy smoking – it was Europe, after all. But when we went to dinner, everyone in the restaurant smoked constantly and I struggled.

I'm not being precious but it was disgusting: the air in the restaurant was heavy with thick, painfully acrid smoke. It was like having dinner in a burning furniture warehouse. Drakoulis took me on to a fantastic Rembetika club (a type of traditional Greek gangsta folk music) but my head throbbed and my eyes stung. I felt guilty leaving during the players' first break but I had set and reached my limit.

Effie had also set me up with an AE (Amicable Ex). **Joseph (Date #20)** was a tour guide and since his first group arrived at 10 a.m., we'd arranged to meet at the fish market for an 8 a.m. breakfast date. If it worked out and he didn't mind, I thought I might go on the tour with him afterwards?

But I'd had five hours sleep in two days and woke with a start at 8.30 a.m. I repeatedly called his mobile as I scrambled to dress and get to the market on the off-chance he was still there. But his phone rang unanswered and there was no sign of him at the market.

Forget it: he'd probably drive you as crazy as he drove me, Effie replied breezily to my apologetic email. *Though it would have been interesting to hear why he split up with Claudia?*

Damn her: Joseph obviously wasn't an AE at all. He was a UE (Unresolved Ex) and Effie was using me to get an update. As I left for Italy, I silently congratulated myself on avoiding what sounded like unfinished business.

Verona was the home of Romeo and Juliet, arguably the world's most famous lovers. Some might argue that a couple whose poor communication skills resulted in joint suicide were perhaps not the best relationship role models? But up to 5000 people a year saw it differently, writing to Juliet's house and tomb, asking for her advice about their own love lives.

Local poets and writers have been responding to the letters since the 1930s, but in 1975 Verona intellectual Giulio Tamassia founded The Juliet Club and organised for ten unpaid, multi-lingual 'secretaries' to answer the letters. In addition, he established the Dear Juliet Award, which is presented to the most romantic letter writer each year.

I'd been emailing Eleanor, the secretary responsible for Italian, Spanish and English correspondence. With the explosion of the Internet and online dating, I wondered if people were increasingly emailing Shakespeare's heroine?

Now, we do receive some emails, but mainly letters; writing by hand is more intimate, especially if you talk about love, feelings and emotions . . . We answer all the letters, by hand.

Eleanor had been a huge help, not only arranging for me to meet this year's Dear Juliet winner but also for me to stand on Juliet's balcony and date 'Romeo'.

Whatever the outcome, I reasoned, it would be interesting to see what dating two of Italy's most romantic men was like. As terrible as it sounds, I suspect I would find dating an intensely romantic man a bit claustrophobic and annoying: all that fetching and carrying and fussing around would get on my nerves. Either that or I'd assume they'd done something really bad and were overcompensating.

I know, why I'm still single is a mystery to me too.

This year's Dear Juliet winner was Davide, a Verona man in his thirties. As we waited for him at the Juliet Club offices, we watched a group of women chatting amiably around a huge table sorting hundreds of letters into different piles. Eleanor told me it was easy to spot which country a letter was from: 'French people are very passionate, very romantic. Italians and Spanish like flowery phrases, like South Americans, they are verbose: using a lot of words to say just one thing.'

I wondered if it was mainly the Latin countries who asked for advice about their love lives? Was there some truth in that stereotypical hot-blooded image?

'No, no,' Eleanor shook her head vigorously. 'We get letters from China, Japan, Russia . . . all over. Latin people tend to be extremely forthcoming about their feelings. Americans are the other extreme: they'll write just a five-line letter saying, "She's blonde, I like her, what should I do?" It's very frustrating. I want to tell them, say a little more: do you know her, does she like someone else? It's difficult to give advice when you know so little.'

British people are resigned to scoring badly in any kind of international personality contest, but I went ahead and asked Eleanor what the British were like. She thought for a moment before answering carefully: 'Reserved at first, but then – since they are writing – they become very deep and introspective. It takes them a while to open up, but when they do it is heartfelt.'

Apparently, some think that Juliet is a saint or goddess of love: 'People often don't go into that much detail because they think Juliet already knows their problem. And if their problem is resolved, people come and thank Juliet for her help. An Italian lady left a message at Juliet's tomb last month saying she had come three years ago single and here she was now, with her new husband. She saw this as a miracle and wanted to thank Juliet for helping her find love.'

Italy is reputedly one of the most romantic countries in the world, yet even here finding a decent boyfriend is considered a miracle. That didn't sound good.

Then **Davide (Date #21)** arrived. Just under 6 ft tall with short dark hair, he had large, soft brown eyes, like huge chocolate biscuits ready to be dunked. Davide didn't speak English, so Eleanor was going to translate for us.

I hadn't had a chance to read Davide's letter; I wondered what had made it more romantic than any other that year?

(All translated by Eleanor.)

Davide: 'It is not easy to tell people my story, so it took effort to write to Juliet. I had to be sure I was writing to someone who would understand. It started eleven years ago at a moment in my life when I was very alone and sad.

'I was walking through a cemetery and noticed a tomb full of dust that no one had taken care of for many years. I started cleaning it, and as I cleaned I uncovered a picture of a young woman on the grave. I saw by the inscription that she had died in 1927 when she was twenty-three, my age at that time.

'I have always believed in another life, but, as I cleaned, I had a strange and powerful feeling that Elena – the young woman in the grave – was calling me to take care of her.

'So I did.

'And, little by little, in addition to the sense of compassion that compelled me to look after her grave, over the years another feeling for her developed: one of true love.'

Davide stopped talking and looked at me shyly. I realised that the entire time he had been telling his story, I had been holding my breath. I inhaled sharply and blinked hard. I couldn't believe what he was telling me but I knew I had to say something or he'd close up.

'So you fell in love with Elena after you stumbled across her grave?' I clarified in a neutral tone. 'Why were you in the graveyard in the first place?'

Davide explained he was there because he was in love with a real girl who sold flowers outside the cemetery. The feeling wasn't reciprocated, he admitted with a gentle shrug.

As Davide and Eleanor talked, I quickly read a translation of Davide's letter for the first time. When they finished talking, I showed Davide the translation. 'In your letter – which is really beautiful – you say: ". . . her angelic face was covered in years of dust. I was moved and saddened by her image so I cleaned up her grave and bought some flowers."'

I wondered if he'd ever bought flowers for Elena's grave from the flower seller as an excuse to talk to her? He said at first yes, but as he fell in love with Elena he'd forgotten all about the flower seller and stopped buying from her.

I asked how much he knew about Elena's background?

Davide explained he'd visited the records office in City Hall and read up on her family, initially with the intention of contacting them to let them know how neglected the grave was. He found she'd been born on the same street as Juliet in the centre of Verona. Her father was a trader, she had two brothers and one sister. All were dead now.

As Davide explained, I watched him closely: for the last 11 years he'd been in love with a girl who'd been dead for nearly 80. Did that make him mad? He looked normal and sweet but was this the sign of a lonely man or something more sinister?

But as easy as it would have been to dismiss his feelings out of hand and ridicule his situation, I didn't want to do that. It felt very important that I kept an open mind about what he was telling me. What if he really did love her? And what if loving her didn't make him mad or deluded but actually incredibly brave to recognise and honour his feelings?

Rather than making assumptions and judging him, I wanted to hear what he had to say. I asked what his friends and family thought of the situation? Also, 'When you go to parties and people are there with their partners, don't you wish you had someone with you?'

Davide shook his head. 'Although my family knows, I don't tell my friends as most wouldn't understand. I just say "I'm alone, maybe I will find someone one day." And anyway . . .' he continued . . . 'when I go to parties, I don't mind that nobody "real" is there: I am quite happy.'

I asked what it was about Elena that made him happy? Davide considered the question for a moment then said: 'I feel a deep sense of joy and peace. Even though she can't speak, she communicates with me. I feel her presence, otherwise this wouldn't have gone on for so many years.'

He paused, then said simply: 'I believe we all have a Soul Mate – just one – either in this life or the next. Sooner or later you meet: this is how I feel about Elena.'

I was moved by Davide's devotion, though I didn't agree with his Soul Mate theory. As I see it, when you are young, you go through a lot of fast-changing stages. As you get older, the stages change more slowly and you are in each for a progressively longer time. I believe there is a Soul Mate for each stage. If you are lucky, you find them. If you are luckier still, their stages coincide with yours and you stay and grow together. I suppose that's why I can be positive and believe there is a Soul Mate out there for me.

With luck, I will find them.

But what if you believed there was only ever going to be one Soul Mate for you, and you found them after they'd died? How incredibly strong or lonely would you have to be to be true to them anyway? Would you live like Davide and be true to your Soul Mate – no matter how hard – or would you just give up and settle for the easier option of a 'live' mate?

I asked Davide how he knew she was The One?

Davide told me that although he felt connected from the moment he first saw the grave, it was only little by little over the years that he realised how deeply involved he was with her. 'She leads me,' he said simply. 'She gives me signs.'

'What kind of signs?' I asked.

'Like encouraging me to write to Juliet,' he said. 'I am convinced she wanted me to tell the world about us. I wrote to Juliet about our relationship and the letter was awarded the prize. After the letter was published a lot of my friends and colleagues saw it and congratulated me. I had done the right thing.'

I asked if he found loving Elena easy?

'No,' Davide replied gravely. 'You must feel ready, otherwise it is impossible to live this life. But, if you have been lonely and suffered with that loneliness, you find love where you thought you never would.'

I didn't want to judge Davide or patronise him with my pity, but it sounded a hard life and I did feel sorry for him. I thought back to the Love Professor observing that when you've been single for a long time, after a while anything will do. I asked Davide if – having experienced such a deep love with Elena – he thought the experience would make him more receptive to loving someone living?

He shrugged: possibly, but that person would have to accept his huge love for Elena, otherwise it would not work. Part of his heart would always be devoted to Elena.

One of the things I loved about being in a relationship was coming home and relaxing together, chatting about our days, having someone to share moments and thoughts with. I wondered how Davide and Elena's relationship worked on a daily basis?

Davide explained that he led a normal life; he took fresh flowers to the grave often but not every day. Either way, he always felt connected and close to her. 'I've always been very reserved, I don't have many friends. Every time I feel sad or down, I turn to her and she gives me comfort and love.'

I suddenly noticed a ring on Davide's left hand. 'Oh, is that a wedding ring?' The question just popped out.

Davide smiled proudly and touched it gently with the fingers on his right hand: 'Yes, with her name inside.'

I wasn't prepared for this and was deeply shocked. An involuntary groan escaped before I could stop it. I tried to turn it into a more appreciative noise: 'Ooooh, did you have one made for her too?'

Davide nodded and explained that in Italy, after a certain period of time has elapsed, it's legal for people to dig up family coffins and rebury the remains inside a smaller casket. Davide had dug up and reburied Elena last year. Inside the new casket, alongside her remains, he had placed his wedding ring to her, his name engraved inside.

'Right . . .' It took me a moment to collect my thoughts. '. . . So, when you put the ring in with Elena's remains, was that your wedding as well as her reburial?'

'Yes,' he confirmed. 'By then our relationship had been going for ten years. I was sure of how I felt and wanted to give her a sign of my love, a symbol.'

'Davide, did you invite anybody else along to the wedding or was it just the pair of you?' I asked evenly.

'My mother came. She knows all about Elena and is fond of her.'

Davide went on to explain that his mother was at first extremely uncomfortable about the situation with Elena but 'when she saw how happy Elena made me, she accepted and grew to care for her too'. Initially after the reburial they felt bad *for disturbing her sleep*, but now they were happy: she was no longer neglected and was being taken proper care of.

As Eleanor translated, Davide reached into his pocket, took out his wallet and tenderly removed a small black and white photograph. It was Elena. He looked at the picture fondly, before holding it out proudly for me to inspect. It was a copy of the original photograph on her gravestone. A young girl stared shyly out. She looked polite and neat, her hair was bobbed short, her face heart-shaped and pretty.

I felt incredibly moved that Davide was showing me the picture but also unbelievably awkward. I knew I needed to say something complimentary about it, but, honestly, it felt more like I was being shown an old family photograph of someone's grandmother rather than the 'wallet shot' of someone's wife.

'She looks very fun-loving and open,' I said after the briefest pause. Were people 'fun-loving' back in 1927? I didn't want to say the wrong thing and offend Davide, but he seemed fine, obviously happy to be able to include her in the conversation: 'Her sweet eyes look beyond time and life; I fell in love with her look.'

'She looks lovely, thank you,' I said, handing back the photo. I caught sight of my watch: it was time to go.

'What are your plans for the future?' I asked, as we all got to our feet. Davide said he just hoped for a good life, to find a good job.

'But if you are asking about my heart, I am happy now: fulfilled. And even though people don't understand and even if I meet someone else, Elena will always be a great part of my life. I feel happy with that.'

So I wished Davide and Elena luck and we all said goodbye. Eleanor drove me back to my hotel. Lost in our own thoughts, neither of us spoke much.

In the alleys off Via Cappello, in the shadow of Juliet Capulet's house, pairs of Italian teenagers fall in love. Heads close, they talk and laugh quietly, locked in a private world of mutual desire, delighting in each other's company. Randomly, conversation gives way to urgent kissing, moped helmet dangling from one hand, mobile phone from the other.

Out on the main street, cumbersome knots of American

and Japanese tourists mill by oblivious to the teenagers. They are making their way to the structure symbolising the only kind of Italian teen-love that interests and moves them: Juliet's balcony.

In Verona everyone seemed wrapped up in their own desire. In a city famous for lovers who would rather die than compromise their feelings, maybe this was appropriate. Davide's story had saddened and perplexed me though: even if he was happy, I felt troubled for him.

Unable to distract myself by shopping (all the clothes were either too small, too expensive or too white), I felt preoccupied and restless. I didn't want time on my hands with three gelaterias right outside my hotel ('BRITISH TOURIST DEAD FROM FREAK ICE-CREAM OVERDOSE') so I rang Eleanor and we went out and got really drunk instead. It was great.

There was a courtyard around Juliet's beautiful fourteenth-century house. Over the years, the courtyard walls had accumulated such a collection of graffiti that people now wrote their love poems on wads of chewing gum which coated every inch of wall, like rubbery, multi-coloured tiles.

Under the balcony was a bronze statue of Juliet. Folklore had declared it lucky (though possibly not for her) to touch Juliet's right breast. The statue of the fourteen-year-old girl – breast corroded a pale orange by the acid sweat of a million would-be Romeos – looked on stoically, as a hundred stamping and baying tourists took turns being photographed groping her. Like the audience of *Blind Date* transported back in time, with each squeeze the crowd roared their approval.

I watched with a huge hangover, knowing that in about ten minutes, I was going to have to put on a velvet gown and dress up as Juliet.

Despite my misgivings, Eleanor took me into the house and persuaded me to go into the fuse cupboard and change into the dress. It was a heavy red velvet floor-length outfit, laced up the front, cinched round the waist with a jewelled belt and topped off with a red spongy headdress.

As I emerged, the crowd spotted me immediately. They poured in from the courtyard, pushing inside to get a better look, roaring replaced by quiet, rapt expectation. 'The first person who tries to rub my breast will quickly discover they are anything but lucky,' I thought grimly.

Actually, as the dress trailed across the floor, I felt my spirits (and hangover) lift. I immediately understood the attraction of dressing like this: so voluminous and red I could have spent my whole life living off marmalade croissants, gelati and pizza and nobody would have been any the wiser.

Then 'Romeo' **(Date #22)** arrived. Sporting a deep red velvet tunic, green tights and a codpiece that made me instinctively avert my eyes, he was a hyperactive mid-thirties Italian called Solimano. He looked vaguely consumptive and a foot too short but with a mischievous smile. Solimano marched across the courtyard into the hallway and through the parting crowd, like Moses on a mission. Stopping directly in front of me, Solimano sank down onto one knee, snatched my hand and kissed it passionately.

To my astonishment and the delight of the crowd, he declared: 'I am here, your Romeo. Now we will be together forever.' He finished with a flourish, then, jumping to his feet, vaulted out the window, onto the balcony. 'Come now, my

Juliet,' he commanded. 'Come to the balcony, so I may speak of my love for you.'

'Oh, Sweet Jesus,' I sighed to myself. My head was starting to throb again, the spongy headdress was itching uncomfortably. Back out in the courtyard, however, the remaining crowd had no such misgivings. Hands paused in mid gumming and groping, they let out a collective sigh. This was the romance they had come for: the floor show had begun.

Fortunately Eleanor took one look at my face and pushed through the crowd to where Solimano was now waiting expectantly beneath the balcony. 'Come along, Romeo,' she said briskly. 'Jennifer knows that bit of the story already. Let's find somewhere more private for your date.'

Solimano looked dejected but trailed obediently after her. The crowd followed with their eyes, mutinously disappointed, like children told they could not throw their pet from the window to see if it could fly.

Eleanor found us a couple of thrones on the first floor and the date began.

Solimano was fun, sensitive without taking himself too seriously. We chatted about life on the road. He travelled all over Italy performing, but always played Romeo when he was home.

'Don't you ever get bored of it?' I asked. Unexpectedly a look of guilt and frustration stole across his face. Solimano quickly looked away to compose himself then turned back: 'I love Romeo,' he protested, 'but the problem is that he is young and his emotions are not . . .' he waved his hand around searching for the word '. . . developed.' He leant forward and lowered his voice in a conspiratorial manner: 'I am not telling anyone this yet, but I am thinking maybe now I am more interested in Mercutio.'

He looked deep into my eyes, watching my reaction to his confession for signs of . . . I have no idea what. Outrage? Ridicule? He was clearly going through a bit of a character crisis and my question had unwittingly opened the floodgates.

Actually, most of my 'Romeos' seemed to be at a crossroads, 'going through something' (hey, who wasn't?), but it never occurred to me that even *the* Romeo would be.

Fresh from my intense meeting with Davide, I knew how to keep a poker face. I also knew a reaction was expected. 'So, why Mercutio?' I asked conversationally.

Solimano looked troubled, then, leaning in close again, pausing to assemble the words before speaking, he answered: 'Mercutio is – how you say – the central pillar of the play.'

All around us, cameras flashed incessantly as groups of tourists stood inches away posing for photos with us. I slapped away hands that tentatively snaked over my shoulder (this was the first date where I was actually more concerned about being groped by the passers-by than the Date). Of course the crowd had no way of knowing that they were not witnessing perfect love in action. Juliet was halfway through a rejection – Romeo didn't want to be with her, in fact he didn't even want to be with himself.

But Solimano was unaware or immune to the crowd and he continued to unburden himself: '. . . You see, at first it is a play about life. But then Mercutio dies and it becomes a dark, brooding play about death.' Solimano sat up straight, his speech gathering in momentum and intensity. 'Mercutio is the play's turning point; he is so strong, he can change the play from day to night, light to dark . . .' Solimano spoke with a feverish passion, he clenched his hands and arched his body in the chair. '. . . He is the most powerful person in *Romeo and*

Juliet and I want to be him. I am sick of love, I want power. I have had enough of being Romeo. I want to be Mercutio.'

Reaching the climax of his speech, Solimano cried out this final pronouncement. He paused, suspended in the intensity of his realised feelings. Then a huge smile lit up his face and he collapsed back in his chair, sighing deeply, all tension gone from his body.

But I was busy having a revelation of my own: I'd come all this way only to be proven superfluous. Romeo was cutting Juliet out of the deal altogether and going straight to the afterlife on his own, as Mercutio. Love was passé; Death was in.

No wonder Davide had won the bloody Juliet prize, I thought bitterly. When it came to the most intense relationship, it seemed nobody beat Death.

'Thank you, Jennifer,' Solimano breathed. 'I have never told a soul this and now I have told you. You were sent to me: I know now what I must do. No more Romeo, I am to be Mercutio.'

The cameras continued to flash and Solimano leant back, spent and content with his revelation. I sat with my mouth slightly open, trying to work out what the hell had just happened.

I said goodbye to Eleanor (without whom I very much doubt I would have got out of Juliet's house alive) and embarked on a long cross-country train journey via Bologna to Florence. After two hours by bus through the soft green hills and vineyards of Tuscany, I arrived in Siena.

I had a date with **Umberto (Date #23)**. He ran the traffic dating website www.motoristmail.com. I knew from our emails that the idea had come out of Umberto's frustration of being cut up in traffic:

```
One night while I was driving inside a tunnel a
fast car cut me off, and I couldn't contact it
(to tell him 'how smart you are'), so I thinked
what a beautifull idea if I could write to its
license plate numbers by an Internet site.
```

But Umberto was a businessman and he soon realised his website could be put to better use as one of the *labour-saving devices* for busy single people. It was now a dating website custom-built for Italians who spent most of their lives stuck in their cars in traffic. Rather than registering the numberplates of bad drivers on the website, it now allowed you to register your own numberplate if you were single and looking to meet someone. So if you saw someone you fancied in a traffic jam but couldn't get to talk to them from your car, you just went to Umberto's website, and, if their details were registered, emailed and asked them out on a date.

The idea had caught on, and Umberto's site now got 6000 posts a day.

This and all Umberto's other businesses kept him so incredibly busy, however, that he could only spare the time to date me over lunch. So we met at a teeny pizzeria and chatted at a table outside in the bright Tuscan sunshine. I was fascinated to hear about the site and really liked Umberto, who was shy but charming. But he seemed a total workaholic. I was sad for him but not surprised to hear he didn't have a girlfriend. 'I'll get one when I have more time and lots of money,' he said matter-of-factly before having to rush back to work.

• • •

After our pizza date, I caught the train to Pisa and flew to Berlin. As the plane taxied for takeoff, I took one last look out the window at Italy. Another country done. It had been fascinating and I had met some lovely people, but I was now over 20 dates into my journey – a quarter of my potential The Ones met – and I was still no closer to finding my Soul Mate. Was I doing something wrong or was it simply that I hadn't yet achieved the critical mass that statistically contained my new man? What were my Soul Mate odds: one in how many?

How many more before I met him? Was I close? What more could I do to speed up the process, or be confident I was even on the right path? If I held my breath until we took off; if the man next to me finished his chapter before the captain said we could undo our seat belts, would I meet my Soul Mate in Germany? Was our meeting a matter of such superstition or random luck?

Did I have to work harder at finding my Soul Mate or did I have to work harder at trusting Fate? I wasn't exactly losing hope but it was a surprise that so many people had yielded – and I don't mean this in an unkind way – so little. And in the meantime, I seemed to be loading up my romantic mystery tour bus with a huge number of people who all quite understandably expected my energy and attention. Was I in danger of becoming so busy picking up passengers that, when the time came, there wouldn't be room for the one person I wanted on board?

This was a very real possibility.

Although Berlin had regained its status as capital of Germany, most airlines had yet to build this into their schedule and fly direct. As a result, although travellers might just make the tight connections, their bags generally weren't so lucky and lost luggage had become the norm.

Sure enough, I got to Berlin but my bags didn't. And I'd made the mistake of agreeing to meet **Ede (Date #24)** in Arrivals. Even on a normal day, I like to arrive at my own pace. Today, with make-up and dating clothes in my lost bags, I felt particularly unprepared.

Ede was waiting with a single yellow rose (which unlike Willem in Holland he gave me straight away) and didn't seem at all troubled by the fact that we couldn't leave until I had reported my bags missing. There was a huge line at the Lost Luggage office, so we went for a coffee.

It was to be my first – and hopefully last – airport date.

I sneaked a look at him as we queued: mid-thirties, tall and slim, with long legs and a slightly mysterious air. He was nice and easy to talk to, but I struggled to concentrate on the conversation: all I could think about was my bags and if I'd ever see them again.

Four hours later, we finally made it to the front of the Lost queue. The clerk assured me that my bags would be delivered to my hotel by 5 p.m., although 'there may be a delay as all streets are being closed for the Love Parade'.

Yes, I knew all about the Love Parade. It was the reason I was here.

Since 1989, Berlin's Love Parade has been the world's biggest techno street party. It might take two to tango, but it took up to two million to techno, as big-name DJs on flamboyant carnival floats pumped up the volume in Tiergarten Park, surrounded by huge crowds of ravers. I wanted to see if I would be lucky in Love in Berlin?

Ede was lovely but he didn't have my attention. It was no one's fault. I liked him and in a different situation think we might have clicked, but not this time. I felt bad when he dropped me at my hotel: I half-heartedly said maybe I could see him later but secretly hoped he wouldn't be too disappointed when I didn't get back in touch.

I was staying in Prenzlauer Berg. Part of old East Berlin – one of the few areas to resist Hitler's rise to power – this was where the radicals, intellectuals and students lived. It felt like a place only you know about, and it was fascinating to stumble across quirky galleries, stark buildings with beautiful features, plus loads of funky bars and cafés.

I was staying here, but apparently my bags weren't: there was still no sign of them.

I went out to see an art installation in the cavernous and scary basement of a water tower up the road. When I came back, there was still no sign of my bags. I went for a long walk round the Berg, poked round shops, found a great bar and settled down with my book until 11 p.m. The bags were still not at the hotel when I returned. 'Maybe midnight, maybe tomorrow?' the receptionist answered without looking up from his paper.

I knew there was no point in getting angry: it would just give me a headache and the paracetamol were in my lost bags.

I came down to reception the next morning. 'Any sign of my bags?' I asked in a monotone.

'No, we have no idea where they are,' the receptionist replied cheerfully.

Sometimes I think there is nowhere more foreign than Europe.

I went back to my room, drank some coffee, turned my knickers inside out, then set off in two-day-old clothes and no make-up to join some of the most beautiful people in the world dance for joy.

It was a shame I wasn't at my best, as I had quite a tricky dating day ahead of me. I was to go to the Parade with **Paul (Date #25)**, a raver I'd met via one of the Love Parade websites, then date **DJ Frank from Holland (Date #26)** on his float, then **Franz-Philipp (Date #27)** on his float. I knew from my Radio 1 days how incredibly resistant club people are to being nailed down: any arrangement was going to be fluid.

At school, I was always very sporty. Love Parade gave me an insight into how it must feel when no one wants you on their team.

I made myself up in a department store using the testers on the cosmetics counter. I then met Paul, who was very young and completely hyper on E. Ten minutes into the date, he scaled a lamppost and that was the last I saw of him (I was wearing a skirt and two-day-old knickers: I wouldn't have joined him even if I'd been able to). DJ Frank's float had been detained at the Dutch border and the bouncers on Franz-Philipp's float took one look at my appearance and refused to even pass on a message saying I'd arrived.

And the whole time, a psychiatrist called Wolfgang followed me around asking me out for a drink. I was worried that since I'd had a couple of no-show dates, Fate might think I wasn't living up to my side of the deal to date 80 men.

So to appease the Numbers God, I went for a coffee with Wolfgang. Apparently he had just moved from Brussels and didn't know anyone. He'd come to the Love Parade because 'I'm at a crossroads and I thought I might meet someone here?'

I felt a bit sorry for him but also worried that, in his own way, maybe he felt just as sorry for me. Did I also appear an unconnected outsider, randomly jumping into the slipstream of other people's fun, hoping to be swept up and carried along with them?

I'd given it my best shot, but every fibre in my body told me that as hard as I tried, I was not going to find my Soul Mate hanging with the ravers at the Love Parade. I'd tried it, it hadn't worked. It was time to go home and regroup my energies and those of my Date Wranglers for the next stage of my journey: America.

Oiled and toned in leather bikinis, plastic dresses and pink fur boots, ravers blew their whistles and savoured the narcissistic tang of dancing and being watched dancing. I let the crowd push past me as I forced a path through the oncoming tide of revellers, back to the station and my hotel. 'Oh, Ms Cox, good news: your bags have arrived,' the receptionist beamed at me as I walked into the lobby.

'That's lovely,' I responded with an empty smile. 'I'd like to check out please.'

I flew back to London. As I walked through passport control at Heathrow, one of the officers asked where the flight had just come in from?

'Denmark,' I replied blankly. The man behind me laughed:

'You're a bit lost, love, it wasn't Denmark, it was Germany. Sounds like you don't know where you're going.'

Everyone laughed, except me. I was just too tired. Too tired to laugh, too tired to talk, too tired to explain why I had no idea where I was. He was right, though: I had no idea where I was going, I was just ploughing ahead blindly. And when I thought of how much more travelling was still ahead of me, I wondered if it was really worth carrying on?

CHAPTER SEVEN

London

But I felt better as soon as I got home: it was the perfect tonic at just the right time. To be able to shut the front door and feel the stillness and silence slowly soak into my bones, like milk gently colouring black coffee caramel, drop by drop.

Until I had to leave for the US two weeks from now, my time was my own: no dates, no travelling. It felt an impossible luxury. And in the meantime, I could see my friends, sleep in my beloved bed, pick any outfit from my entire wardrobe and do all the things I'd missed so much about my daily life in London. I was off-duty and I was going to relax.

Except I couldn't.

My brutal Date & Go, Date & Go schedule had become ingrained and there was still so much to be organised before I'd be ready to leave again. I was completely incapable of switching off.

Plus there was the backlog of London dating traffic that had been accumulating in the time I'd been travelling through Europe. I haven't really mentioned this before but despite deciding to travel in search of my Soul Mate because London seemed such a dating desert, for some reason I couldn't bring myself to give up on my home city altogether. I'd been in low-impact email contact with about six or seven people from London (and about six or seven hundred everywhere else in the world) whilst I'd been away. Nothing serious, just gentle *seeing if we get on* chat.

I'd vaguely agreed to meet the friend of a friend; replied to a few people from a dating website I was on; plus I'd been asked out on a couple of regular dates just before I left on the first leg of my trip.

I'd been completely honest with everyone and explained the reason for being away. There was an unspoken agreement that if I was still available when I got back to London, we'd meet up. Inadvertently I'd committed myself to a significant amount of home dating.

And now I was back, feeling frazzled and a bit *dated-out*.

hi there are you back? I was just wondering if
you were around to meet up for a quick coffee?
Patrick

It would be lovely to see you, either in
Greenwich or the West End if you are free/in this
country! Love, James

I can't remember when you said you'd be back?
Give us a call — can't wait to meet up. Cheers,
Chris

Karl was a Swiss man I'd found on an Italian dating website, when I was looking into dating in Rome. As it turned out, he now lived in Egypt but we'd stayed in regular contact, partially as there was no reason not to go to Egypt for a date (even at this point my route wasn't confirmed) and also because we were both working away from home and had struck up a rapport via email.

But suddenly Karl was coming to London:

```
I will probably come back around the 3rd for a
couple of days before I head off to Cairo, will
you be around then? Otherwise I am also in London
on 14th for three days, how about then? How is
your quest for the perfect match going, have you
met someone special yet? Karl
```

I desperately needed a break from dating. But at the same time, what if one of these men turned out to be what I was looking for? My journey would be over and I could stay in London. I could neither afford nor bear to ignore this possibility.

Clearly, I did need time off though. The job of keeping all my *date balls* up in the air had utilised my professional skills as I had anticipated. But whereas in the past, I'd run a department to get the job done, it was now my family and friends who were helping. And I was in danger of treating *them* like staff.

My mother observed very gently on the phone that I'd become *a bit bossy*. I was mortified to hear it but knew she was absolutely right. In fact, I'd become bossier than ever. I'd had to be to make all the elements of my journey come together. But I was home now and I'd missed my Date Wranglers as the regular friends they'd always been and wanted to hear what they'd all been up to in the time I'd been away.

But it didn't quite work out that way, precisely because I'd asked all my friends to help me with my quest. Now I was home, they understandably wanted me – in accordance with the International Girlfriend Charter – to act out the high- and lowlights of the 27 dates they'd been instrumental in setting up. I was torn between my friendship and obligation to them and my need, for reasons of self-preservation, to switch off and recharge my batteries before the next big push.

I arranged to see my friends and family anyway though. Belinda and I caught up as we crawled around the floor with her young daughter Maya; Paula and I watched John Cusack films and talked about music; Eddie asked lots of questions and was as dry and funny as ever; Eleanor and I chatted as she pushed Alex along the Thames path in his pram; I did the crossword with my parents in the village pub.

It felt good to see everyone but it was frustratingly one-sided at times. I was trying not to bore on about my journey but it seemed all anyone else wanted to talk about. And as selfish as it made me feel, I did need to talk.

But it wasn't all *ooohhs* and *aahhhs*. Although interested and supportive, some had observations I found hard to hear.

Charlotte was my *other best friend*, and, like Belinda and Toz, had watched my Relationship Empires rise and fall over the years. As she fed Poppy and watched Daisy, Charlotte listened to me list the reasons why so far none of the dates had been right: 'Oh, Jennifer,' she said sympathetically but with characteristic bluntness. 'Your problem is you've become too picky.'

Charlotte didn't mean to hurt my feelings and I think her reaction – talking with a woman who had access to virtually every single man in the world and was still complaining none was suitable – was quite understandable. But it stung. I was bossy and picky? Would I have found a suitable man amongst my dates if I'd been less judgemental and given them more of a chance? (*Everyone* thought I'd been too hard on Olivier in Paris.) And if this was true, was it possible my Soul Mate had been in London the whole time and it was my bad attitude that had been keeping us apart?

I gave it serious consideration, then decided no, that wasn't the case at all: when it comes to finding your Soul Mate, there is no such thing as too picky. I wanted a boyfriend who made me happy and I could make happy in return. I didn't think I wanted children (or maybe I did? I don't know); I had my own money, house, friends and adventures. I didn't need anything from the relationship other than the relationship itself. If I didn't like them and couldn't enjoy their company, what other reason did I have for being with them?

Being forced to examine these issues – although difficult – was incredibly useful: it helped me re-establish how important the journey was to me and my belief in the value of the search. It was another very old friend, Ian, who finally cemented my commitment to the journey I was undertaking.

I was talking to him about how hard it was to pull everything together and what if I didn't meet anyone and was my bossiness spiralling out of control and god, I looked tired and rubbish . . . Ian just hugged me and said calmly: 'Jen, this is the trip of a lifetime and it'll be over before you know it. Stop putting yourself under so much pressure and just enjoy what you're doing while it lasts.'

And I knew he was right: a bit like the Love Professor saying you had to like yourself before anyone else would, I had to enjoy the journey if I was going to get anything out of it. So I stopped moaning and got on with setting up the US leg of my trip.

• • •

Out of all the places to set up dates, the States was the hardest. Although relating to my mission, Americans seemed a little reluctant to get involved. I'm not saying they weren't helpful, it's just that it rarely got us anywhere. The situation was most acute in LA. My friend Olaf explained why:

As you know, LA is a very demanding city: men
already feel under so much pressure. I think
perhaps they don't want the additional stress of
competing with all the other men who are dating
you?

I found this a worrying observation: were LA men too stressed to date per se or just too stressed to date me? After I looked at the small ads in the online papers, I started to realise just how different a culture I was dealing with:

FUN STRAIGHT GIRL SEEKING FRIENDS
Be slim and pretty, to hang out with at all the hip new clubs, shopping, movies, lunches at hip/trendy restaurants and of course rich man hunting. Please be sincere and fun. (SFV/LA) Call Box # . . .

I assumed these ads were for prostitutes but my friend Ellie put me straight:

Sweetie, LA is about what you do and how you
look. Making friends is super hard, so we have
Activity Buddies instead: clubbing buddies; movie
buddies; gym buddies . . . LA is more about what
you do than who you do it with.

Yikes.

But maybe because it was so hard to form any kind of relationship – romantic or social – the American online websites were full of the most gorgeous-looking men ever: all plaid shirts, strong arms and bold smiles directly into the camera. They described themselves using words like smart, active and curious. There was a real energy and sense of manliness about them.

In contrast the British websites were all receding hairlines, Next casual shirts and smiles so forced they looked like they'd been photographed at gunpoint. The profiles were dispiriting too: '*I don't really know where to start . . . ,*' '*my friends say I'm caring and supportive*' (always followed with a self-deprecating '*but they would, wouldn't they?*'), '*After 7 difficult years . . .*'

Going online late, after a night out with my friend Cath, I saw I had a couple of emails from a dating website. The first man looked quite normal (though he did use the phrase *open-minded* twice when describing himself) but when I looked in the photo section he was draped across the bonnet of a red sports car, wearing leather trousers, his shirt open to the waist.

The second man told me he liked to travel but: *that was in the days when my knees both worked at the same time . . .*

Happily, I had already decided to give up on London dating by then: there simply wasn't the time to date, socialise and relax.

I did think I'd try and meet Karl but he lost patience when I struggled to find the time. I explained:

```
It's not that I don't want to see you or you're
unimportant, it's just I won't know until the end
of the week when I'll be free.
```

Who knows, maybe I was procrastinating because I only really wanted to see him on the road, not on home turf. Either way Karl wasn't happy:

For a person travelling the world dating, you seem surprisingly afraid of committing to meet up. I take it those you actually do see meet some criteria I'm not aware of. I guess it's time to call it quits, don't you?

I didn't blame him for being angry. He got back a few days later and said he was sorry for getting annoyed: he liked me and felt frustrated we couldn't meet. We awkwardly made up – just one example of how insane meeting through a dating website is: we'd never even met but we'd already had our first row.

In the meantime, I was still flat out trying to set up the US dates. I felt I needed to approach the situation differently: rather than have a succession of rushed one man/one night dates, I thought staying in one place with the same group of people would mean more time to get to know them.

I was going to Missoula for a few days to date a smoke jumper (basically a parachuting fireman), a rodeo rider and some friend of Jo's. It was a teeny town in the American Rockies and the kind of community where I thought I'd fit in. The experience of the Burning Man Festival, camping as part of the Costco Soul Mate Trading Outlet, was another strong possibility.

Costco had its own intranet site where all 40 of the campers seemed to email each other constantly. Although logging on to find up to 90 emails a day from them was a bit mind-boggling at times, they seemed a really fun and interesting group of people:

Absolutely, bring the kissing hammock, Rico had told a man called Gambo approvingly.

I chatted with Rico a lot via email: we talked about Soul Mates and work and life. He seemed a lovely man, though we did argue sometimes. He told me he was deeply in love with his partner Rite Aid Annie and he hoped I would meet someone who would make me just as happy:

```
I want to see you get your ass kicked by love.
```

You don't say.

```
What am I, some kind of a love slacker? Rico, I
want to be in love too, and have taken pretty
drastic steps to try and make it happen. But it
takes more than just wanting and looking you
know: Fate and chemistry need to show up and play
their part too.
```

Meanwhile, there seemed to be a strange new phenomenon at home. As word of my homecoming had spread throughout my group, old boyfriends and The One Who Could Have Beens were getting in touch. To try and rewrite history?

```
Was lovely to see you. The freckles are gorgeous.
Am definitely up for hot date. Not in the least
worried to be one in eighty.
```

And Would-Be Dates (WBD) were trying to use me to settle professional rivalry scores.

How's your round-the-world dating going? Let me
know when it's my turn! By the way, is ********
going to be a hot date as well? He wrote a nasty
review of my ******* book in the *******. Cut him
off your list!

The Date Wranglers were having a bit of a moment too.
Hannah rang from Budapest to ask if I thought I was going to
get on with the friend she'd set me up with in Bangkok. I quite
understood why she was having second thoughts but what
could I tell her? That I'd never met him but she knew both of
us and so was clearly the only person who could make that
judgement call?

Posh PR Emma had set me up with Jake, her friend who
worked as an A-list photographer in Vegas. Newly divorced, he
lived a larger-than-showbiz life: gold bath fixtures and his last
two ex-wives' implants in the fridge (cold eye-masks for
reducing puffiness before a photo shoot). He sounded extraordinary. But so far his emails had been a little disappointing:
more blank than bling.

Out with Jo, I mentioned my concerns about Jake and she
shrieked: 'Oh god, Jennifer, he's Emma's pet project. She set
me up with him too, and he's DULL, DULL, DULL. You
think he'll have all these really interesting stories and he
doesn't: he's just really, really boring.'

I don't want to sound unkind, but I wasn't the dating arm of
the Samaritans. I was looking to meet my Soul Mate and it was
important I didn't get rerouted into other people's dating
agendas. I know that sounds mean, but I just didn't have the
energy to spare. I learnt this the hard way when Paul asked me
to go down the pub.

It had been a long and trying day: trying to firm up the hotel in Vegas; work out if a tattooist two hours north of San Francisco was worth the drive, as well as attempting to get the New York Fire Department to take me just a little more seriously. ('*Like I tell all of you ladies calling to date our boys, put it in writing.*') The dating website that based your matches on which books you read just highlighted that men and women read different books: thankfully, the site that based your matches on what you like to watch on TV was looking more promising.

Paul rang to say that a group of our friends was going down the pub and did I want to go? I was frazzled but thought I could do with a break, so agreed. When I arrived an hour later, Paul was the only one there.

'Oh, are we early?' I asked as I plonked myself down at the table.

'No,' he replied cheerfully. I was confused but thought I must have misheard him. While Paul was at the bar buying me a drink, my phone chirped. Jo was texting me:

Let me know how it goes?

How what goes?

Paul came back from the bar and we settled down and chatted for about half an hour. He was unusually attentive, also quite tense. 'Is everything okay?' I asked him, concerned he might be having a bad time about something and wanted to talk about it. 'Yes,' he replied anxiously, 'I'm just pleased to see you.'

It was then it dawned on me. 'Paul, are we on a date?' I asked, trying to sound conversational. He nodded and squeezed my hand.

I could have killed him.

He was a nice guy but there was no way I would have agreed to go on a date with him, especially at the moment when I was dated to the max. And he'd tricked me into it by pretending our other friends would be there – probably knowing it was the only way he'd get me to say 'yes'. We walked to the railway station together at the end of the evening, and I had to execute an advanced Quick Peck and Hug manoeuvre to avoid his persistent advances.

Back in my little flat, I thought how good it had been to spend time at home. But the fact was, by involving all my friends in my Soul Mate quest, I'd made my home life too chaotic. And if I stayed here any longer, things would only get more complicated and out of control. But my two weeks were up anyway. And in my upside-down fairytale world, I'd really enjoyed it: working quietly, eating nothing but toast and living in knackered old T-shirts and frayed jeans every day. Now the clock was striking midnight and it was time to squeeze those glass slippers back onto my feet and whirl and twirl across America, in search of my Prince.

CHAPTER EIGHT

USA – LA

Weird, bloated stomach; indecisive and easily confused; tired and craving sugar . . . jet lag is the PMS of travellers, without the payoff of knowing you're not pregnant.

But I was in LA, low-fat, low-sugar capital of the world, and I was determined that it would be the inspiration for a new healthy me. I was going to get back in shape: eat properly and start working out again. I'd feel and look better, as well as having more energy for my quest.

I was staying at the Best Western on Sunset Strip, much nicer than it sounds and incredibly central, especially as my first date was with a comedian across the road at the Comedy Store, called Lowell. My friend Lizzy had given me his number but suggested I catch his show tonight and ring him tomorrow if I liked him. I knew my Date Wranglers well enough by now to know I'd live to regret not taking their advice when it was offered.

Date #28: Lowell – Sunset Strip, LA, USA
It was open-mike night at the Comedy Store: 24 comedians each with three minutes to be funny. Such rapid turnover

meant that the audience never got to know or care about the comedian, they looked for quick laughs instead. Faced with such performance pressure, most comedians first lost their confidence and then their audience, whose wandering attention made them chat and heckle.

Watching the audience smell the blood of a dying comedian, then finish him off with brutal indifference, was a chilling sight, like a gladiator fighting for his life in front of a jaded mob.

I missed Lowell's entrance on stage: an Australian impersonator (he impersonated a swallow by holding the mike to his throat and swallowing) was asking me if the audience hadn't laughed because they couldn't understand his accent?

Instead of answering, I turned my attention to Lowell, who was a few moments into his act. He had an electric presence: tall with a tense, sinewy body and short, dirty blond hair, Lowell spoke with a deep southern drawl. There was nothing languid about him, though, his act was deeply offensive, performed with the furious belligerence of a drunk being bundled into a police van at midnight.

He did what virtually no other comedian had managed though: he got the attention of the crowd. After telling one of the sickest jokes I have ever heard spoken aloud, his three minutes were up and Lowell stormed off-stage to such howls of outrage and abuse that for a moment I wondered if *stage-struck* actually meant someone coming up on stage and punching you.

Although appalled, I actually thought he was a pretty good comedian, but there was no way in the world I was going to date him (and I suspect Lizzy knew this). I drank a beer and watched a few more of the acts, before deciding to call it a night.

Outside in the car park, a knot of spent comedians paced in distracted agitation, like a gang of street fighters licking their wounds after a violent clash. Lowell was amongst them. He didn't know I was Lizzy's friend, still, he caught my eye as I passed. 'Thanks for coming,' he called out.

'I admired your act,' I said over my shoulder as I continued to walk.

'Really?' he asked, running to catch up. He walked a couple of paces ahead, then turned to face me. 'It gets me right here,' he said, hitting his fist on his chest, arrogant yet clearly stung by the reception he'd just received.

'I thought you were funny,' I told him honestly.

'Really?' he asked again, his need for approval naked and demanding. 'I thought it was a disaster.' He looked shocked, whether at his act or the audience's response, I couldn't tell.

'You're original,' I said evenly, 'you weren't like the others: you weren't trying to please, you stood out.'

Behind him, the strung-out comedians continued to pace, ebbing and flowing around each other as the adrenaline surge slowly abated. 'Will you be coming back?' Lowell asked.

'Maybe,' I shrugged as I walked off. But I knew I wouldn't: funny was what these men did, not what they were.

Date #29: Brian – CBS TV Studios, Fairfax, LA, USA

Brian wasn't what he appeared either.

When I'd told Ellie about my difficulties in finding a date in LA, she promised to find me someone and, sure enough, her friend Brian was coming on a TV date with me.

I wanted to go on a TV date to test a theory. As I see it, once you get past the initial mutually obsessed and introspective stage of a new romance, it settles into something cosier, and that generally involves staying in and watching a fair amount of TV together. Since LA is where most sitcoms are recorded, I thought watching TV on a date – or, to be more specific, sitting in on the recording of a TV programme on a date – would be a good way to see if we were compatible.

Sadly, my theory went untested as there were apparently two CBS studios in LA and we ended up going to the wrong one.

Brian picked me up from the hotel in his car and we made the short trip over to Fairfax. Tall, with short dark hair, huge blue eyes and a body gymed to perfection, my first impression was that he was cute . . . and gay.

Needless to say, I kept this thought to myself.

When we arrived at CBS and were told we were at the wrong studio, Brian was upset and apologised profusely: 'Oh, Jennifer, I am such an idiot: I really wanted to see it too.'

He looked genuinely disappointed but rallied quickly. Grabbing my hand, we raced from the car park to the scariest and most fabulous second-hand clothes shop I'd ever seen. None of the genteel manners of Help the Aged: people pushed trolleys around the racks, shopping here because they had to.

And in the shop I discovered that Brian wasn't Brian and that he was indeed gay.

The Thrift Store had no changing rooms, instead about twenty mirrors were mounted close together on the long back wall. I modestly disrobed behind a stack of quadraphonic cartridges and a wall of Harold Robbins novels. Brian had no such hang-ups: a pile of clothes at his feet, he unselfconsciously stripped off in front of the mirrors (and a crowd of admiring young men). His stomach was so flat and his muscles so hard that, if lost at sea, you could have flipped him onto his back, gripped his nipples and surfed to shore on him.

I stared at his buffed body and blurted out: 'Brian, you have the kind of body gay men would kill for.' Much to the disappointment of his audience, he stopped rippling his washboard stomach and looked sheepishly at me.

He held my gaze for a moment, then said quietly: 'You know, don't you?'

'Well . . .' My voice trailed off and I shrugged awkwardly (which considering I was balancing on one leg, an apricot satin jumpsuit halfway up the other, was quite an achievement).

We left the clothes in a pile on the floor and went next door for coffee. Brian was a friend of Ellie's, and also a friend of Marc, who apparently was the man I was having coffee with right now.

'Jennifer . . .' he said with a pained look on his face. 'No question, I was going to tell you, I was just waiting for the right moment. You must be really mad at me, huh?' Marc went on to explain how Brian had had to work late, but Marc – his flat mate – was a huge fan of one of the actors in the programme, so volunteered to come along instead. 'We figured this way, at least you'd have a date for the night,' Marc (aka Brian) reasoned wretchedly.

I'd missed my programme and my date was gay, but I genuinely couldn't have been happier. To go shopping was always a treat, but to be taken shopping by a sweet man who knew where the best designer bargains in LA could be found . . . in that respect Marc really was my Soul Mate. Brian/Marc paid for the coffee and we went right back to our shopping. It was a wonderful date.

Dates #30–50: Speed Dating – Redondo Beach, LA, USA

I read on the in-flight magazine coming over that 74 per cent of men know after the first 15 minutes of a date if they are interested or not.

Fifteen minutes? That long?

Women know instantly if they are interested or not. Like playing a slot machine, in those first, dense dating moments, the tone of voice, content of conversation, appearance, body language, dress sense, height and general vibe all spin around women's heads until the barrels fall into place. They are then either predominantly cherries (put more money in and keep playing) or lemons (stop playing and leave the machine for someone else).

That's why the theory behind speed dating – 20 dates each lasting three minutes – makes so much sense. It might be hard on the men – whether comedian or dater – but women can learn a lot in three LA minutes.

My friend Ian cynically accused me of wanting to speed date just to get my numbers up, but I was genuinely curious. Less convenient than online dating – it's at a set time and you have to travel to a venue – there are however real advantages. A face-to-face meeting means you quickly discover if you like them or not, plus you see straight away if there's any chemistry between you, without feeling obligated or involved. You'll also find out how accurate their profile is – in my early online days I spent two weeks having fabulous e-chats with Martin, before meeting up and disappointedly discovering he was in fact *10 Per Cent Too Small Martin*.

So I went speed dating.

. . .

Arriving at a packed bar in Redondo Beach, organiser Styve (it's LA) smiled with pleasure and relief at the sight of me: 'Oh thank goodness, another woman, we're running so short.' I looked around the bar and sure enough there were five little tables, with a harassed-looking woman sitting behind each one, a swarm of impatient men surrounding them, checking to see no one exceeded the allotted three minutes and edging forwards in anticipation of their own.

Part of me thought I should feel intimidated by the pressure and the incredible air of competitiveness that permeated the room, but instead I was delighted. LA is a social barometer for the rest of the world: was this the future of dating? Single men outnumbering women five to one?

Styve gave me a badge with my name and a number, pushed a clipboard into my hand, and told me to write down the number of any guy I was interested in. They would email me the results (like some kind of weird dating pregnancy test: *Congratulations, Jennifer, you're going to have a boyfriend*) in a couple of days.

God, I suddenly realised I hadn't thought up a story: what reason would I give the Dates for being here? I didn't want to tell them about my quest as that would take the whole three minutes. But if I told the truth – I was here for two days and wanted to meet someone – even in therapy-hungry LA, that was going to scream relationship issues.

As it turned out I needn't have worried: with so few women and so few minutes, the Dates did all the talking.

Date #30 told me Jesus didn't mind us doing this and asked which church did I attend? **Date #31** was an analyst of something I didn't catch because he muttered (his username was 'no_talking'. I felt like replying 'no_kidding'). **Date #32** worked in defence: 'I can't tell you anything else until I get you security cleared.' I asked **Date #33** if he had ever been to one of these events before? 'Last night,' he replied. 'I'm ready to have children and need to meet my wife.' **Date #34** was German and desperate to talk to another European. **Date #35** was a sweet, lonely Vietnamese man: 'I've decided I need to chill out and meet more people. It doesn't have to be dating – I just want some friends.' **Date #36** was a management consultant who talked about how much he enjoyed Nepal. 'Why?' I asked. 'They floss their teeth in the street,' he replied. I liked **Date #37**, though he shouted at 2 minutes 59 seconds, 'I have two children,' as **Date #38** dragged him away from my table by the chair.

I felt slightly overwhelmed by the time I'd completed **Date #50** and couldn't get away fast enough. Like being on a quiz show and having the audience shout '*cuddly toy, cuddly toy*', I thought there had to be a less stressful way of getting the prize.

As I arrived back at the hotel, Lizzy rang from London to see how it had worked out with Lowell. I told her he was a little too intense for me, but he was Parker Knoll laid-back compared with some of the speed daters I'd just met.

We laughed about it and Lizzy commented: 'Jennifer, this is the first time I've heard you sound really happy in ages. I was worried it was all beginning to get to you.' I hadn't thought about it but she was right: I felt excited and alive in a way I never had in Europe.

'For some reason, I found it really hard to get under the skin of the dates in Europe,' I confessed, realising for the first time that this was true. 'I always felt like an outsider. Maybe because American culture is more like ours or everyone loves my accent here and wants to talk to me . . . ? I feel part of what's going on rather than just a spectator.'

It could also be that, rested from a spell at home and now with quite a few dates under my belt, I was more experienced at handling the 'workload'. It had felt incredibly intimidating when I'd started out, but now there seemed to be a natural rhythm and order to events. It was easier to know what to expect and be prepared.

'You know, I actually feel excited to be here: in fact I'm even looking forward to dating. I don't know that I ever did in Europe: there always seemed so much of it.'

We then chatted about normal stuff – how her baby Connie was, the fabulous pair of boots I'd bought on Rodeo Drive – before saying goodbye.

Although it was late I felt really cheery and full of energy, so popped next door to The House of Blues to catch Arthur Lee & Love. It was good, simple, loud fun: talking was impossible; I smiled and shrugged at the guys who tried to engage me in conversation. Encoring with a scorching version of 'Smokestack Lightning', Lee removed his sunglasses for the first time and croaked to the audience: 'Hey, ya'll do me a favour: love each other.' So different to the hard-nosed comedy crowd across the road, the audience cheered and danced wildly.

This felt like a good omen and I cheered and danced along with everyone else. Lizzy was right, I felt happy and flirty, and seemed to be getting chatted up like mad as a result. I can't explain why but for some reason I knew I was on the right path, doing the right thing. My Soul Mate was getting closer; things were going to change, I could feel it.

'So where are you stripping tonight?'

It took every ounce of willpower I possessed not to turn and

see who in the Southwest Airlines check-in queue had just
been asked that question.

It cleared one thing up, though: why so many big-haired,
big-boobed, teeny-outfitted blondes were walking around LA
airport. One woman wore a small (and I mean tiny) red T-shirt
and red plastic shorts that covered just the top half of her
bottom. As she bent over, struggling to lift her heavy bags onto
the check-in scales, she oozed from her shorts like peanut
butter out of a sandwich. The queue watched, helplessly transfixed, unsure whether we should call a porter or a gynaecologist
to help.

Thursday afternoon was obviously when all the strippers
travelled to work: we were catching the Red Thigh to
Vegas.

'You wanna see a show tomorrow, ma'am?'

The top-hatted ticket tout waved flyers energetically at the
fifty-something woman and her husband ducking into the air-
conditioned sanctuary of New York New York to escape the
searing heat of the Strip.

'We're going to a wedding tomorrow,' she barked back in a
thick Brooklyn accent. 'That's the biggest show there is.'

Las Vegas is famously both the wedding and gambling
capital of America. You've got to wonder if there's a relationship between the two? Apart from legalities (i.e. it's quick and
easy), why do so many people get married in Vegas? Is it
because, a theme park in the middle of a desert and cut off from
the rest of the world, Vegas brings out a 'what the hell . . . ?'
impetuosity? Or having bet and won in the casinos, do people
feel more prepared for the ultimate gamble?

And if relationships are a crap shoot, could I learn anything helpful from a professional gambler? How much was luck and how much was knowing and playing the system? I'd arranged to meet Chester through a third-generation Date Wrangler. Aware this could be a little dicey, we were having a drink in my hotel bar so I'd feel more secure on 'home territory'.

The problem was my usual hotel, the Alexis Park (cheap but really homely, with three swimming pools and huge comfortable rooms) was full at the last minute, so I had to stay at the Days Inn off Strip.

It wasn't a bad hotel; actually I grew incredibly fond of it by the time I had to leave, but it was threadbare and in a very dodgy neighbourhood. A dark bar ran the length of the lobby, a cluster of slot machines were behind it and a large, basic diner was through an alcove off to the right. All was guarded by a one-armed maintenance man in his seventies called Neville.

The place was full of old people, all either waiting for the slots to pay out or the macaroni cheese to be served up. Outside it was more lively. On the first night I was chased by a gang on chopper bikes. The second, I narrowly missed getting hit with a chain in a fight between rival chopper gangs. On the third night a punch up between rival chopper gangs exploded onto the hotel porch where I was sitting quietly. The Days Inn was like an old people's home in a cul de sac off Armageddon.

And it was here that Chester came for our date.

Date #51: Chester – Professional Gambler, Vegas, USA

Chester, a big man in his late forties, with dark hair and an expanse of Desperate Dan stubble, and I sat at the bar. He immediately became engrossed in a poker game on TV and stayed engrossed for the duration of our date.

Poker is huge in America. Not only are the games televised (including a long-running series of celebrity poker), special wrist-cams have been developed so you can see the hands of star players and follow their progress.

Chester didn't want to miss the big tournament currently underway and after several failed attempts to engage him in conversation, I resigned myself to sitting and watching with him. I set a two-drink time limit: if the programme was finished and we'd talked by then, great, if not, I was going to my room to catch up on email.

The game wasn't particularly interesting but I found the intensity of the players utterly compelling. Chester did too: 'Look at his hands,' he said, nodding up at the screen, 'they're shaking. That means he's got a good hand.'

'Really?' I asked, impatience immediately forgotten. 'How do you know?'

'You can tell a lot about a player and what they're holding by their body language,' he replied, his eyes never leaving the screen. 'See him stare at his cards, that means he's got a good hand. When they stare at their chips, that means they've got a bad hand and they're wondering how much they can afford to lose.'

This was what I had come for. 'So that man tidying his stack of chips, does that mean anything?'

Chester didn't answer immediately, lost in the game again, but then with distracted impatience snorted: 'It all means something. If you're going to gamble you've got to study your opponent: you can be damned sure they'll be studying you. Man who tidies his chips? He's probably a real careful player:

thinks things through, don't take a lot of risks. Man who leaves them loose, he's aggressive and harder to call. And look how they're sitting: see the guy just sat back in his chair? He's about to fold, knows he's out the game . . .'

And sure enough, the man laid his cards down and the dealer swept his chips away into the centre of the table.

This was fascinating. I had witnessed similar body language amongst the speed daters. The mumbling analyst had leant right back in his chair, whereas the management consultant/ street flosser – presumably more confident of his hand – jutted forward, his face pushed quite intimidatingly into mine.

After the intense flurry of insights Chester was silent again, engrossed in the game, acting as if we were two strangers at a bar (which of course we were). I took tiny sips of my warm beer, half watching the game, half watching Neville slowly clean the frayed carpet. Chester suddenly let out a big sigh. I turned back to the TV: the game had finished and Chester was slumped slightly, the tension he'd been holding for the duration of the game leaving his body.

You'd think gambling or comedy would be fun jobs, but so far they were some of the tensest people I'd met. Is this how I'd seemed to people when I was working?

'The thing about gambling,' Chester explained, turning his stool to face mine for the first time, 'is that it's not a game at all: it's a job. You've got to work at it and take it seriously. You can't put it down to luck and go in unprepared.'

He was obviously very serious about it, as were all the people I'd met when it came to their profession. And where did that leave Love? Was I right to approach my Soul Mate quest like a job, or could you be lucky in Love?

'What about beginner's luck?' I asked.

'Just that,' he replied dismissively. 'It doesn't mean anything and it doesn't last.'

'So what do you need to play well?' I asked him. 'What makes a good player?'

'Well,' he replied, blowing out a little more of the tension before taking a swallow of his whisky and coke. 'A good player has done half his work before he even gets to the table. Are you in the right frame of mind; have you set your limit; who's the opposition?'

Although I could see parallels, so far gambling was about winning at any cost. I didn't want a man at any cost, I wanted the right one. But being able to read my Dates would help me decide if I was on the right track.

'I know this sounds stupid, but is it always about winning?' Chester looked intrigued by my question: like I'd graduated from basics and made it through to the next — but still basic — level.

'You have to think about what you want: I mean obviously you want to win, but you have to think about how much you want to win and how much you have to lose. You have to set your limit and when you reach it, get up and walk away; never throw good money after bad.'

That made sense: I'd never set a limit with Kelly, I always thought I was in too deep to go back and if I just tried a little harder, gave a little more, we'd be fine.

'That must take a lot of control?' I said humbly.

'Playing is all about control,' Chester observed bluntly. 'You don't play angry, you don't play drunk. It's not just your cards you're playing, it's people. And at the exact same time, they're playing you. You need a clear head to think through that, then imagine yourself winning.'

'Imagine yourself winning?' I repeated, perplexed. 'Wouldn't that make you overconfident?'

'Not at all,' Chester disagreed. 'It's called "positive visualisation", like being a runner: see yourself making it across the finish line, you pace yourself better, run a better race too. See yourself winning at poker, you make the winning calls. See yourself as a loser, you've not got the self-belief or determination to play well, no matter how much money you gamble.'

I was shocked to hear the words of the Love Professor echoed by Chester: like yourself and you'll win; think you're a loser, and sure enough you'll end up losing.

'That's why none of these weekend gamblers got the first clue,' Chester said, showing emotion for the first time. 'Gambling takes patience: before you even sit down at a table you have to watch, study and learn. You make all the moves in your head first: you can't just rush in.'

Although I thought Chester was right about being prepared, I also thought he was being overly harsh: weekend tourists weren't professional gamblers, they were people enjoying themselves. And surely that was okay? Like all of us obsessed with our careers, Chester was assuming that everyone took gambling as seriously as he did.

'But surely most people coming to Vegas just gamble for fun?' I countered.

'Yes, ma'am, they do,' Chester agreed. 'And there ain't nothing wrong with fun.' And with that, he leant over and kissed me.

I was absolutely not expecting this. I mean, not remotely. Not like when Frank in Holland kissed me and I wasn't expecting it, because Frank and I had spent the whole day chatting and had got on really well. Chester had hardly even spoken to me, let alone established any kind of a rapport.

Horribly afraid that Neville was watching, I grabbed the edge of the bar to stop myself toppling backwards off my stool and slid sideways, away from Chester's kiss. He smiled good-naturedly: 'Sometimes you just gotta take a chance,' he said.

In a fluster, I got up and thanked him for his time. I didn't say what I really wanted, which was: 'Oh, so suddenly now you believe in luck?' It seems when it came to romance, even professionals forgot the theory and followed their heart (well, one of their organs anyway).

The next day I thought about what Chester had said. The body-language tips had been useful, so had the one about setting limits (though I had learnt this in Paris). What I found completely invaluable were his comments about positive visualisation. This was one step on from the Love Professor's *like yourself* philo-sophy: it implied that once you liked yourself, you should then imagine what the lovely new you wanted and deserved.

I booted up my laptop and reread my Soul Mate Job description:

> . . . *old-fashioned enough to want to feel 'ladylike' . . . someone who makes me smile; lets me read them bits out the newspaper . . . tells me interesting things I didn't know . . . you'll believe that life is short and you should make the most of it . . . sense of fun and adventure essential.*

God, whoever he was, he sounded lovely. I concentrated on the job description and imagined us together: making each other laugh; arguing about politics; getting lost in exotic countries; curling up in front of the TV. I smiled, a little sadly, wondering if I would ever meet him, then remembered I liked myself and was meant to be positively visualising him. He was out there and I would meet him: I would.

And suddenly I realised I actually believed it. Not because I was meant to, but because in my heart, I truly felt it.

The next morning I came downstairs as a couple of other Days Inn-ers – Earl and Rhea – were heading off in a coach with their friends to renew their wedding vows. They were going to the famous Little White Wedding Chapel and, seeing *that cute Briddish gal*, asked if I wanted to come along too. They'd been married 50 years and clearly relished each other's company (in a teasing, mock eye-rolling way). Rhea looked lovely in a peach-coloured silk suit, Earl resplendent in a '*If it's got tits or tyres it's gonna git you into trouble*' T-shirt.

Known as the Wedding Queen of the West, over the last 40 years, Little White Wedding Chapel owner and marriage aficionado, Charolette Richards, had married everyone from Judy Garland, Frank Sinatra and Joan Collins to Britney Spears and, umm, Blue Oyster Cult. Staff included ex Bluebell girls and a vast array of impersonators from Sammy Davis Jr to Dean Martin. And, of course, Elvis. I got separated from the party after they decided to hire a stretch limo and do the wedding as a drive-through. Trying to stay out the heat, I got chatting with Roseanne, Charolette's second in command, instead.

We retreated to the cool of the staff room and a piece of wedding cake was pushed into my hand as Roseanne told me that 25 per cent of all the ceremonies were renewals. I found this, and everything else about the place, really uplifting. The room had the atmosphere of a feel-good musical: Sammy Davis Jr laughed and spun as he showed another Sammy Davis Jr how to do a complicated move. Flower arrangers danced around the huge fridges that kept the blooms chilled, as Elvis teased and serenaded, begging them 'Don't be Cruel'.

'Is he practising?' I asked Roseanne.

'Oh no,' she replied cheerfully. 'He just loves to sing. Once he starts, he don't stop.' With newly married couples popping in, bursting with happy tears and heartfelt thanks, it was an emotional and joyful atmosphere. Before long I had told them about my quest and we were swapping stories and advice about love and marriage.

It was a wonderful day. Everyone hugged and kissed me goodbye, as Dean Martin prepared to drive me in a stretch limo to Bellagio's. The wardrobe mistress – a tiny Italian woman, choreographer to Michael Crawford in *Barnum* with the unquestionable authority of a Sicilian Godmother – walked me to the car. 'You wanna know the secret to a successful marriage?' she asked, poking her finger sternly into my chest. She hand-tailored fairytale wedding dresses and had herself been married 53 years, so I said yes without hesitation. 'Meet the family,' she said in a tone that brooked no argument. 'Because when the sex is all gone, the family will still be there.'

When I got back to my room, Frank had emailed from Holland:

i was wondering where on earth you are at this moment, wich number of date you are dealing with,

and . . . how many guys you have been kissing
untill now. am i still the one and only lucky
lips?

Although I had had a few kisses since Frank, he'd been the
most fun and I emailed him straight back, reassuring him that
he was still the #1 Kisser.

For now.

I loved Vegas. Everything about it: my dodgy hotel; the
crushing heat; the incessant tackiness; the relentless beep of the
slot machines. It should have been repellent but it was the
opposite. Apart from the chopper gangs, everyone was really
friendly and the tack was so well done, wandering around the
imaginative air-conditioned interiors of the hotels and casinos
was a real pleasure.

Over the next couple of days, I dated **Elvis (Date #52)** (real
name Dean Z) who had mesmerising turquoise eyes and a quiff
as high and solid as a well-baked granary loaf. Sadly, he was too
young, at just 20 years old, but he was gorgeous, clever and
extremely interesting. He'd been Elvis since he was three; his
grandfather had been a drummer in the Fifties with a big-name
British performer: 'Maybe you have heard of Max Bygraves?' he
asked politely.

Rob (Date #53) was nearly as good-looking as Anders
without being as scary. He was determined to prove I could have
gone Around the World without leaving Vegas. So he took me
for drinks in Venice, dinner in Paris, a stroll around the

Pyramids and side streets of New York, shark watching on the Mandalay Reef and finally drinks again, this time in Morocco. Rob couldn't sit still for two minutes and long-term I would have found that too distracting. But we laughed and teased each other and at the end of the night, he stole Frank's title.

Betty's Outrageous Adventures was a funky, lesbian social club in Vegas. I'd found them on the Internet a while back and had been in regular email contact with their president Nanc ever since. She seemed lovely and I was looking forward to meeting her and the other **Bettys (Date #54)**, at one of their regular picnics out of town:

We tend to sit around and chat, and often run off to hike because the area is so beautiful and less hot than Vegas. Feel welcome to come along. I would love to hear about your travel adventures.

Nanc picked me up from the Days Inn late the following morning, with another Betty called Elizabeth. We set off in her four-wheel drive for the mountains, 40 minutes outside of Vegas.

In her mid-thirties, Nanc was pretty, blonde and petite but also incredibly gentle and kindly. We all felt a little awkward and Nanc was at pains to make me welcome. Elizabeth, on the other hand – late thirties, slim and very fit-looking – was a non-stop acerbic wit from the moment she opened her mouth. She was a tough and successful journalist and grilled me relentlessly as we drove through increasingly heavy rain to the mountains.

It was a brilliant drive. Not just because we were all single so the subject of my journey was close to our hearts, but also because Nanc and Elizabeth – naturally – responded to everything from a lesbian perspective. It was a completely fresh angle for me to consider my position from.

'How do you know if they're your Soul Mate if you only have one date with them?' Elizabeth demanded.

'Oh come on,' I retorted, really enjoying sparring with her. 'Where's your sense of romance: have you never just looked at someone and known they're The One?' She begrudgingly admitted she had; I confessed in return that it made me uncomfortable and perplexed when men expected me to sleep with them on the first date.

'But they're men,' Elizabeth snorted, 'that's why they're dating you. And they only have one date, what else do you expect them to do?'

'Lesbians have different priorities to straight couples,' Nanc observed gently. As she spoke she kept her eyes firmly on the road, by now bouncing with huge hailstones and illuminated by the piercing forks of lightning flickering ahead. 'First and foremost, we want friendship,' she continued. 'If that works out, the next priority is a long-term partner. Some, but very few, lesbians feel sex is their most important priority: it's way down the list.'

As Elizabeth and Nanc fell into a conversation about one of the Bettys for whom sex was a priority and the mess she was in at the moment, I considered Nanc's statement. Those weren't just lesbian priorities: I am sure they were most women's. They were certainly mine. I knew I wasn't gay, so where did that leave me and my search? Trying to meet my Soul Mate in a situation where our priorities were polarised.

But now wasn't the time to be introspective. We had arrived at the spot for the Bettys' hike and picnic. On the side of a steep hill, staked by huge, shaggy pine trees, 23 lesbians sheltered in a five-woman tent as hail and rain thundered all around. Grabbing our pot-luck contributions, Nanc, Elizabeth and I splashed through the mud and sprinted towards the tent.

It had been erected around one of those outdoor wooden picnic benches and any surface not taken with huge bowls of tuna salad, white wine or chocolate cookies had a drenched Betty sitting on it. Nudging our way into the shelter was like squeezing into a lesbian elevator: there was not one spare inch of room.

Under these circumstances it was incredibly easy to make friends, and – like the Wedding Chapel yesterday – we joined in with the laughing and storytelling that was already well underway. Hearing the reason for my journey, Hettie and June, a couple in their sixties, wished me luck in my search. They were Soul Mates, June told me. Not that I needed to be told: as the Love Professor had predicted, they mirrored each other's body language and unselfconsciously finished the other's sentences.

There was nothing cringy or schmaltzy about them: sitting huddled in the pouring rain in their soaked hiking jackets, they looked like they were made for each other.

'We've only been together three years,' June confided. 'But our entire lives were leading to our time together,' Hettie added with conviction.

June smiled and squeezed Hettie's hand.

I smiled too and told them both about Chester's positive-visualisation theory. 'Yes,' Hettie nodded thoughtfully, 'you've got to believe it will happen, but just as importantly, when the moment comes, you have to be prepared to take that leap of faith.'

I hugged them both, touched by their story and acknow-ledging the truth in Hettie's advice.

CHAPTER NINE

USA – Black Rock City, Nevada

The woman motioned for me to kill the engine as she stepped from the checkpoint and swaggered through the searing desert heat towards me. Eyes protected from the harsh elements by diamanté-studded goggles, she was naked but for a pair of large greying y-fronts and a golden sheriff star painted onto each of her nipples.

Walking up to my side of the car, without saying a word, the *Greeter* stuck her head through the open window and kissed me long and hard on the mouth.

Straightening up, she then stared at me calculatingly. Without breaking eye contact, I reached behind me into the cooler on the back seat and pulled out a six-pack of beer. In silence I handed it to her. She smiled for the first time, then, rolling the icy cans across her bare stomach, threw her head back and let out a shriek of pure joy. 'You're my kind of girl,' she laughed, pulling her goggles back and beaming at me. 'It's a pleasure to have you in Black Rock City. Welcome to Burning Man.'

• • •

At the end of every summer, The Burning Man Festival set up camp on the Playa, a blistering, barren section of the Nevada desert, two hours drive northeast of Reno.

Started in San Francisco in 1986 by Larry Harvey and relocated to the desert in 1992, it was less a festival and more a radical exercise in personal expression and communal inter-dependence. Nothing grew on the Playa, there was no shelter and you couldn't buy or sell anything (with the exception of ice and coffee). Life on the Playa was about bringing everything you needed for a week, then sharing it with a community of up to 30,000 people.

The result is Black Rock City (BRC): a well-organised collection of theme camps – arranged in vast concentric circles – that challenge you to experience thoughts and activities ranging from the spiritual or political to the physical, artistic or just plain silly. Feel underdressed? Walk into that marquee and help yourself to a ball gown from the racks. Can't cope with your dust-encrusted body for another moment? Go to the hair-washing or the feet-washing camp, or just forget the dust altogether and go to the Picasso Painting camp and get your body *arted*.

I was here to work at the Costco Soul Mate Trading Outlet, the Playa's dating camp. As I drove very slowly along the dusty roads between the neighbourhoods of tents, temples and giant structures, trying to avoid the naked cyclists, I searched for the Costco banner to help me locate them.

'Hey slow down,' I suddenly heard someone shout. Although I was going only five miles an hour, I braked hard and peered with alarm at the group of Rangers (the volunteer BRC law enforcement) standing by their bikes (the site covers 25 kms, so once you're parked, you cycle everywhere).

As a teenager growing up in rural Essex and attending a hippy secondary school, I've been to a lot of weird festivals, where it was the norm to stand around naked or hang out of trees at 4 a.m. playing the saxophone. But because this was an American festival, it was outside my own festival culture. Self-consciously English, I was scared I'd commit a *festival pas* and do something embarrassingly uncool.

'I'm really sorry,' I called out apologetically to the Rangers. I had no idea what I'd done. 'Was I going too fast?'

'No,' one of the group called back grinning. 'But you're in a car so we're experiencing some difficulty in checking you out.'

I rarely blush but I did now. Deep, deep red.

They didn't notice, however, because they were too busy talking amongst themselves. 'Oh fuck, is she British? Hot and British?' They all nodded wide-eyed at the Ranger who'd spoken to me. 'Hey, cute Brit chick . . .' he called out, handing his bike to another Ranger and walking over to my car.

Although still blushing, by now I was giggling too. 'Where are you camping, sweetie?' he asked, resting his arm on the open window and leaning in, letting me admire his green eyes sparkling mischievously against his tanned skin.

'Umm, I'm with Costco,' I replied, flustered and self-conscious but unable to stop laughing. 'But I'm a bit lost. Do you know where they are?'

He replied, of course he did, everyone knew Costco and pointed me towards BRC's centre. 'But hey, one more thing . . .' he said sternly as I started the car.

'Yes?' I asked, turning anxiously to face him.

'Just remember this . . .' he told me, and, leaning into the car, he gave me a long, lingering kiss that gently wiped the desert dust from his face onto mine.

When he finished, he raised one eyebrow and touched a finger to my cheek: 'I'll be watching out for you, Hot British Chick,' and, rejoining his group, cycled off around a large group of naked people cartwheeling through the burning sand.

I watched him go and decided to take a moment to organise my thoughts. I had known Burning Man was going to be crazy – as many of the dates were in their own way – so had automatically slipped into my standard *whatever* travelling state of mind. What I hadn't expected was there to be so much kissing, but – do you know what? – it was nice. I was okay with this. In fact, I liked it: it was *sport kissing*, no-agenda fun. Feeling I had taken an emotional litmus test and the results had come back all clear, I started the car up again and drove slowly towards the Costco camp.

I was soon to discover this was barely the tip of the kissing iceberg: I was Captain of the *Titanic*, powering full steam ahead towards a vast ocean of puckered lips.

Date #55: Garry – Burning Man Festival, Nevada, USA
Dusk settled on the cracked desert floor. The earthy scent of wood smoke mixed with the pulse of music and the sound of hundreds of camps hurrying to assemble their tents, as the long fingers of fading light brushed passed them, leaving the Playa suffused in a soft, inky darkness.

As I loaded up with supplies from the boot of the car (gallons of water, eggs, tequila) and started walking towards the Costco camp, I felt a deep and growing sense of excitement.

I'd been in contact with Rico for eight months by now and couldn't wait to finally meet him. I had a sense of most of the other 40 Costco-ers too, from reading their daily email exchanges on The List (the Costco intranet).

There'd been a lot from Garry – the Seattle guy Rico had put me in contact with months ago – as he was the camp cook so had to tell The List what supplies to bring. I felt I'd left it too long to get back in contact with him after our initial exchange but I paid close attention to any email he posted to The List. They were always funny, affectionate and full of energy; he sounded like a good guy, a little mysterious as well. I was curious about him, as well as feeling slightly intimidated.

There was also Annie (Rico's girlfriend), plus OB, Jennith, Kenzie, Leopard Head, Hank, Brenda and Jefe, Age, Elvis (a lovely woman called Rachel), Vanilla, Shakes, BillnotDave, Reverend Johnny, Cute Steve, Lello, Princess, Angel and Kirby, Abelicious and Boy Toy . . . and a whole ton of others, all of whom I met the moment I walked into the Costco camp.

I stepped over a guy rope, into a clearing full of dusty sofas. One of the couples draped across them looked up as I walked in and smiled at me. 'Hi,' I said, peering over an armful of water bottles. 'I'm Jennifer, I'm camping with you guys.'

It was like I had triggered some kind of Code Red security alert. As soon as the words were out of my mouth, the couple jumped to their feet, ran into an area behind the sofas where three large marquees backed on to each other and yelled at the top of their lungs: '80 Dates Jen's here! 80 Dates Jen's here!'

I jumped in surprise and struggled not to drop my supplies as people poured from the marquees and ran towards me. Their faces were lit up with smiles as they exclaimed, 'Oh my god, she actually came: it's 80 Dates Jen!'

I had no idea why everyone was so happy to see me (or indeed until this moment that I was called '80 Dates Jen'), but it was one of the nicest welcomes I'd ever received and I burst out laughing. 'Yes,' I grinned, accepting my title, '80 Dates Jen has arrived.'

As the group gathered around me, over their heads I noticed a man standing in the doorway, staring as if sizing me up. I had no idea who he was but – although looking a little harassed – I didn't mind the attention: he was tall and utterly gorgeous with bleached blond hair, startling aquamarine blue eyes and a broad smile on his stubbly face. Shaking his head, he walked over. 'I'm in the middle of cooking but I had to come and see this for myself,' he told me. 'So you made it, huh? 80 Dates Jen, welcome to Costco. I'm Garry.'

And he kissed me.

It wasn't a long kiss, but it was knowing, playful and sexy. Pulling away, he grinned: 'Okay, gotta get back to the kitchen,' and walked back towards the marquee.

I didn't get the chance to react: as soon as he turned and walked away, every single person in the camp stepped up to introduce themselves in the same way. I felt like the UN of Kissing as a multitude of mouths descended on mine. About 20 kisses in, a voice shouted: 'Hey, has anyone offered 80 Dates a drink?' A man with a sunburnt face half concealed by a dusty mop of curly hair and a pair of black horn-rimmed glasses beamed at me. I knew straight away it was Rico and we gave each other a big hug. 'Come on, 80 Dates, let me introduce you to . . . the bar.' And, putting his arm affectionately around my waist, Rico steered me into a marquee.

Inside the tent, I found myself behind the bar, being served cocktails from a blender by Age, the barman. Rico and I sat and chatted, too happy to see each other to be shy. He introduced me to Annie, tiny and beautiful, like a gorgeous, dusty

Tinkerbell; Jennith, resplendent in a leopard-print dress, not to be outdone by Leopard Head, who was outfitted – head to toe – in leopard print . . . Costco staff washed in and out as over the next couple of hours I sat in the bar – too excited to eat – and finally met my co-workers at the Costco Soul Mate Trading Outlet.

As the campsite became engulfed in darkness, Rico made a speech welcoming me to the camp. 'Costco staff come from all over the world, and although we shouldn't be impressed that she's travelled from England via virtually everywhere else to be here with us, we are. Welcome, 80 Dates Jen.' And everyone cheered and raised their glass to me.

'Hey, has she been welcomed *officially* with Age's chilli vodka?' OB shouted from the back. I raised my eyebrows, having no idea what this welcome entailed. The doubt must have shown on my face, as Age squeezed my arm reassuringly.

'Don't worry,' he said. 'You can nominate someone to drink it for you.'

For the last 15 minutes, Garry had been standing a few feet away. He'd smiled at me quite a few times but hadn't yet come over to talk. I'd been dying to talk to him but had been inundated with people introducing themselves and wanting to chat, plus – if truth be told – I was feeling a little shy, so I'd contented myself with returning his smiles.

I knew this was my opportunity.

Without stopping, for fear I'd change my mind, I spun around to Age and said: 'I'd like to nominate Garry to drink it for me.'

Garry, who'd obviously been keeping track of our conversation, gave a groan and rolled his eyes but came straight over. Without a word, he took the brimming shot-glass from Age and, fixing me with a steady look, put the glass to his lips and downed it in one, then pulled me to him and gave me a long, deep kiss, holding me tightly against his chest. As the chilli set my mouth on fire, the kiss set my heart racing. I had no idea what was going on but I didn't want it to stop.

But it did stop with Jennith, Lello and Kenzie suddenly tugging at my shoulder and urging, '80 Dates, come with us: we're going to play on the Playa.'

I felt dazed as Garry and I pulled apart, but I nodded and told them I'd love to go exploring. Turning back to Garry, I blurted: 'Would you like to come too?'

Garry smiled and said: 'Maybe I can organise the grand tour?' He disappeared for a moment and came back with two bikes. Handing one to me, he asked: 'Shall we?' and together the pair of us cycled off into the night to explore BRC.

Cycling around the festival by the light of the moon was the physical equivalent of lying in bed at night tuning a radio. Spells of intense darkness were suddenly interrupted by unconnected voices or music that suggested an incredible story you'd grasp the edge of, before the darkness sucked it away and engulfed you in silence once more.

Sharing this experience with Garry was intimate and intense as – rattling along the bumpy desert floor in the dark – we could hear but not really see each other. There was the additional danger that if you looked away for a moment, you ran the real risk of running someone down or getting knocked off yourself.

There was so much to take in, it was almost overwhelming. But this wasn't the only new experience. From the moment

Garry and I had left the Costco bar and cycled off on our own, it was almost as if the chilli kissing was forgotten. The focus was off us and on the wild nightlife of the Playa. We set off like wide-eyed truants, stowing away together on the first train to London.

Paradoxically, as the seething mass stripped, slapped, danced and paraded around the Playa, Garry and I were on a wonderfully old-fashioned date. We'd get off the bikes in busy areas and people-watch or inspect one of the many intricate pieces of art. Like the 100 ft model of a chandelier that – perfect in every detail – appeared to have crashed from the sky, shattering in pieces across the Playa floor. Or the roller-rink full of naked skaters laughing and crashing into each other. Or the Thunderdome, where – like *Mad Max* – two fighters suspended from a 50-ft metal dome by bungee ropes beat each other with padded baseball bats as the crowd roared and screamed for their champion. At the remote Temple of Remembrance, people sat quietly reflecting and remembering lost loved ones.

Garry and I shared it all.

I was really attracted to him but I also loved the way he was always concerned for me: whenever we rocketed over a bump in the desert or a crowd would crash into us, he would check I was okay. He was gentlemanly without being macho. And he was really good company: he talked just as much as I did and made me laugh a lot. We talked about ourselves, old relation-ships, family and friends, life in London and Seattle, our plans for the future. As he spoke, I was absorbed in what he was saying; I didn't feel bogged down in detail the way I had done on the other dates.

We seemed to like and dislike the same things. We spent a

long time with the Deities living in the base of the 47-ft pyramid temple on which the 32-ft Burning Man stood. Taking time out from cycling, we curled up together on a sofa and watched a rather uneventful-looking film, which suddenly turned into scary 1960s porn. The man graphically thrust his hand in and out of the woman as if searching for car keys in a glove compartment. We were both frozen to the spot with embarrassment: this was not first-date material but we were both too self-conscious to laugh it off. Garry managed to break the tension: 'Did you want to carry on watching *Bad Core* or shall we make a move?' he asked with a wry smile. I scrambled gratefully to my feet and we cycled onwards.

I know this sounds clichéd, but being with Garry was effortless. It wasn't awkward or stressful; I didn't feel like I was trying to behave in a certain way or pushing myself to be more this, less that. And it wasn't just because we liked the same music and places and food. I was relaxed, like I already knew him.

Being with Garry felt like coming home.

I know, I know: it sounds completely pathetic and I don't blame you for wanting to slap me really hard, but I couldn't help it: I was smitten. Completely and utterly. And even though I'd suspected from his emails to both the List and me that I would like him, I hadn't seen this coming. I mean, in theory Garry wasn't even a date. I had spent the last eight months cajoling and bullying the Date Wranglers into coming up with an array of the internationally available and here I was, meeting someone on my own, just like that.

But I wasn't thinking about any of this because I was having such a brilliant and funny time. I wasn't thinking about Soul Mates or about dating or about what number I was up to and how many more I had to go. I was just here, in the desert, with a man who made me want to tell him my secrets and listen quietly as he told me his.

It had been a long day for both of us. As dawn transformed the Playa from a peek-a-boo playground of the twisted and the inspired into a parched wasteland of all-night revellers, we both felt the need to get some sleep.

Cycling back to the Costco camp, as we stacked our bikes against the others, Garry asked: 'Did you get a chance to pitch your tent earlier?'

'Oh, I don't have a tent,' I told him nonchalantly. 'I'm going to sleep in my car.'

Garry looked appalled and stared at me with real concern. 'Jen, you can't sleep in your car: that's crazy.'

I asked him why: 'I've got some hotel towels to sleep under and it's pretty quiet where I parked. I'll be fine.'

My *whatever* travelling attitude was so firmly in place, sleeping in the car genuinely didn't bother me at all. Garry, however, seemed to feel strongly to the contrary. He bit his lip in exasperation as if trying not to say what he was thinking, then ran his hand through his dusty blond hair. 'Look,' he said awkwardly, 'I really don't want to tell you what to do, but I won't be able to relax knowing you are out there somewhere sleeping in your car.' He frowned deeply and took my hand in his. 'Jen,' he said, 'please sleep in my trailer.'

I raised my eyebrows but he ignored the look and continued, 'You can have the bed, I'll sleep on the floor. There's plenty of space and I'm not trying to . . .' He trailed off, shrugging uncomfortably but with a look that suggested he was going to keep insisting until I said yes.

I thought about it. I really didn't mind sleeping in the car – it was no big deal – but, for me at least, that wasn't what this was really about. I remembered Hettie's words in Vegas: '. . . when the moment comes, you have to be prepared to take that leap of faith.'

I wasn't going to over-think this: I liked and trusted Garry. I felt safe with him, cared for rather than hit on. The idea of sleeping in his trailer – although a little scary – felt right. I knew it was time to take that leap.

'Thank you,' I said quietly. 'I appreciate the offer.'

I thought I could sleep on the floor and he could have the bed. But when we got back to his trailer it felt the most natural and wonderful thing in the world to climb out of our dusty clothes and slip under the covers together.

We were woken a couple of hours later by the sounds of the Costco crew breakfasting in the communal area outside. I felt a sudden pang of anxiety: would they all think me a total slapper for jumping straight into bed with Garry?

Propped up on one arm, I confided my fears: 'I haven't even come close to sleeping with anyone else on the trip,' (I sort of glossed over Frank) 'what if they think I sleep with all my Dates?'

Pulling me back down into the bed, Garry kissed me, then shook his head reassuringly. 'They're not like that,' he said. 'Everyone will just be pleased for us: why wouldn't they be?'

And sure enough, as we dragged ourselves out of bed and stood in the doorway of the trailer, squinting into the ferocious morning sun, the Costco-ers sitting around the breakfast tables spotted us and started clapping and cheering. Garry and I smiled at each other sheepishly. The crowd laughed and cheered even harder. By now we were laughing too and – pausing at the top of the steps to take a bow – holding hands, we joined our friends for breakfast.

The next five days were magical.

The rest of that day passed in a blur. I had to work in the Costco Store (where old Soul Mates were traded for new) and Garry had to organise dinner for 40 people that night.

This was a good thing, partially as it gave me a chance to get my head around the last 12 hours and also because the desert by day was very different to the desert at night.

The heat was overwhelming. Dust storms would sweep across the Playa, blinding and choking you. The dust was abrasive and invasive: it coated your body and hair, got in your mouth, your eyes, made your nose suddenly gush blood. You had to constantly remind yourself to drink as the heat brutally sucked moisture and minerals from your body, leaving you dizzy and disorientated. Sometimes I'd get terrible cramps. On the worst day I was so overwhelmed by heat, I couldn't remember what I was saying, and sentences would just trail off. Some people collapsed; everyone kept an eye on everyone else, alert for the first signs of dehydration and ready to share precious water.

Twice-a-day trucks would drive along the main roads spraying water behind them in an attempt to keep the dust down. That was always a carnival-like atmosphere: people would stream out of their tents, running naked behind the trucks, cooling off in the al fresco shower.

Over the next five days, I'd see this all from The Store as I worked to help people find their Soul Mates.

The way it worked: people brought in a Soul Mate they didn't want and both answered questions on a form that would help us find one they did want. The forms recorded where they were camping (vital if Soul Mates were to find each other) and included questions like: What do people say is your most annoying habit? What's the one class you regret not taking at school? and Are you or have you ever been a slut?

Using their answers, Interviewers would further probe the applicants. They would then pass their conclusions on to the Matchers, who would use all this information to identify the applicant's ideal Soul Mate from amongst the hundreds of other interviewed applicants on file. People would return the next day to find out who they'd been matched with and then go to their Soul Mate's camp to introduce themselves.

Costco was one of the oldest and most popular theme camps on the Playa: every day hundreds of people turned up to have a fun experience but also seriously hoping we could help them find their Soul Mate.

And we took it just as seriously.

Working in two shifts from 10 a.m. until 6 p.m., we sat every day in the sweltering tent, literally sweating over the completed forms of hopeful applicants. Tears welled up in the kohl-rimmed eyes of a dreadlocked pixie as she confided how she hoped to find a man who loved welding as much as she did. A French woman told me she had been matched with a fabulous *Playa Lover* last year and wanted one just as good this year. Naked but for a Viking helmet, one man suddenly got really upset after 20 minutes of banter and told me he just wanted a woman he could trust.

I was surprised by how similar the hopes and needs of the people here in BRC were with those I'd already dated on my travels.

As countless people, dressed as fairies or undressed as nudists and every possible combination and permutation in between, sat across the table and talked, I heard the same heart-felt story each time. It didn't matter that some had extreme tastes or habits: whatever the personality, the aims were the same: to find someone who was like them. They wanted a companion who shared their interests, someone who would understand and cohabit their world.

More than anything, people didn't want to be alone.

Listening to people talk honestly and vulnerably about what they hoped for in a Soul Mate was exhausting but humbling. Of course I knew exactly how they felt (with the possible exception of the man looking for a Soul Mate who would lock him in the boot of his car) and I wanted to do all I could to help.

Sometimes this worked, for example with the lovely artist guy and Welding Woman. They came to see me at the end of the week, still delighting in each other's company, and thanked me for helping them meet. Sometimes it didn't work, like the nervous mid-thirties teacher, who anxiously told me that he was always unlucky in love. I was so convinced he was gay it didn't even occur to me to ask.

As I happily told him I had the perfect man for him (a sweet scientist from the day before), his face crumpled; his chin jutted in and out dangerously, like a cutlery drawer possessed by demons.

'But I'm not gay!' he told me incredulously.

'Are you really sure about that?' I wanted to ask, but his eyes beseeched me to say I had made a mistake. I wanted to help him find happiness (with his gay Soul Mate), but seeing him look so miserable I lost the courage of my convictions. Patting his hand, I guiltily told him I was sure we had a ton of suitable women for him.

He sniffed tearfully, still looking shocked and upset. Quickly scanning his application form in the hope of changing the subject, I hit the Talents section and started talking as I read. 'Oh that's interesting,' I said heartily. 'It says here, you do an extremely life-like impersonation of . . .' my voice trailed off, '. . . a . . . ummm . . . frog?' I finished weakly, looking up to check I hadn't misunderstood.

The man looked at me steadily. Still swathed in misery, he nevertheless cleared his throat and – wobbly at first, then louder as his confidence grew – started to impersonate a frog. He sat staring at me, unblinking. Croaking. Although he still looked completely wretched, he clearly had been unable to resist the opportunity to show off his party piece. Watching, I struggled to arrange my expression into one that (I hoped) conveyed both enjoyment and admiration.

After a couple of minutes, his croaking crescendoed, then came to an end. I thanked him for *sharing* (a popular ritual in America) and told him we'd do our very best to find him his Soul Mate. Revitalised by his impersonation, he thanked me sincerely and left the marquee. I reached for my water bottle and took a deep swallow. Perhaps I was suffering from heat exhaustion and had just imagined the entire episode?

The days were filled with incident like this and interspersed with a kaleidoscope of impressions and adventures shared with the other Costco-ers.

One day, Jennith and I ended up on the Spanking Machine.

I had never tried or even been curious about S&M, but as Jennith and I came across the Bike Mistress sitting on her saddle, hard wire bristles radiating out from the front wheel, we thought *why not?*

I went first. Standing in front of the bike, the scary wheel a few inches from my bottom, Bike Mistress demanded in a strict voice: 'How bad have you been?'

Even though I've never experienced recreational beating, I knew instinctively my reply would impact very directly on what happened next. I thought carefully before answering: 'Well, on the whole, actually I've been pretty good,' I prevaricated, 'but . . . you know . . . possibly a bit bad towards the end?'

Hoping I'd said the right thing, I heard Bike Mistress turn the pedals over. And as she started to pedal, the wire spokes gently slapped against the back of my combat shorts.

As Bike Mistress began cycling harder, though, I could feel the wires start to sting. I let out a gasp: it hurt. Bike Mistress was in her element by now and pedalling faster and faster, the wire switches started slapping and biting hard into my skin.

As the pain increased, I opened my mouth and let out a shriek that grew louder and louder as the bike went faster and faster. By now the pain was intense, and I shrieked unreservedly, like a kettle boiling near to the point of death.

Then it stopped.

I stumbled forward from the sudden change in pressure, then, realising it was over and how much my bottom hurt, I started laughing. I don't know why I found it so funny – maybe because why anyone would do this for pleasure was now truly a mystery to me, or because I was happy I'd tried something new.

I turned around and saw Bike Mistress looking at me with respect: 'That was really awesome,' she said. 'You did well.'

I grinned and looked at Jennith, who – in complete contrast – looked mortified: 'Come *on*, 80 Dates,' she said, grabbing my arm and hustling me away. 'You're making *so* much noise.'

'But, Jennith . . .' I protested in astonishment. 'You're next. You're going on too, aren't you?'

Pretending she hadn't heard, Jennith was already on her bike and cycling determinedly away. I gingerly climbed onto my own saddle and pedalled after her, shouting unconvincingly: 'It didn't hurt that much. Come back, you baby . . .'

I loved having these experiences with the Costco-ers: they were warm, wonderful people, a community I instantly belonged with.

The time we all felt this most strongly was at the communal dinners each night. Dinner was always accompanied by speeches: Rico thanking us for all our hard work; Garry and the kitchen-ers being told what an amazing meal they'd made; Hank sharing an experience he'd had in the Store; Elvis telling us about a fantastic theme camp she'd discovered. It might sound gushing and sickly, but having a brilliant time in an ultra-extreme environment was only possible because everyone worked so hard as a team; sharing a good meal and making speeches was a way of acknowledging that.

And I especially loved this time of night because Garry and I were off-duty. We'd pop in and see each other during the day, but, busy working in the kitchen and Store respectively, it wasn't until the evening that we could spend more than a couple of minutes together.

Some nights we'd stay with the whole group, dressing up in

ball gowns and going to the Prom a couple of camps down, or cycling around with OB and showing each other parts of the site that had been built that day; watching the world go by from the dusty comfort of one of the Costco sofas.

It'd always end up just the two of us, though. Caught up in conversation with each other, we sometimes just didn't notice when the group moved on. Other times, we wanted to be on our own, to hold hands and walk through a neon maze or marvel at the people scrambling over vast granite obelisks impossibly suspended from thick iron chains.

And the whole time we'd be talking about everything and nothing; laughing at silly jokes we now shared; stopping in the dust and kissing each other with a hungry passion.

And of course we talked about my journey. Garry understood absolutely why I had decided to embark on it. Being a career junkie himself, he'd started to lose hope of meeting anyone he really cared about too. 'Until now,' he told me as we sat by the Temple of Remembrance, looking up at the stars over the desert.

After just four days together, it seemed crazy to say that I had met and was falling in love with my Soul Mate. But that's how it felt. We'd clicked instantly, in a way that was powerful and very real.

But I was also painfully aware that I was going to have to leave soon. As well as a dating past, I had a dating future.

I couldn't quite get my head around how I was going to incorporate the fact that I had met Garry – potentially my Soul Mate – into my journey, but I knew I had to. I was committed to my Dates: they weren't just numbers, they were people I was involved with now and I didn't want to treat them badly. And I *wanted* to meet them, as well as do all those things my DWs and I had worked flat out to pull together. And besides me and my Dates, leaving here would hopefully give me a chance to think about Garry and put everything that had happened between us on the Playa into perspective. Who knows, maybe I was just in denial and marching on with a *business as usual* attitude because I didn't know how else to handle this new minefield of feelings?

Garry seemed much calmer about it all: 'Don't worry, Jen,' he said reassuringly, 'I know you have to do this.'

I think one of the reasons he was able to be so reasonable was because our experience was so intense that we weren't really able to imagine anything beyond it. Everything about *now* felt so right. Leaving Garry and the Playa seemed impossible, like this was our home and we'd stay here forever. Leaving Garry – the man I'd travelled the world to find – to go date other men seemed too bizarre for words. Like a parallel universe.

But I thought again of the couple in Vegas united through the dogged efforts of Fate: 'Our entire lives were leading to our time together,' Hettie had told me.

Well, Fate had brought me on this journey and had led me to Garry; it would seem she had plans for our future too.

Back in London, when I'd finally settled on my route through the US, I had decided to go from here to Missoula, then from Missoula on to Seattle.

Seattle was where Garry lived.

After I left the Playa, I'd see Garry again in Seattle five days later and stay with him for the duration of my stay.

• • •

We slept less as the time to leave grew closer. It wasn't that we were consciously trying to cram in as much time together as possible, it was more that the better we got to know each other, the more hours we wanted to spend together.

The morning I had to leave, we'd been up all night.

It was 5.30 a.m. After a tearful goodbye with the lovely Costco-ers the night before, Garry and I walked along the dusty road to the car with armfuls of my belongings that item by item had taken up residence in Garry's trailer.

Usually when we went out onto the Playa together, we'd always be nudging each other to look at an incredible sculpture; an interesting theme camp; a crazy costume (or lack of it). But now we walked in silence. We didn't notice the pink dawn blossom around us, or the dancers or the cyclists or the art. We were both quietly wondering how we were going to say 'goodbye'.

Over the last week, I had lived in my boots, combat shorts and bikini; I'd almost been embarrassed changing out of them into my regular jeans and a T-shirt half an hour earlier. Here for another three days, Garry was still in his crazy shorts and a Burning Man necklace whilst I was dressed for the real world and feeling as if I already had one foot out the door.

We dumped the stuff in the boot of my dusty car and Garry walked me to the driver's side, opening the door for me. I threw my bag onto the passenger seat and turned to face him.

We looked at each other in silence. Neither of us wanted to say the words, so we said nothing at all. Garry reached out and took me in his arms.

'I am not going to cry, I am not going to cry,' I told myself.

But strangely, in a way, I felt sort of all right.

I'd been on 54 dates and met no one. What were the

chances of me meeting anyone else? In fact, considering the odds, I thought myself pretty lucky to have stumbled upon Garry at all. Also, I had talked so much to Garry, I now needed to talk *about* Garry. I wanted to ring and email my friends and tell them I'd met someone amazing; give them a blow-by-blow account of how gorgeous he was; what he'd said; what he was like; how he made me feel. Girl stuff. And I'd see him in five days.

Okay, I'd talked myself around: it was all right; it was all going to be fine.

'It's all going to be fine you know,' I said gently, moving my head from Garry's shoulder and looking up at him. 'We'll see each other in five days and you can show me Seattle.'

But Garry didn't look fine: he looked tired and sad. I could tell he was thinking about how it was going to be when I was gone. But he forced a smile and narrowed his eyes, studying me intensely. 'Yes,' he said quietly. 'Yes. It'll be fine.' Then, determined to be strong, he straightened his shoulders and stopped frowning. 'Now you drive safely and have a good flight.' I nodded dutifully. 'I've got your hotel number in Missoula,' he continued. 'I'll call you on Monday when I'm on the way back to Seattle.'

Now that he was suddenly fine, I started getting upset. The tears ran down my cheeks as I buried my face in his shoulder.

We held each other tightly as all around us BRC geared up for another hot day on the Playa. But I had a long drive to Reno and a plane to catch, so with one last kiss and one last promise to call, I got in the car, got out the car, gave him another kiss and a hug, got back in the car. And drove away.

I kept looking up at the rear-view mirror. Garry stood on the side of the road and watched for a long time as I drove out of BRC, past the Greeters and away. A part of me was saying, 'Oh bugger the Dates, I'm staying,' and thinking of turning back. But I knew I couldn't. And I knew I mustn't. Garry lived in Seattle, I lived in London.

If we really were Soul Mates, this would be the first of many goodbyes.

CHAPTER TEN

USA – Missoula, Montana

In the heart of the Rocky Mountains that run southeast from Alaska all the way down to Mexico, Missoula was one of those places where it was hard not to have a good time. The University of Montana's campus was here, so there was always a decent band playing, plus with all the rivers and trails dotted around, you could pedal, paddle and promenade to your heart's content.

That was one of the reasons I'd planned to come here on my dating tour: Missoula has always been one of my feel-good places and, even before I'd met the Love Professor, I'd known that happy people are luckier in love. The other reason was a bit sillier but no less heartfelt. Nicholas Evans's book *The Smoke Jumper* was based on the Missoulian firemen who fight the huge fires that ravage the surrounding area each summer by jumping out of planes directly into the path of the blaze.

It was a classic, sappy love story full of fearless, athletic yet imperceptibly vulnerable men doing a real and dangerous job. I was in a romantic daze as I read it and – since it was set in my beloved Missoula – wanted to see for myself if the real smoke-jumpers were just as dreamy.

Of course, all this was before I met Garry.

For the ten hours I'd been travelling I could only think of two things: how much I needed a bath and how much I missed Garry. The notion that I had Dates waiting for me at the end of the journey (the smokejumper plus a rodeo rider and possibly Cam, an American friend of Jo's) was not so much unwelcome as unimaginable.

Descending the steep mountain pass from the Interstate 90 highway down into Missoula, I was struck by the eerie brown pall engulfing not just the entire town but the mountains all around it too. I already knew from conversations with the Missoulian Smokejumpers' headquarters that this summer's fires were some of the worst on record: over 3,300 wildfires already burning out of control across 665,800 acres, with new fires taking hold every day. It was only now I was here that I understood just how serious it was and I felt guilty for having taken such a flippant attitude.

Parking the car, I walked up the steps of the Holiday Inn, admiring the pretty Clark Fork river and bike trails that ran behind the hotel and along the edge of town. Down in the valley it was a fabulous sun-trap but the smoke from the burning mountains that surrounded us made the hot sun hazy. I couldn't actually see the smoke but my eyes were streaming and my throat stung; people checking in ahead of me were coughing constantly. The town really was in the grip of a disaster.

I wasn't surprised, therefore, when reading my messages up

in my room, to see one from Tim Eldridge, my contact at the
smokejumper HQ and the man who Nicholas Evans's main
character had been based on. He wanted to warn me that the
date probably wasn't going to happen as all the men were
working back-to-back shifts trying to control the fires. He
invited me to meet him at HQ the next day and he'd do the
best he could. I left a message immediately asking him to please
not worry about the date: I hoped everyone was safe and yes I'd
love to meet him tomorrow.

I opened up my laptop. On the Playa there had been no
mobile coverage, no emails, so I hadn't been in contact with the
outside world for five days. But as AOL popped onto the
screen it quickly became clear that the outside world had
indeed been in contact with me.

There were 378 emails. From Dates who had been; Dates
who were to be and friends checking the details on Dates who
might be. There were confirmations from hotels; invoices for
reserved flights; details for hire cars to be collected. There were
also work emails: could I do an interview about this; was I free
to write an article about that; did I have the notes for a
conference I was chairing next month?

My eyes blurred as I struggled to take in the details and I
finally gave up and ran a bath instead.

After five days in the desert – where I had barely washed,
knowing not to waste a single precious drop – I now marvelled
at how freely the water gushed from the taps. It seemed an
extraordinary extravagance to be able to lie in a huge tub of hot,
clean water.

Undressing, I was shocked when I caught sight of my
reflection in the mirror: tanned a deep brown, my face was
sprinkled with freckles and my body was caked with sand and

dirt from the desert. My hair was rigid with dust, my plaits sticking out almost at right-angles. It took me a moment to work out why I had angry red welts and black bruises on my bottom, until I realised I was inspecting the handiwork of Bike Mistress.

Exhausted from the last week's excitement and lack of sleep, I caught myself dozing off in the bath, so had to drag myself out and dry off. Crawling into the impossibly huge and impossibly clean bed, I slept like a dead person for 14 hours.

The next morning, feeling stunned like I had jet lag, I walked to one of the downtown coffee shops. Armed with a couple of strong black coffees I planned another attempt at reading my emails and getting my thoughts into some sort of order.

'A grande Americano with space please,' I asked the thirty-something woman busy taking orders behind the counter – a black coffee, cup not filled to the top. Starbucks has taught even us Brits the universal language of coffee ordering: *Espresseranto.*

She took my money: 'I'm not sure what kind of spice you want, hun,' she noted helpfully, 'but we have cinnamon over there by the milk.'

I looked at her blankly. 'Spice?' I repeated slowly, then realising she'd misunderstood my accent, I laughed and said: 'Not spice, s-p-*a*-c-e,' putting heavy emphasis on the offending vowel.

Now it was her turn to stare blankly. Another woman, making the coffee, sensed a problem and came over to the counter. 'Everything okay?' she asked brightly.

The first woman turned and said: 'She wants spice but we only have cinnamon.'

'Oh, I'm sorry,' the barista apologised. 'What kind of spice was it that you wanted?'

I was a bit too tired for this, but persevered. 'I don't want s-p-i-c-e,' I explained, enunciating for all I was worth, 'I want s-p-a-c-e.' Now both looked at me blankly. I tried another tack: 'Room. I'd like room in the cup, please.'

Upon hearing my request, both women stiffened visibly and regarded me with open disapproval. 'We don't have a licence to serve alcohol, ma'am,' the barista said with a sniff. 'I'm afraid you'll have to go to a bar if you want to drink.'

This really was too much. Putting both hands flat on the counter and leaning towards them menacingly, I hissed through gritted teeth: 'Not RUM, r-o-o-m!' A caffeine-withdrawal meltdown was barrelling irrevocably towards the surface, like a great white shark with a stomach unexpectedly full of cork.

'She wants a black Americano with space,' the man behind me called across the counter. *'That's what I just SAID,'* I thought to myself. But his American accent made all the difference and the cloud perceptibly lifted from the countenance of both women. They beamed, as all anxiety over serving the alcoholic foreign lady vanished and they busied themselves with my order. I turned to thank the man, but he spoke first: 'It's Jennifer, isn't it?'

That threw me: could today be any more disorientating?

'Ummm, yes?' I replied, as if unsure myself. 'Errrr, how do you . . . ?'

'I'm Cam,' he interrupted, seeing my bewilderment, 'Jo's friend? I swung by your hotel to ask if you wanted me to show you around a little. They said I'd find you here.'

God, it was a Date. I was on a date and I hadn't even had a flaming cup of coffee yet.

Date #56: Cam – Missoula, Montana, USA

Cam was a friend of Jo's. They'd met at a Buddhist retreat in California, where he lived. Although I was grateful he'd rescued me from my coffee debacle (it turned out to be terrible coffee, for the record), he scared the bejesus out of me right from the start.

With a shaven head and extraordinary cornflower-blue eyes (I felt like I was on *The Amazing Eyes of America* tour – all the men I met seemed to have them), he sat across the table from me, talking about kayaking but giving me a direct and unnerving look that said: 'I will take all your clothes off here and now, if you just say the word.'

It was all too much. I hadn't yet mentally prepared myself: I was still loved up and back in *Garryland*.

Every year, Cam came to Missoula to take a ten-day rafting trip along the Lochsa River. He'd got back from it just the night before and was excited and energised by the adventure. 'Moving with the elements allows you to harness the energy of nature,' he told me, his face feverish with excitement. Apparently he'd come away believing more strongly than ever that: 'You can't waste that energy. You have to store it up and channel it through everyday life; channel it through the people you meet.'

It was no good: I wasn't in the mood for Cam and his channelling. 'Cam, it's lovely to meet you,' I said, trying to stem the flow. 'And I'm glad you had such an exciting trip but . . .' And I told him all about Burning Man and Garry and how I needed a couple of hours simply to absorb and understand what had happened to me. I was sorry and was very much looking forward to our date, but could we maybe have it a little later?

Cam smiled. 'That's beautiful, Jennifer,' he said, taking my hand in his. 'And I can feel this man has affected you deeply: I have to tell you that you are generating some very strong, spiritual energy right now.' I nodded, relieved. 'In fact,' Cam continued, now trailing his fingers across my palm and circling them around my wrist, 'perhaps there is a way that you and I can channel our energies together?' Giving me *that look* again, he edged his chair closer, sliding his leg slowly and deliberately against mine. 'It would be a very powerful experience for us both,' he added in a low voice.

Wriggling my hand out from Cam's grip, I lurched unsteadily to my feet as I attempted to disentangle my legs from his whilst grabbing my laptop from underneath the table and snatching my cardigan from the back of the chair.

'So, umm, Cam, thank you for coming out to find me,' I stammered, backing away from the table and pretending I hadn't understood his suggestion. 'I'm pretty busy whilst I'm here and actually, may have to go early. But, you know, I've got your number, so if there's time, I'll . . . uummm . . . give you a call.' And with that, I fled the café and went straight back to my hotel, leaving a message at reception that under no circumstances was I to be disturbed.

Back in my room, I threw myself onto the bed and stared up at the ceiling for inspiration. What was I going to do? Where could my dating tour go from here? I mean, forget about Cam and his energetic overtures, could I carry on dating any man when all I could think about was Garry?

It felt like sitting down to dinner having already eaten: I wasn't hungry for more dates. I wanted to see Garry, pick up where we left off. I felt embarrassed to be missing him already

– it was only a day since I'd seen him, for chrissakes – but it wasn't just that I missed his presence: I missed the way I felt when I was with him.

But what if it was just Playa Love?

What if, outside the extraordinary, emotionally live environment of BRC, we met in the real world and . . . there was nothing? No spark, no wonder?

Should I give up on my trip or should I keep dating?

If I stopped dating, Garry and I would have the time to get to know each other and see if this was for real. But would I then feel I'd let my Dates and Date Wranglers down? And if I didn't complete my journey, would there always be a quiet voice whispering *What if?*

From a positive perspective, would continuing to date be the test that proved Garry and I really were Soul Mates? But did I have the confidence in me, Garry and me, and in Fate, to believe our relationship could survive the rest of my journey? Or was I being naïve and selfish even imagining that a relationship could be that flexible? Would I inevitably push Garry's understanding too far and lose him forever?

Ugh! It was all going round and round in my head. I wanted to do the right thing, but I had no idea what the right thing was. Then it hit me. I sat up on the bed and dragged my laptop onto my knees.

This was a question for the Date Wranglers.

My Very Dear Date Wranglers,
    I'm sorry to be so me, me, me (though you all know me well enough not to be surprised), but, as the inner circle of my Date Wranglers, I am in urgent need of your advice and counsel.

55 dates in, I've met my Soul Mate and I don't know what to do.

I met Garry at the Burning Man festival last week and it was pretty much love at first sight (see attached pic). From the moment he took me on the moonlit bike ride through the desert — romantic and magical — we were inseparable.

He's my age, works in radio, lives in Seattle and is funny, kind and utterly gorgeous :) I'm going to stay with him in Seattle next week to see how we get on in 'real life'.

But in the meantime, I'm in Missoula and the last thing I feel like doing is dating the rodeo rider or smokejumper whilst I'm missing him so much. I still have loads more dates to go and don't want to drop everything at the first sign of SMA (Soul Mate Action) but at the same time, he's just great and I don't seem to be able to think beyond that.

Please tell me what you think I should do?

Sorry to be so melodramatic — this has completely thrown me. I always assumed I'd meet someone in Fulham when I got home! Hope you are all groovy and well. Kisses, Jxxx

PS. Jo — we need to talk about Cam!

The moment I sent the email I felt relieved: I knew I'd done the right thing. The DWs would give me some perspective and good advice; the situation felt too big for me alone and for the millionth time I was grateful to have such good friends to call on.

And, seeing that the decision was now percolating through the system, I felt free to get on with my day. Grabbing a coffee from reception, I jumped in the car and drove the seven miles west out of town to the Missoula Smokejumper HQ.

Tim wasn't there but he'd left another message saying he was sorry he couldn't make it, he was out fielding calls. As he'd predicted, all the men were out fighting the fires, so getting me a date **(Date #57)** had proven impossible.

To be honest, I felt relieved, and that was nothing to do with my feelings about Garry. The fires were so bad, crews were being called in from neighbouring states to help. This was clearly the wrong time for me to be turning up looking for a fun night out.

Latching on to a passing tour, I noticed a visiting crew were just finishing a tour of their own and were preparing to drill. Liz, our guide and a student volunteer, explained that drills were vital: from the time the siren sounded to being airborne, the crew had less than 12 minutes to drop everything, scramble into their 110-lb packs and suits, and be in position onboard the plane. To do this, the smokejumpers had to be fit (able to do 7 pull-ups, 45 sit-ups, 25 push-ups and run a quarter of a mile in less than 11 minutes) as well as organised.

We walked through the locker room (a sign on the wall declaring Stupid Hurts), passing a couple of men at a bank of sewing machines making their own parachutes, out into the workshop where yet more parachutes were stretched over long benches, smokejumpers hunched over them painstakingly inspecting their condition. A two-way radio sat on a shelf, surrounded by multiple containers of eye-wash and the largest collection of indigestion tablets I'd ever seen.

It was clearly a stressful life and the room crackled with testosterone, boredom and restless tension. The men were certainly manly, but Liz gave me a sobering insight into how life with a smokejumper would be.

Watching the visiting crew doing pull-ups on a bar, one of the women in our group asked Liz if she fancied any of the crew? 'No,' Liz replied, looking uncomfortable. 'I know all the wives, who spend every day wondering if this will be the day their husbands don't make it home.'

Back at the hotel, I logged on and was amazed to see that 21 of the DWs had already got back to me. All had clear and strong opinions as to what I should do. Some qualified their advice before giving it, like Paula:

```
I want you to know that what I know about boys
can be written on the back of a very small
postage stamp to a very small island . . .
however . . .
```

Reading through the suggestions, I felt like a contestant on some kind of reality game show where everyone was ringing in and voting on my next move. There were two unanimous reactions. Firstly, thrilled I'd met someone I liked so much:

```
OOOOOHHHHHHH MMMMMMYYYYYYY
GOOOOOODDDDDDDDDDDDDDDDDDDDDDD!!!!!!!!!!!!!!!!!!
   For real? He looks damn cute, that's for sure!
Grainne xxxxx
```

Secondly, demanding to know which of them could claim the Date Wrangler crown, having pulled off this coup:

I'll be interested to know how the date came about (or to cut to the chase . . . WHO gets the credit?). Lots of love, Hec and Ang xxx

PS. Call IMMEDIATELY if you find yourself serenading complete strangers with songs by The Carpenters and declaring yourself to be 'On Top of The World' to anyone who'll listen...

However, on the dating question of should I stay or should I go, the DWs were split down the middle.

The No Girl - Stop Dating camp was all female, and romantic:

Wallow in it. Even if he is the one and you spend the rest of your lives together, it'll never been the same as it is for the first ninety days together . . . I'm thrilled for you. Lots of love, Alison

inventive:

You've had 55 dates around the world, can't you do another 25 with Garry? My advice is give it a go and forget about the singing cowboy or whoever you had lined up for subsequent dates. If you don't, you'll kick yourself. Sarah xxxxx

and considerate:

No need to travel any further. It would not be fair on you, it would not be fair on Garry, not to mention those poor fellows who are waiting to meet you. Malgosia xxxx

The Go Girl - Keep Dating camp was a mix of male and female, and practical:

No matter how lovely Garry is, don't give up now.
If it's meant to be, and if he's the guy for you,
he'll wait for you. Simple as that. Lyn
xxxxxxxxxxxxxx

sensible:

when you're rolling round in the desert with
exciting people, art installations and dusty
nipples at every turn (and I'm taking this
directly from you, girl), most people look
attractive/sexy/cool . . . but when you see him
doing the washing up or queuing to buy a coffee .
. . well, that's the test. The mundane stuff.
Cath xxx

and extremely direct:

Coxy — put the relationship on hold till you've
finished or do the rest REALLY FUCKING FAST!!
Love, S

My advice would be to stay with your Soul Mate in
Seattle & let me carry on the dating game for
you! Okay, that wasn't very helpful, but you
can't give up: what if a month down the line SMA
turns into GOOMFYP (Get out of my face, you
prat!)? Good luck, sweetie. She MacB xx

Some brought their expertise to the problem:

Being an obsessive astro-chick — what's his star
sign/date/time of birth? If he's an Aquarian, don't
get too excited too soon: they fall head over heels
every couple of months . . . Glam Tan xxxx

Others brought their own problem to the problem:

Can't talk about Cam or anything else now . . .
am having trouble with Ryan AGAIN. Saw his ex at
the pub, who 'really wants to be friends again'.
Of course, we had a huge fight. Why does he get
pissed off with me when SHE'S the bitch who broke
his heart? Ah yes, Love . . . that used to be a
nice feeling. Jo xxx

It was Belinda who gave the advice that was practical as well as
romantic:

. . . You've worked so hard setting up this trip:
you won't be happy unless you see it through to
the end. Garry has to trust this isn't about you
looking for another man: it's about you having
your crazy adventure. If it's going to work, he
needs to appreciate that that's who you are and
love you for it, as we all do. Love B xxxxx

The jury was split.

Which actually was fine with me: they'd given me tons to
think about and ultimately it *was* my decision. So I shut down

the computer, put on a pair of shorts and went and hired a mountain bike.

I think better when I'm on the move, and now, as I cycled along the trail that followed the Clark Fork River east to the university, I mulled over my situation.

I hardly noticed the American Football teams dashing up and down the field, their coach sweating as he shouted instructions; or the couples – also on bikes – chatting comfortably as their dogs bounded up and away; or even the early-twenties girl dressed in black, sitting strumming her guitar in the shade of a broad tree. I was pedalling hard and thinking harder.

As *I* saw it, this was my situation. I'd presented Fate with a challenge: I'd find and date 80 men around the world (okay, 79 dates with 79 men and one date with 25 women) and in return she'd give me my Soul Mate. I felt pretty sure Garry was The One, so Fate had delivered.

But of course, life is never that simple.

Rather than giving me my Soul Mate on Date #1 or Date #80, Fate had come through in the middle of my journey: Date #55. It was brutal timing and one that presented no end of problems, but the fact was: Fate had delivered.

And maybe there was a reason for it happening this way: maybe I'd met Garry halfway through the Odyssey because Fate had an additional purpose for my journey that I had yet to discover?

It might sound ridiculous but my instincts told me that I had to stick to my plans, that if I didn't honour my side of the bargain, I'd lose Garry; if I reneged on my end of the deal, Fate would renege on hers.

I had no choice: if I wanted to keep Garry, I had to keep dating.

I'd need to ask Garry what he thought. I'd also need to tell the remaining 25 dates how my circumstances had changed (and accept that some might not want to see me as a result), but I'd made up my mind: I was going to keep dating.

Going back to the hotel was hard: now that I was clear about what I needed to do, I really wanted to talk with Garry and try and explain my reasoning. I wanted to talk to him anyway: I missed him and now that the pressure of *the next step* had lifted, I wanted to hear his voice and know I hadn't just imagined the whole thing (and that he hadn't changed his mind!).

The message light was flashing as I entered my room. My heart leapt: even though I knew Garry was still at the festival, was it possible he'd found a way to call me?

But the message was from Chip, a friend of Tim's and a fellow smokejumper. He was getting married this weekend, had heard my story and did I want to come and have dinner with him and his fiancée tonight? They lived a way out of town. I checked my watch: I'd been cycling for four hours and it was now too late to go over. I rang Chip to explain.

He was incredibly friendly and down to earth. The wedding – a barbecue in the paddock overlooking the river, everyone drinking and dancing to a local band – sounded fantastic and I was sorry I wasn't going. Chip in turn was fascinated by my journey and the lengths I had gone to meet a Soul Mate. 'You shoulda done what I did,' he told me over the phone.

'Oh, what's that?' I asked intrigued, imagining a barn-raising or a moonlight hike through the forests, or maybe even a dramatic rescue from the heart of a ferocious fire.

'Go on the Inner-net,' he told me, breezily shattering my

fantasies. 'That's the way we meet our Soul Mates in these parts.'

Cheered by my conversation with Chip, I took my book down to the hotel bar. It was full of petrol-heads from the Mustang Car Convention, which was currently making parking impossible outside. Aware I was a date down, I let one of the exhibitors buy me a beer as a sacrifice to The Numbers God. But my heart wasn't in it: I felt guilty and all I could think about was Garry.

The next day was the day I was going to hear from Garry and time wouldn't pass fast enough. I wanted him to be the one to call but feared I'd be weak and ring him first (which as much as I liked him was obviously out of the question). I needed a distraction: it was a good day to get back on the Dating Wagon.

First, I sent an email to my Seattle Dates letting them know that there had been a change in my date status: one to Jason, the President of the Ukulele Association of America, and the other to Ted, a friend of Posh PR Emma's.

```
Ted! :)
  Hey there, matie, how are you? How's it been
since last we spoke? I'm good, really well thx.
  Now, I have some good and bad news! The good news
is I'll be in Seattle from Thursday. The bad news —
I've met my Soul Mate and he lives in Seattle!
  I'd still really love to meet you, though —
finally put a face to the typeface!! Let me know
what you think?
  Take care, Jx
```

I know, I know: an insane amount of punctuation and far too hearty and fake-cheerful. But let me ask you this: how do you tell a man you've never met – but have been in contact with for two months because you're dating 80 men around the world – that you've met someone else but hey, did he still want to meet up and go on a date?

And then have to do it another 24 times over?

And I still had to tell Garry about popping across to Australasia and completing my dating tour.

I'm not asking for sympathy. Just observing that, for some, the course of true love ne'er runs smooth. For me, the course of true love had not so much failed to run smooth as mounted the central reservation, taken out three lanes of oncoming traffic and was now burning out of control on top of a hot-dog stand on the hard shoulder opposite.

Or maybe it just seemed that way to me.

Next, I rang Sandy. She was my local contact and would be able to tell me where I was meeting Cleete, the rodeo rider **(Date #58)**. He had apparently thrown himself into rodeo riding after his wife had left him and I was curious as well as slightly nervous to hear more about his life.

'Oh, I was just about to call you,' Sandy said as soon as she heard my voice. Apparently the date was off. 'Cleete's recovering from surgery,' she told me apologetically. 'It's an occupational hazard when you ride those bulls. He punctured a lung and broke his back in seven places.'

I murmured my sympathy: clearly Cleete had thrown himself into rodeo in every sense of the word.

'He's been quite depressed,' she continued in a motherly tone, as if explaining why little Billy couldn't come out and play football, 'and really isn't up to dating at the moment.'

Reassuring Sandy that I understood (which I did: why he would choose to do something so dangerous was what I was struggling with), I noted her suggestion to visit Bill and Ramona Holt. They ran a rodeo museum on their ranch out of town and had been in the business themselves for over 40 years.

The Holt Heritage Museum housed a huge and fascinating collection of wagons, saddles and folk art from the Nez Perce Indians (who developed the appaloosa horse) and the cowboy ranchers who settled here alongside them. It also celebrated rodeo riding, a sport with a following as big and fanatical in the Western States as football in the UK.

For years Bill Holt was one of the sport's top announcers and Ramona Holt, his wife, one of the country's leading barrel riders (where tiny women hurtle at breakneck speed on horseback around a course of barrels).

Ramona let me inspect the wagons, rescued and restored from the turn of the twentieth century. Cowboy life looked organised but hard: families were isolated and forced to be self-sufficient (noting my squeamish reaction to hearing people sewed up their own wounds, Ramona told me she'd sewn up all her children's wounds: 'When you live in the country, that's just how things are,' she said with a shrug).

Cowboy ranching – close-knit families tending cattle on horseback – was at the heart of rodeo. Like ranching, rodeo was a family affair. Rodeo riders weren't contracted to a team: they mostly came from ranching families, the parents and wives acting as their support units (driving the horses across the country, maintaining the equipment etcetera).

Rodeo was divided into five major events: steer wrestling,

team roping, tie-down roping, barrel racing and bull riding. Showing me around a barn full of intricately tooled leather saddles, Bill told me rodeo was a serious business: 'It's a professional sport and the competitors are professional athletes,' he said gravely.

Bill stressed that the sport had standards. A heritage too: 'It's the only sport that's grown out of an industry,' he said proudly. 'The cattle industry. Rodeo represents ranching and the Old West.'

It made sense that rodeo had evolved from ranching. Like being a turn-of-the-century-cowboy's wife, life with a rodeo rider sounded a hard, extremely full-time job. I doubted that I – riding skills limited to cycling to Starbucks every morning; animal-wrangling skills limited to a pet hamster when I was eight – would be a natural fit. I explained to Bill I'd been due to date a ranch cowboy but he'd been too damaged (something I generally didn't discover until the date) to make it.

'When you say he had a punctured lung,' Bill said, waving his hand dismissively and snorting with contempt, 'well, he wasn't wearing a protective vest. You're telling me straight away he's not a professional.' Like a father comforting his stood-up daughter on prom night, he patted my arm reassuringly: 'I'm sure he's a wonderful guy, but sweetie, he's just an amateur.'

Amateur date promptly dismissed, Bill and Ramona showed me around their collection of cowboy boots.

It was fabulous: a vast array of boot couture featuring the cream of C & W instep royalty, from John Wayne, Johnny Cash and Clint Eastwood to Patsy Cline, Dolly Parton and Loretta Lynn. I teased Bill when he showed me Tom Selleck's boots. Shiny and showy, they were the cowboy boot equivalent of a Porsche.

'They're surprisingly small,' I taunted mischievously.

'No ma'am,' Bill replied firmly, without hesitation, 'I think you'll find you're wrong there.'

I left the ranch in no doubt that – from head to toe – rodeo men were Real Men.

As I walked into the hotel lobby, one of the receptionists called me over. 'Ms Cox, you have a visitor. He's waiting outside on the terrace.'

A visitor? My heart sank: *Oh please, don't let it be Cam.*

With a huge sense of dread and trepidation, I walked through the side doors onto the terrace that looked out across the river. But I didn't recognise the man sitting quietly on the bench, his eyes closed as if asleep. He wore a cowboy hat and leather chaps. He also wore an extremely uncomfortable-looking corset, which reached from his waist up to his neck, holding him in a rigid upright position.

Oh no. This had to be Cleete, the rodeo rider.

As he heard my feet on the path, Cleete turned awkwardly, winced, tried to stand up, winced again and miserably eased himself back into a sitting position on the bench.

'Oh my god, Cleete, is that you?' I asked, sitting carefully next to him, fearing he'd try to stand up again.

'Yes, ma'am, it is,' Cleete replied through gritted teeth, sweat trickling down his face, either from the heat of the corset or the pain of his injuries.

'Cleete, whatever are you doing here? Sandy said you were recovering from surgery,' I asked, horrified.

Unable to turn, Cleete wiggled the fingers on his left hand, as if they were doing the talking. 'Couldn't have no Enger-lish lady thinkin' rodeo riders let a little biddy bit o' pain git in the way o' their datin','' he wheezed, clearly in agony.

This was crazy.

'Cleete, how did you get here? Did Sandy bring you?' He wiggled his fingers: I took that to mean yes. 'Is she here now?' Again he wiggled his fingers. Asking Cleete to excuse me, I ran into reception, borrowing their phone, and called Sandy on her mobile.

She answered straight away. 'I know, I know, Jennifer,' she told me in a fluster. 'But he just wouldn't listen to reason. He insisted on coming to meet you.'

'Sandy, you've got to come and pick him up,' I told her sternly. 'The man should be on anti-inflammatories and pain-killers, not on a date.'

'I'm just pulling into the parking lot now,' she said, sounding more harassed than ever. 'I'll be with you in two minutes.'

Four minutes later, Sandy and I were loading Cleete into her truck.

'Don't be leavin' on my account,' Cleete winced as Sandy gently buckled the seatbelt over his surgical corset.

'It's not you, it's me,' I lied, wanting him to get home but with his pride intact. 'I have a bit of a headache.'

Rigid with pain, Cleete was clearly having trouble focusing. He stared vaguely from the back seat as if a hundred miles away. 'Ma'am, I sure am sorry to hear that,' he mumbled politely. 'I have some pills here that'll git rid of that problem for you real fast.'

But Sandy had started the truck and was shouting her goodbyes. I thanked Cleete for coming to see me and waved them off.

That poor man: if bull riding was helping him forget the pain of a broken heart, his heart had clearly taken quite a thrashing.

Back in my hotel room and still no message from Garry. Like a plate, I couldn't spin forever: my resolve not to call wobbled precariously.

I mean, it was fine: I knew he would call and it was still only 5 p.m. But in the meantime, waiting for the call was like needing to go to the toilet really badly: until it had happened, it was impossible to do or think about anything else.

I turned on my laptop hoping to distract myself with Date Traffic. I thought Ted and Jason might have got back to me. I felt curiously guilty: almost as if by meeting Garry I'd cheated on them. I wanted to check they were okay with my change in date status and that their feelings weren't hurt.

Scrolling down the emails, I caught up with the news from my world around the world. Things were calmer (for now) between Jo and Ryan; Cath had just got back from Antarctica; Belinda's baby daughter Maya was walking; my Thai date was happy I'd met someone but still wanted to go ahead with our date. I opened an email from a woman whose name I half recognised:

Hello, Jennifer — How are you? Things are excellent though extremely busy here: we are setting up another conference and I wanted to ask Kelly to speak. I bumped into him and his girlfriend at a party last week but don't have his email address. Could I trouble you for it? All the best, Sue.

My heart started to beat really fast as I read the email. I felt my mouth go dry and I put my hand up to it, as if fearing my heart was going to leap right out.

Kelly had a girlfriend.

You never know how much you're really over your ex, until you hear he has another girlfriend. Yes, I know I was dating stacks of people, I had met Garry, and I know it was now nearly a year and a half since Kelly and I had split up. But the shock of someone casually talking to me about him and his girlfriend was still immense.

I forgot to turn the computer off, I just scooped up my sunglasses, grabbed my bag and went straight out into the smoke-hazed, late afternoon heat. In a daze, I got on the bike and cycled across town to the Iron Horse microbrewery. I needed a drink.

I found a table in the corner of the terrace and sat staring out across the other drinkers without noticing a single one of them.

Kelly had a girlfriend.

I hated that it hurt so much. And the fact that it did took me by surprise. For me he was an appalling boyfriend; I was glad we weren't together any more AND I'd just met the most amazing man ever. So why did it hurt that Kelly was with someone else? I thought I'd got him completely out my system; why was there still undigested Kelly clogging up my emotional colon?

All these thoughts jostled around my head, fighting to be the one that made me feel the worst. I took a sip of my honey ale and pushed my sunglasses up my nose to hide the tears that were threatening to spill over my lower lashes.

Not wanting to cry in front of anyone made me more aware of the people on the tables around me. Two women in their late twenties sat close by. Both had huge manes of bleached blonde hair, billowing magnificently out like breaking waves sculpted from candyfloss. They leant close together, talking and smoking furiously.

They had boyfriend problems. The woman on the left stubbed her cigarette out, keeping on stubbing long after the glow was extinguished and the cigarette crumpled into the filter. '. . . I mean I was only out of town for a week,' she said bitterly, 'it really pisses me off.'

My heart sank further as I eavesdropped. Comparing their cheating boyfriends' misdemeanours, they complained it was hard to be a woman, yet both were standing by their man.

Two more women singing in Tammy's choir.

Was this the course of all relationships: starting out thrilled that you'd found your Soul Mate; ending up hating yourself for being a doormat? And if that was the case, did I really want to be in another relationship? Was Garry going to turn into another Kelly? Could I trust him or would I always be bracing myself, waiting for the telltale signs it had all gone wrong?

I took a long sip of my drink and thought hard. Suddenly I felt a surge of irritation with myself for being so melodramatic: *Oh, get over it, Jenny*, I told myself crossly.

If I'd come all this way only to get cold feet, well, I didn't deserve the support of my friends, let alone to meet someone as lovely as Garry. Not everyone was a cheater. I mean, I'd cheated on poor Peter with Philip when I went to Australia but I'd never been unfaithful again.

Let Kelly have a girlfriend (poor woman); I didn't want him back. I didn't want to keep looking back either. I wanted a better boyfriend and I could stay here and keep brooding about it, or go and find out if I'd just met him.

Jumping up and resisting the temptation to tell the women to dump their loser boyfriends, I headed for the door. Bugger being cool: I was going to the hotel to call Garry.

I cycled across town like a maniac, weaving in and out of traffic. I shot through two lights that stayed red far too long. Dumping my bike in the hotel reception, I paced agitatedly as a crowd of new arrivals slowly tried to work out the best way to fit all their luggage into the lift. Too impatient to wait any longer, I ran up three flights of stairs to my floor.

Hurtling into my room, the first thing I saw was the message light flashing on the console.

YES!

Snatching up the phone, I dialled into the answering service. An automated voice thanked me for calling and gave me the news that:

You have two messages. First message, left today at 5.23 p.m. Message one:

'*Hey Baby, so I finally made it off the Playa. I am totally tired and dirty. Make me jealous: you're clean and sleeping in a real bed, huh? That'll be me in another seven hours. Call me when you get this message, I want to hear your news.*'

As soon as I had heard Garry's voice, I sank down onto the bed, a huge smile taking up my entire face. God, he sounded gorgeous: American accent, voice gravelly from the desert dust and lack of sleep. Ummmmmm.

Second message, left today at 7.09 p.m. Message two:

'Five crazy days on the Playa and you've got me thinking about you. You're really something, British Girl. Call me.'

And I did.

I curled up on my bed in Missoula; he lay on the bed in his roadside trailer somewhere between Reno and Seattle. And we talked and talked. For two hours we talked about the Deities in the base of the Pyramid; the Booth of Bad Advice telling people not to apply sunscreen and drink less water; we talked about what our Costco friends had been up to after I left . . . We talked about my continuing to date and what that meant for us. He was supportive and understanding, leaving me reassured that I was doing the right thing. And we also talked about Seattle and the time we would have together in his city.

Meeting in the desert had been magical and dramatic: it had been larger than life, like something out of a film. But now, as we talked and laughed and teased each other over the phone, I realised we could have met at a bus stop or a bar or on a blind date and I still would have found Garry intriguing and entertaining. It wasn't the Playa or BRC that had captivated me: it was him.

You know, I blame Hector for putting Carpenter lyrics into my head, but I had the strongest feeling that Garry and I . . . *had only just begun.*

CHAPTER ELEVEN

USA – Seattle, Washington & San Francisco, California

If you're having one of those days when happy people make you want to randomly punch strangers, feel free to skip the next few pages.

I was excited but extremely nervous when I arrived at Seattle airport two days later. One look at Garry told me he was just as nervous, though, and I immediately felt relieved: it wasn't just me that needed a little time for romance reacclimatisation.

But we had too much to talk about and got on too well to stay self-conscious for long, and the days that followed (. . . I warned you this was coming) were complete and utter bliss.

I'd never been to Seattle and although I expected an interesting city, I hadn't expected such a beautiful setting. Seattle is actually a rash of islands, with the city sitting on a lick of land between Puget Sound and Lake Washington. Mountains run around three-quarters of the horizon like a mandarin collar: the Olympic Mountains to the west, Mount Ranier to the south and the Cascades to the east.

Although a native Californian, Garry had lived in Seattle for seven years and made an excellent guide. He took me to all the funky areas, buying me drinks in the coolest bars, waiting outside as I ran riot in the clothing boutiques and cosmetic stores in Fremont and West Seattle.

At Ballard Locks, we made up stupid stories about each of the salmon trying to work out how to use the fish ladder. The sun was hot as we walked along Lincoln Beach holding hands, constantly stopping because we were laughing or kissing.

Incidentally, I know this sounds sugary and sickly but I want to make it absolutely clear that we weren't one of those slobbery, big-tongue-action-in-public, 'hey, get a room!' couples. We were electrified with newly minted romance – it pinged out of us like static from nylon sheets – and we couldn't get enough of it or each other.

Garry had a comfortable house in a quiet, forested area overlooking Puget Sound. He was an incredible cook and happiest when creating impressive gourmet meals as I perched on a stool with a glass of wine chatting or rifling through his CD collection. Other than perhaps toast or spaghetti, I've never had a man cook for me before. Once Garry finally managed to persuade me that he enjoyed making barbecued pizza with red onion, pesto and goats' cheese or baked snapper with chilli and mango salsa and I didn't need to keep offering to help, I was surprised by how much I liked it.

It did take some getting used to, though. Garry was clearly someone who liked to be a gentleman: he insisted on paying for everything; holding open doors; giving me his jacket if I was cold and generally being kind and considerate. As much as it thrilled and amazed me (I felt like I'd picked the best ride at the

Relationship Theme Park), I struggled with it, a little at first and more so as time went on.

It was really the *paying for things* part. Although I knew Garry enjoyed treating me, I was extremely conscious of not wanting to take advantage of him or cruise along on his generosity. Plus, I had little experience of being treated this way: I had my own money and expected to contribute. I genuinely didn't know how to deal with it. So I kept trying to pick up the bills and Garry kept saying no.

On the third night it came to a head.

We'd spent a lovely afternoon wandering around the touristy but entertaining Pike Place Market, and were now having early evening drinks at Anthony's on Belltown harbour. As the sun set, we drank martinis and watched a sleek, chic, sixty-something couple confidently moor their boat (elegant, opulent and the size of a small city), looking every inch like an advertisement for the wonders of Viagra.

Garry looked up as the waitress came to take our food order. 'Jen, I know you don't like oysters,' he said, prodding tentatively at the minefield of my dietary foibles, 'but they're so good here, why don't you try one?'

I hate oysters. They have a hellish texture and aren't even vaguely filling: eating them has always seemed a pointless exercise in combining the traumatic with the superfluous. He asked so sweetly, though, so two cocktails later our perky waitress ('Ohmigosh, are you Briddish? Oh man, I just love your accent!') brought us half a dozen kumamato oysters, served on a bed of pink champagne and cracked-pepper sorbet. Gary showed me how to fork a tiny amount of sorbet onto the oyster, and top it with a squeeze of fresh lemon.

I was determined not to think as I popped the oyster into my mouth and chewed gingerly. The rich, creamy, salty flavour filled my mouth and wrapped itself around my taste buds. I was amazed to find I loved it. And glad. Not just that Garry had talked me into trying them, but also that for once I'd been undogmatic enough to say yes. But when the bill came, things took a sudden turn. As we tussled as usual over who was paying, Garry suddenly sat back, thought for a moment and then took my hand in his. 'Jen,' he said slowly. 'I know you're used to paying your way and that's why you keep offering to pick up the tab. But here's the thing: you're only here for a few days and you're my girlfriend: can you please just accept that I want to take care of you and let me do it?' He looked both firm and sincere but I was too scared to say anything for fear I'd burst into tears. It was the most romantic thing anyone had ever said to me in my whole life.

As the sun set across the bay and the early evening crowd strolled across the boardwalk next to us, I felt lost in my emotions. Was he for real? Was this for real? Did Garry have a wife, 27 children and a job in a lawnmower repair shop in Iowa and that's why he could say and do the things he did? Also, I don't want to sound contrary here, but much as I wanted to make changes to my life, could I allow someone to give – what felt to me – so much and not feel weird or diminished by the loss of control?

I looked at Garry, still sitting quietly waiting for my answer. He looked incredibly handsome: those crazy, deep blue eyes fringed by dark lashes so long they made me jealous, his face tanned and smooth from the desert heat. I loved being with him so much: he was funny, generous, a good storyteller, and with just enough self-doubt to make him seem a little vulnerable and utterly loveable.

And he seemed completely smitten with me.

It was no good, I'd held off for as long as anyone could possibly have expected me to. The tears started rolling down my cheeks.

Garry, of course, had no idea what was going on. He just knew he'd challenged me and now I was sitting here silent and in tears. He looked completely mortified. 'Oh God, Jennifer, I didn't mean to upset you,' he said, the anxiety clear in his voice. I sniffled and, one hand rifling through my handbag for a tissue, the other still in his, 'No, no . . .' I spluttered between tears. 'You haven't upset me at all. Quite the opposite: it's the most wonderful thing anyone has ever said to me. I'm crying because I'm happy.'

Garry looked unconvinced but gradually his expression changed from one of horror to one of *never try and understand women* instead. I wiped the last of the tears from my cheeks and gave a wobbly smile. 'Thank you, Garry, it's a deal: you're buying.'

I extended my ticket so we'd have ten days together in Seattle. I was flying back to London out of San Francisco so we decided to spend three days on his parents' boat in the Bay Area too (Anders' floating sauna had begrudgingly opened my mind to the possibility that maybe *some* boats may be okay).

As time sped by, real life started to reassert itself. Garry had to go to work, doing audio for the Mariners baseball games on TV, and in theory I was meant to be seeing Ted and Jason.

Turning on my laptop, I spotted emails from both of them amongst the deluge. I was surprised and happy to see one from Nanc in Vegas as well and I opened it straight away:

Well, he sounds very interesting. Maybe you
should get us his driver's license identification
and Elizabeth can run his background for us (just
kidding). I am very happy for you. But I still
think Elizabeth and I should interrogate
him. Seattle isn't far from Vegas. Send him to us
and we'll take him to dinner and let you
know. Miss you kiddo. Nanc xx

I laughed when I read the email: Nanc might have been joking
about the background check, but Elizabeth would be
completely serious. I was incredibly touched that Nanc and
Elizabeth were looking out for me and thought – not for the
first time – how many unique and genuinely special people I
had met on this trip.

I replied to my old friend Eddie, who'd emailed asking for
my phone number in Seattle (another subtle vetting ploy as he
could easily have called me on my mobile). I then got to the
emails from Jason and Ted to check they were still okay to meet
up now I had met Garry.

So . . . are you serious? You've actually met
your Soul Mate and he lives here? That was fast!
What happened? Okay, I'll admit that I'm a little
disappointed but I'm obviously very happy for
you. Of course we can still go hang out. I'd love
to finally meet and hear all about Burning Man
too. I'll be around this week, is there any time
that's good for you? Take care, Jason

I felt relieved: the last thing I wanted to do was upset anyone.

And I was pleased that Jason still wanted to meet up. Although I'd suspected he wasn't The One, I'd enjoyed echatting with him – mainly talking about music – and could tell he was a good person.

I'd got Jason through the usual network of relationships maintained via email. Randy was a second-generation Date Wrangler. He knew my friend Paula from the time he worked in Amazon's British office, but before that he worked at their head office in Seattle which was how he knew Jason. Randy now lived in New York but was still in regular email contact with both Paula and Jason (neither of whom knew each other). When Randy had got my Soul Mate Job Description, he'd emailed Jason, who in turn – as I was in the middle of *A Date for Europe* – emailed me.

The other Seattle date, Ted, was a friend of Posh PR Emma's. He ran a thriving dotcom company and warned me from the start (nearly three months ago) that although he had *no time to email, wait until you get to Seattle then I'll impress the hell out of you.*

Well, here I was in Seattle, though admittedly under different circumstances to the one Ted and I had originally anticipated. Opening the email, instead of impressing, Ted *scared* the hell out of me:

Jennifer, you are kidding right? I have had Saturday marked off on my calendar for two months. I sent my Director of Operations to the Tokyo conference in my place because you and I had this engagement. This is not acceptable. Meet me and I will change your mind (I am considering the possibility that defaulting on your promise

constitutes the breaking of a contract between
us, the honouring of which on my part could
subsequently result in the loss of earnings for
my company). Please call Janelle my secretary to
confirm on telephone # 206 – . . .

I read it and reread it. The first half was bad; the second half
read like some loan small print where the company reserved the
right to eat your parents should you miss a payment. Ted had to
be joking, he couldn't be serious. But what if he was serious?
What if America had become so litigious and work-obsessed,
you could be sued for wasting someone's time and emotional
energy by falling in love with a third party?

I hit reply then closed down the empty email about five
times, each time wanting to get back to him but each time
being at a loss as to what exactly I should say.

In the end, I decided to forward it on to Posh PR Emma.
Much as I was grateful to the Date Wranglers for all their hard
work and support, it was like a dinner party that was a guy short
at the last minute. If the guy you brought as a favour went on
to get drunk and threw up in the hostess's fish tank, favour or
no favour, it was your job to sort out the mess. Whether she
liked it or not, Emma was going to have to get Ted's head out
of the tank and give him a good talking to.

Meanwhile, Garry was upstairs in his office getting on top
of his own life. I could hear his fingers clatter across the
keyboard as he emailed and talked on the (constantly ringing)
phone. People called to talk about work, catch up after Burning
Man and find out about his new British girlfriend (I heard the
term *New British Girlfriend* so many times I started feeling like
some political initiative).

He was very sweet, and as he talked I couldn't help but overhear how proud and happy he sounded. Most people were clearly delighted for him: a few less so. When Garry told one woman in particular about us, she was so upset I could hear her reaction ('*NOOOOOO!*') from where I was sitting down in the kitchen. ('Don't be like that,' Garry reasoned, clearly taken aback by her response.)

But I was soon to meet the female who would pose the biggest challenge to our relationship. She was called Hal, and she was so much a part of Garry's life, she was already in the house.

Garry had to work the Mariners baseball game but – worried I'd be bored on my own – suggested I drop him off and keep the truck for the rest of the day.

I was touched and slightly overwhelmed. That he trusted me to drive his huge truck was kind but a bit of a responsibility. That he thought I would make it home without ending up in Vancouver was lovely but possibly expecting too much from my navigational skills. That I would be able to make my way back to where he worked, from the house – 20 minutes of twisting and turning roads, in the dark – felt like madness.

But, whatever, I'd make it or I wouldn't.

When we arrived at Safeco Field, the Mariners' home ground, OB and some of Garry's other workmates came out to say hello.

It obviously wasn't just my friends who were vetting for suitability: Garry's clearly wanted to make sure I was good for him too. And don't forget, they all knew Garry and I had met because I was travelling the world dating 80 men. That made them doubly protective of him and doubly curious about me. (In the likelihood I was an International Slapper, what guy wouldn't want to come and take a look: *Roll Up, Roll Up, Ladies and Gents, see the freakishly loose woman . . .*) They teased Garry mercilessly and made me feel really welcome. I was touched they cared about him so much, and it felt good to have their seal of approval, because no matter how we met, Garry was my boyfriend and I wanted his friends to like me.

I did end up getting hopelessly lost trying to find my way back to Garry's house, but I didn't mind as I ended up in Alki Beach. Full of pert inline skaters and deal-breakers walking their dogs and barking into their mobiles, it's a little corner of LA in Seattle.

I managed to make it home at last, intending to spend a quiet evening catching up on emails and American sitcoms. It was all going well until I started to get cold.

I mentioned Hal. She was the Home Automated Living (HAL) computer system that allowed Garry to operate lights, heating and burglar alarms remotely when he was on tour. Garry had shown me a couple of days ago how to operate Hal through his computer, also by speaking to her via a microphone wired into the system.

I was sitting in front of the Hal programme now, trying to turn the heating on. But as I scrolled through the various options, I couldn't for the life of me remember how to make it work. There was no way I was going to ring Garry and admit that, though, so I had to figure it out for myself.

As I drummed my fingers in irritation, I jumped in shock as, out of the blue, a woman's voice queried: 'Yes?' The microphone on the desk had picked up the sound of my tapping fingers and activated Hal's listening programme. 'Yes?' she asked again, sounding imperious and resentful, like a beautiful cat left cooped up too long.

The Hal programme allowed you to select a male or female voice for the system. It also let you pick the pitch and attitude of the voice (polite or curt). Garry had made Hal sound like a sexy woman, who, in my opinion, also sounded high-handed and high-maintenance – I hoped that wasn't how he saw me . . . apart from the sexy bit: I could live with that.

Picking up the microphone and trying to remember how Garry had given voice commands, I addressed the computer: 'Hal, turn the heating on.' Nothing happened. I waited for a moment. Nothing continued to happen. I tried again, this time a little louder, my voice echoing around the large, open-plan, increasingly chilly house: 'Hal, turn the heating on.'

Again, nothing. Hal remained wilfully silent.

Don't tell Garry, my new hi-tech audio-guy boyfriend this, but I thumped the microphone down on the desk in exasperation. It was too frustrating: why wasn't there just a switch on the wall I could turn on, like in a normal house?

The mic was obviously a better communicator than I, though: the sound of it clunking onto the desk got Hal's attention. 'Yes?' she asked again in a bored voice, calculated to inspire impotent fury in the listener (or maybe just this listener). I snatched up the mic from the desk, refusing to admit defeat: perhaps the problem was I'd been speaking too quietly? The advancing cold concentrated my mind; I spoke loudly and clearly: 'Hal, turn the heating on.'

'Did you say "turn the lighting on"?' Hal shot back snootily, her tone suggesting, 'There really is no need to shout: it's quite vulgar and impolite.'

Thank god, the damn thing had heard me: 'No,' I replied,

feeling a little flash of triumph, 'I said turn the heating on.' I made a point of exaggerating the word heating, hoping Hal would feel the humiliation she'd brought upon herself. 'Lights turning on,' Hal chimed smugly, ignoring my contradiction. And with that, every single light in every single room in the house snapped on.

Right.

This was an open declaration of war. That Sim-sucking bitch was wrong if she thought she was going to get the better of me: she was about to discover the hard way that she'd chosen the wrong woman to play computer games with.

Ignoring the house lights, which now blazed as harshly as a fridge opened at 4 a.m., I fixed the monitor with a steady look. In a tone as clear as it was cold (actually, by now freezing cold), my voice rang out in defiance. 'Hal!' I commanded, 'turn the heating on.'

'Did you say turn the heating up?' Hal asked bitchily, by now clearly revelling in my discomfort. Had I asked that? Could the heating be turned *up*, if it wasn't actually *on*? Was this was a trick; was she trying to outmanoeuvre me? I wasn't sure, but didn't want to be caught out on a technicality so I said evenly, 'No, I said turn the heating *on*.'

'I am turning the heating up,' Hal declared, a withering glance at my poker face as she slammed down the winning hand.

For a moment there was only silence. Then, a faint whirring noise stirred in the basement. It grew louder and louder, and as it did the walls of the house started to shudder gently. I looked around nervously, trying to work out what was causing the noise. Then CRASH: with a terrifying roar, air − hot as a breath from Lucifer himself − blasted out from vents and ducts all over the house.

The noise was deafening, and, moments later, the house became unbearably hot. Pausing instinctively to admire the system's efficiency, I yelled, 'Hal, turn the heating off, turn the heating off,' over and over. Maybe she couldn't hear me over the fans as they powered the atmosphere of the Serengeti around the house; maybe she was ignoring me on purpose? Either way, Hal refused to answer.

The house got hotter and hotter, the lights dazzled overhead: I was being cooked to death by a crazed computer-generated housekeeper, unwilling to tolerate another woman in Garry's house.

I shouted and shouted until the heat made my throat too dry to shout any more, but nothing seemed to be working. If I was going to get around Hal, I clearly needed a different strategy. Staggering downstairs to get some water, I threw open the doors and windows to let some cool air in. And then I had an idea. I ran back upstairs through the blasting heat and resumed my position in the computer hot-seat.

Hal obviously wasn't going to do what I asked her, but I bet she'd listen to Garry.

It was tricky. Much as I adored Garry, I didn't really know his voice that well, plus there was the whole accent thing. I rang the house number three or four times to listen to his voice on the answering machine, then took a swallow of water and cleared my throat. 'Hal, turn the heating off,' I said in a deep American accent.

Nothing. Okay, it had been a dodgy accent. I tried again: 'Hal, turn the heating off.' Still nothing.

I tried a variety of pitches; I experimented with placing the stresses in different parts of the sentence; I truncated and elongated vowels. In short, I went deep undercover and immersed myself, blindly navigating the twists and turns of another gender and another culture.

'Did you say turn the heating off?' Hal suddenly enquired sweetly.

Oh my god, I'd done it: she thought I was Garry. 'Yes,' I replied succinctly, not wanting to blow it now I was getting somewhere. 'I am turning the heating off,' Hal replied coquettishly. And with that, the roaring from the vents stopped dead.

The house was filled with silence.

It was like someone had been pointing a hairdryer in my face for 20 minutes and the relief of it stopping was immense. Taking a moment to recover, I took a deep breath, then, trying to recall the winning pitch and accent, I attempted to cajole Hal into turning the lights off too. Three tries later and off they went.

I sat in the dark, quiet, cooling house and let the silence wash over me. Until Garry got home, there was little I could do without lights or heating. Settling back onto the sofa as comfortably as I could to recover from the ridiculous panto-mime, I started pondering for the first time what I was actually doing here. I was besotted with Garry and I thought he felt the same way about me, but, seriously, where would we go from here? How was our hot-house relationship going to survive outside in the real world?

We both lived full and demanding lives a continent apart. I couldn't bear the thought of a permanent long-distance relationship, so where did that leave us? Would I be willing to move to Seattle? It seemed insane to be even considering the question so soon (or perhaps it seemed insane not to have considered it sooner?), but if my answer was *no*, for both

Garry's and my sake I had to end it now before we got in any deeper.

But there was no way I could do that. The more I got to know Garry the more I liked him; even after this short time together I'd miss him too much.

Wrestling to find an answer, I gradually realised that I was expecting too much too soon.

Being with Garry had taken a giant leap of faith. Maybe I was like Neil Armstrong and my giant leap had catapulted me so high I'd be up bobbing around in orbit for a while yet. It was pointless agonising about it all now. I wanted to be with Garry and it felt amazing. That was what was important: anything else would just have to wait until I came back down to earth.

Damn Hal: it was her nonsense that had forced me to think about all this stuff. She was a pretty formidable housekeeper; had all this been her doing? Turning up the heat and putting me under the spotlight, I think she'd been vetting me like the rest of Garry's circle.

'Did you have a good night, sweetie?' Garry asked when I arrived wrung out and exhausted at Safeco Fields to collect him.

'Yes, thanks,' I replied dishonestly. Tonight's events were going to stay between Hal and me. And, whatever else our differences, I suspected this would be the one thing we'd agree on.

The next morning was busy. Posh PR Emma had replied immediately:

```
Darling, Ted can be a frightful bully sometimes
but his bark is far worse than his bite. I've
told him he's got to stop being so silly if he
ever wants to meet a nice girl, but you know men:
love to talk, hate to listen. If you can bear it,
do pop in and see him: he's a total sweetie
really. Let me know. Oh, loved the piccy of you
and Garry — what a hunk! You lucky old thing.
Ciao ciao, Ems xxxx
```

There was no email from Ted (maybe he was out chasing the postman up and down his street). As a sacrifice to the Numbers God I'd probably see him but I'd make him wait a bit first. I was in the middle of emailing Jason when Garry shouted down from his office that there was a phone call for me. I picked up the extension in the kitchen, half expecting it to be Jason and feeling more than a little awkward as Garry had been talking to whoever it was for quite a while. But it was Eddie, my old friend from home. Somehow, I seemed to be the kind of person who – based on no good reason or track record – people came to for advice. Eddie was the person *I* always went to – he was tough and smart and he was also concerned and protective of me, like a big brother.

Eddie had been talking to Garry and I instinctively held my breath, hoping, for Garry's sake, he'd passed muster. 'So, you've found your Soul Mate?' Eddie teased as I picked up the phone.

'Yes,' I replied happily, 'I have. I hope you were nice to him?'

'Tolerably so,' Eddie replied sardonically, then suddenly becoming serious: 'So, apart from fancying the pants off him, is everything okay?'

I took this to be code for *have you picked another loser?* And I smiled, touched by his concern. 'Honestly, Eds,' I replied. 'He really is wonderful. And if you hadn't liked the sound of him yourself, you'd be telling me so by now.'

Eddie never gave ground: the fact he wasn't arguing was his way of agreeing. 'Well,' he said finally, 'I'll meet him when he comes to London so I'll tell you what I think of him then.'

Come to London? When was that happening? 'Oh, I don't know that he is,' I replied, a little defensively.

'Why wouldn't he?' Eddie demanded.

I didn't really have an answer for him: I hadn't even thought about Garry visiting me, let alone talked to him about it.

Eddie and I caught up on news from home before finally saying goodbye. Garry came downstairs: 'Your friend Eddie's very funny,' he said, hugging me and noting my smile.

'Yes, he's a good man. Did you get on with him okay?' I asked, pulling back a little so I could see his reaction.

Garry told me they had, then added unexpectedly: 'He asked when I was coming to London?'

I shrugged awkwardly. 'Yes, Eddie asked me that too. Don't worry, it's fine.'

Garry looked nonplussed. 'Why? Don't you want me to?'

Now it was my turn to look blank. 'Well, yes, of course I do,' I replied. 'But I know how busy you are and . . . you know, it's expensive and . . . a long way . . .'

As I said it, I realised how pathetic I sounded. I trailed off.

Garry looked a bit cross. 'Jenny, London is where you live – of course I'm going to come and see you there. Why would you imagine I wouldn't?'

I was taken aback by how exasperated he sounded, and also by the logic of what he was saying. Garry was right: I was happy to fly halfway around the world to be with someone I cared for, but didn't imagine for one moment they'd be prepared to do the same for me. And that's not all. I was probably being pretty controlling too. I was the one that waltzed in and out of the Dates' lives, deciding when and how they got to see me. It was in their territory but always on my terms. And I kept London for me: a barrier behind which I went *off-duty*, to relax and recharge.

Garry, in London, seeing me on my home turf, meeting my friends, experiencing my life, would break down that barrier. But Garry was different. Shouldn't I be giving him the same kind of Access All Areas into my life that he was giving me to his?

God, why was I suddenly in the House of Questions?

It would be good to ask the Date Wranglers their opinion about all of this, but comforting as the thought was, I knew this was something Garry and I had to work out for ourselves. There was a point when new lovers stopped being public property and made their own world in private (and this was especially true of our *cast of thousands* relationship).

'So?' Garry asked, obviously getting used to the long silences which inevitably accompanied me furiously debating sticky issues with myself.

I snapped out of my inner turmoil and answered him immediately: 'Yes, come to London,' I replied with complete conviction. 'I'd really like you to see my home.'

So, over the next week and a half we settled into a comfortable rhythm of going out, eating in and falling in love. Sharing a space felt easy and natural, uncomplicated and companionable, not like we had to constantly be on our best behaviour.

And when Garry went to work, so did I.

I'd relented and had Janelle schedule me into **Ted's (Date #59)** diary for a coffee. He actually was far nicer in real life and, tall with short black hair and deep brown skin that at times seemed to shimmer golden, he was very good-looking. But he was a complete workaholic: his phone rang constantly throughout our coffee date and although Ted never took the call, each time he frowned furiously, checking to see who it was. That was my old life and I felt a twinge of guilt remembering the many times I'd done exactly the same thing.

Still, date done, at least Ted couldn't sue me now.

Jason (Date #60) was just as much fun as I had hoped. A huge music fan, we talked non-stop over margaritas at a little Mexican place in Belltown. I loved the sound of his life: both that he knew and was so involved with the Seattle music scene, also the more niche activities revolving around his love of the ukulele. He wasn't my Soul Mate but he was very entertaining and we had a fun night out.

Relaxed and comfortable as Garry and I were with each other, as the time approached to go to San Francisco I became increasingly preoccupied. Only three more days together, then I'd be flying back to London. And although I missed London and was looking forward to seeing family, friends and my flat, leaving Garry and going back to my old life filled me with a kind of dread.

Too soon it was time to fly down to San Francisco.

We picked up a hire car at the airport and drove to Andronico's, the upscale supermarket in Walnut Creek, for boat provisions. We browsed amongst the aisles of soft fruit, glossy like multi-coloured cricket balls; rich rounds of ripe, pungent cheeses; broad loaves of crusty bread, knotted like muscular arms; cakes as fussy as Easter bonnets. But as we pressed the spongy flesh of the portabella mushrooms and piled feathery fronds of dill and fennel into our baskets, I was jittery and distracted. And this was nothing to do with flying home.

I was about to meet Garry's parents.

I wanted to buy them something but found myself getting increasingly worked up as I dithered between the walls of unfamiliar wines and the banks of endlessly exotic flowers. Of course, I wanted to make a good impression, but never having met them, I didn't know what they liked.

Garry was no use: 'You don't have to get them anything,' he shrugged.

I narrowed my eyes and sighed in exasperation: 'Garry, your parents are letting us use their boat for three days: there is no way I'm going to turn up empty-handed.'

We left the supermarket and drove to the Bay Area marina where the boat was moored. I was very quiet as we started unloading the provisions and Garry put the groceries down on the ground, wrapped his arms around my waist and kissed me. 'Jen, don't be nervous,' he said, stroking my hair reassuringly, 'my parents are really easy-going. And after tonight, it'll just be the two of us on the boat. It'll be relaxing, you'll see.'

I knew he meant well, but I couldn't keep it in any longer. Trying to keep the snippiness out of my voice, 'Garry,' I said tersely, 'I really appreciate you organising this and I know it's what you find relaxing. But I have a long and well-documented history of seasickness and the thought of spending three days on a boat scares the bejesus out of me. And as for your parents: they're your parents, so I'm sure they're absolutely lovely. In fact, I already know they're lovely because they've given us their boat. But the fact remains, any minute now a conversation will take place where you say: "Mom, Dad, I'd like you to meet my girlfriend", and they'll be like, "Oh, how nice, how did you two meet?", and I'll have to say, "Well, funny you should ask, because I'm going round the world dating eighty complete strangers. Garry was . . . number fifty-five, wasn't it, darling? But no need to worry: only another twenty dates with men I've never met, then I'll be all done."'

Maybe I was being a little melodramatic, but, let's face it, it was the truth and it didn't look good. I was genuinely horrified at what his parents must think. Garry looked at me in astonishment. Okay, maybe I should have said something sooner rather than waiting until, one, I was completely freaked out about it and, two, we were moments from boarding the boat.

Garry took it all in his stride, though. He was calm (which was good because I clearly wasn't) as he pulled me to him, giving me a long, slow kiss. I don't know which stress-management school taught that particular technique, but they deserved a medal: I immediately felt calmer and more secure. Pulling away, Garry smiled affectionately. 'My parents are going to love you as much as I do, Jennifer Cox,' he said.

'Really?' I whispered, crinkling up my face in concern.

'Yes, really,' Garry replied softly.

Hang on. Had Garry just told me he loved me?

Is that what he meant? Or did he mean it in another way? Did he mean he loved – as in was *in love* with – me, or did he mean, he liked me and . . . you know . . . *loved* liking me, and his parents would like me and love that too? Or did it mean something else altogether?

Like a crying child having a stuffed toy thrust in its face, the distraction worked brilliantly. As we walked down the ramp onto the jetty, with armfuls of food, flowers and wine, I was blissfully preoccupied and not in the least bit nervous.

And, of course, Garry was right: his parents were completely wonderful. And the boat, 40 ft of beautiful wood, fantastically restored and outfitted by Garry's dad, was delightful. And most importantly, very still.

Garry's parents seemed one of those couples who enjoyed each other's company, so were relaxed and easy to be around. They went out of their way to make me feel welcome and I liked them immediately. In their early sixties, Gerry and Judy complemented each other. Both fit and energetic, they mirrored the other's body language; instinctively reaching from a shelf what the other was looking for or interrupting each other's stories with gentle teasing.

They clearly were Soul Mates, which felt like a good omen for Garry and me.

Garry busied himself preparing salmon for the barbecue and making some kind of complicated marinade for the mushrooms. So Gerry, Judy and I took our drinks up on deck and sat out in the heat of the early evening sun. We chatted easily about family and work and life in the Bay Area, and life in London.

I didn't know whether to talk about my journey or not, but Judy, perhaps sensing my discomfort, made it easy for me. 'So Jennifer,' she asked in a tone so neutral the Swiss would have begged for the recipe, 'Garry's told us a lot about you; your journey sounds very interesting.'

And with that the floodgates opened. I told them about London and how, although happy with my job for years, my priority had become finding the relationship that would make me just as happy. The journey had been to find my Soul Mate but also to understand why I made the choices that had stopped me meeting him sooner.

I told them about the Love Professor and his theories; I told them about the Vegas Bettys and their insights; I told them about Davide and his dead love in Verona; I even told them about Anders and his amazing floating sauna. As the sun set over the Bay, I told them about my whole journey and how it had brought me into their son's life.

Judy had lots of questions. She asked as a woman as well as a mother: curious about the lengths I had gone to and the people I had met along the way. 'Judy, quit interrogating the poor girl!' Gerry said after a while. But I was glad of Judy's questions: I wanted to tell them my story, but mostly I wanted them to know that Garry was safe with me. And much as it made me hot with embarrassment, I knew the only way was to come right out with it. I checked my glass to make sure I had enough wine for what I was about to say.

But just as I opened my mouth, Garry came up on deck, a beer in one hand, barbecue tongs in the other. Flushed from cooking, he looked relaxed, happy and extremely sexy. Perching on the back of my chair, he draped his arm across my shoulders. 'Hey, what's with all the talking?' he teased. Gerry raised his eyebrows in an *I already tried telling them that* way. Judy and I smiled conspiratorially at each other. 'Are you ready to eat: dinner's a couple of minutes off,' Garry announced, taking a lazy pull on his beer and watching with Gerry as a power boat cruised slowly by.

I wished Garry had been just three minutes longer in the kitchen. Pausing to take a gulp from my glass, I started nervously. 'Look, before we eat, can I please say something really quickly?'

Judy nodded encouragingly.

'Judy, Gerry, it's really nice to meet you. It's very kind of you to invite me onto your boat and I'm having a lovely evening. Thank you,' I told them by way of a preamble. Garry's parents seemed a little nonplussed by my speech and looked over to Garry, whom I felt shrugging behind me as if to say: '*What can I say, she's British, they're very formal . . .*'

Judy reached over and patted my arm: 'Well, dear, you really are very welcome . . .'

'No, no . . .' I interrupted. 'Sorry, I didn't mean to be rude, what I'm saying is – Garry is an extremely special man and I feel blessed to have met him and have him in my life. And although I have to keep travelling and dating . . .' out of breath, I trailed off '. . . I just want you to know, I'm in love with your son and I'm not going to do anything to hurt him or mess it up.'

Garry looked self-conscious but touched. Gerry beamed as Judy hugged me and said: 'Oh, aren't you, darling. Thank you, Jennifer, and don't you worry. We know how happy you make Garry and that makes us very happy too.'

Garry got to his feet, clearly desperate to change the subject: 'So, if everyone's finished *saying what they have to say . . .*' he gave me a pointed look . . . 'can we eat?' And, picking up his beer, he led the way into the cabin. Judy and Gerry stood up and followed.

Feeling emotional and light-headed, I was a little slower. Today I'd flown to San Francisco. Today Garry had (possibly) told me that he loved me. Today he'd brought me to meet his parents. Today I'd told his parents I was dating 80 men and loved their son.

Yes, sitting down to a nice dinner and a number of very large drinks was probably the best way to cope with days like today. I got up and followed them all into the cabin.

The rest of the evening, like the three days that followed, was perfect. As usual, it was an extraordinary meal, and we all talked and laughed until around 10 p.m., when Judy and Gerry left. 'We have so enjoyed meeting you, Jennifer,' Judy told me as we hugged and kissed goodbye. 'You two look so happy together; I do hope it's not too long before we see you again.'

I agreed wholeheartedly.

San Francisco was like a holiday – neither of us worked and we didn't check email once. We had plans to visit some of the Costco crew: Rico and Annie, Brenda and Jefe all lived about half an hour away. Lonely Planet's US office was also in the area and I'd let some of my old friends from the company know we were in town.

But, in the end, we saw no one: we stayed in bed late; lazed on the boat in the sun; drove around with the convertible roof down, singing to Johnny Cash and Def Leppard's request to '*Pour some sugar on meeee . . .*' at the tops of our voices. And, of course, we talked.

We talked about Garry coming to see me in London next month. And Garry was travelling to Japan with Seattle's basketball team, The Sonics. Russia had fallen through but Hector had some dates for me in China: could I go via Tokyo? We got out our diaries: the timing would be tight and I'd have to scramble to set up dates there, but it could work.

These were not always easy conversations to have: we didn't

know what would happen after this point, plus there was the business of my ongoing dating. Plus we were both a little frazzled from our relationship being so fast and intense: it was as if we were *speed-learning* each other, knowing – for the foreseeable future – this was all the time we had together. 'We've fitted three years of relationship into three weeks,' Garry observed as we curled up on deck together under the moonlight, drinking wine. We felt the same way about the situation: incredibly grateful to have met each other, but at times overwhelmed by the pace the relationship was forced to run at.

And to think I'd initially imagined I'd meet my Soul Mate and simply drive off into the sunset, the road straight and easy to navigate.

But, whatever the pressure or complications, I didn't regret it and wouldn't have changed it for the world. And even more perfectly, any time I got scared and thought I was in too deep, Garry would say or do things that made it clear he felt the same way.

We were in this together.

In the end, it was Garry's dad who made the last day easier than it might have been.

He rang to ask if Garry minded giving him a hand with a boat he had to move from a harbour nearby. I think Garry was a little worried I'd get upset since we'd planned a trip into downtown San Francisco, but I was pleased. Gerry was fun, and messing around with fast boats rather than thinking about leaving was exactly the distraction we needed.

So we spent the rest of the morning tinkering with boats

(they tinkered, I sunbathed), then roared around the Bay for a couple of hours.

After saying goodbye to Gerry, we had an entertaining afternoon in San Francisco. We watched a large transsexual shoplifter get chased down the road by police on pushbikes; we played tourist and rode the cable car from Union Square, via China Town and trendy North Beach, out to Fisherman's Wharf. The sunset stained the ocean orange and purple, and as we queued to catch the cable car back we held hands, listening to a soulful busker sing 'Georgia'. Then we drove to Lulu's, a trendy but low-key restaurant, where we ate oysters and made up stories about the old moguls who hungrily watched the starving starlets at their tables.

We got back to the boat late, and got to sleep even later. Knowing it was our last evening together, we didn't want it to end.

Early the next morning, tired from the lack of sleep and a little hungover from the excess of Oregon pinot, we found a diner in the airport and ordered a huge breakfast. Slumping next to each other in the laminated booth, we stared at the taxi-ing planes as we sipped scalding black coffee from chunky china mugs.

Airports are famously rubbish places for saying goodbye: busy and anonymous, there's no room for what's been, only what's coming next. It's one big Hello and Goodbye factory: pairing and parting busy people the length of its production line.

That I was off somewhere new was what I always loved about airports. But not this time. This time I didn't want new: I wanted what I had; I wanted to be with Garry.

Feeling upset and tired, though, neither of us wanted to dwell on what was to come, so we ate instead. I can't speak for Garry, but I wasn't even hungry. That didn't stop us. We ate our way through an insane amount of pancakes and eggs and coffee and toast and French toast and home fries and more coffee. When the time came to say goodbye, I felt unbelievably full and unbelievably sick.

At the departure gate, our arms wrapped around each other with my face buried in Garry's shoulder, I could smell the sour odour of fried food in my hair. We stood for about ten minutes: partially because we were too stuffed to move but mostly because we knew the moment we pulled apart, it would all be over. But we'd had our time together, until the next time we had to accept this was goodbye.

We stroked each other's faces, trying to absorb and memorise every freckle, every lash. 'Thank you for everything, Garry,' I told him. I know that sounds like something from a bland greeting card, but in truth I was grateful for everything. That I'd met him; that he had been so willing to let me into his world, share his house, his truck, introduce me to his friends and family. The fact that he'd let me see so many different parts of his life meant I was leaving not only feeling like I knew a lot about him, but also reassured and optimistic he wanted me in his life. It wasn't just that, after Keep Your Distance Kelly, being with someone who wanted to be with me was very welcome. I also believed Garry and I were similar people: alike in what we wanted and needed, for ourselves and each other. To have found someone like that, who was cute as hell to boot, was truly something to be thankful for.

Even if he lived in America.

When Garry looked up at the monitor and said with a sad

smile: 'Jen, they're calling your plane,' I started to cry. I knew it wasn't fair – we were both trying to be brave and get through this in one piece – but I couldn't help it.

I wanted to tell him that I loved him, but I stopped myself. Nothing had been said since the half-declaration on the boat and a part of me felt it was still too soon. We'd only known each other for three weeks. 'I'll see you soon,' Garry said, looking distressed as he wiped away the tears that now streamed down my cheeks, '. . . London or Tokyo, I'll see you soon.'

'Garry . . .' I said, looking up at him through the fresh tears that clung to the ends of my lashes, '. . . I love you.'

And the tears shook themselves free from my lashes as new ones rose up to take their place. The tears glistened in Garry's eyes too as he pulled me to him, cradling me in his arms. 'I love you too, baby,' he whispered.

CHAPTER TWELVE

37,000 ft (on the way to London)

Exhausted from the lack of sleep and the excess of emotions, I fell asleep as soon as the plane took off.

I slept lightly and my mind flitted around the events of the last few weeks, plucking individual moments from memory like rosy apples from a tree. Garry drinking my chilli vodka shot in the Costco bar at Burning Man; last night on the boat, curled up quietly on deck, his hand stroking my hair, Frank Sinatra on the radio singing 'I Lost My Heart in San Francisco'.

I hated that these were now just memories, that I had to look back to what had happened rather than forward to what was ahead of me. Before too long they would become like gum that had been chewed and chewed until all flavour was gone. They'd become stories and set pieces rather than the rich jumble of sensations, emotions and experiences I could still so vividly recall.

I dreamt about Garry visiting me in London; cutting through the back alleys of Soho; walking along the South Bank from the National Theatre to the Tate Modern and Borough Market . . .

But as I dreamt, pleasure turned to fear and I woke up: what if it didn't work in London? What if our relationship only worked on his home ground, when I was happy and uncomplicated, not distracted by the demands of my London life? Was I going to slide back into old habits and end up a dull workaholic again?

I gave up trying to sleep and slouched tiredly in my seat. I knew it was pathetic but I missed Garry already. Instead of us being together with our *what nexts?*, I was now alone with my *what ifs?*

Arriving back home took the edge off my worries as, once again, the welcome flood of friends, family and a variety of wardrobe options washed over me. And funnily enough, even though he was in America, Garry became part of my London life too. In the morning when I logged on, there'd be an email from him, and most nights (eight hours ahead, so his afternoons) we'd sit on the computer and Instant Message each other or sit on the phone for hours. I loved hearing how his day had gone, what JR had said, where he'd gone for a drink with Doug and his girlfriend Bette. And, in turn, I loved to tell him where The Sonar Sisters (Lizzy and Grainne got so excited hearing about Garry that their voices would get higher and higher until eventually their conversation was only audible to bats, dogs and whales) and I had been the night before; what had happened during my bike ride to Starbucks that morning. I missed him, but technology made it possible to still feel close to each other.

And, as ever, we both had work to do: Garry was preparing for the start of the basketball season and his trip to Japan; I was nailing the final leg of my journey through Australasia, as well as trying to find some dates in Japan. Fortunately, my friend Kylie worked for the tourist board, plus by lucky chance I was on a radio programme with a journalist based in Japan. I emailed him after the interview and he got straight back saying he'd be delighted to date me, though warned:

I've only been here a month, so don't expect me to know anything! Will, emailing from Tokyo

For the first time since I'd made the decision to undertake this adventure, I felt calm and content. Possibly because I'd met my Soul Mate and was now on the home stretch of my journey but also because it seemed that my theory of working your way to your Soul Mate was valid after all. I felt a real sense of satisfaction and achievement and – I have to admit it – All-purpose Flirty.

This isn't a type of bathroom cleaner, it's one of the side effects of falling in love. I felt so happy and good about everything, I think I must have been exuding a sort of cheerful, uncomplicated energy. I don't know which way round it happened, but total strangers were smiling and saying 'hello', holding doors open and generally being lovely. And I was doing it all right back.

It was like the Love Professor said: you get back what you put out there.

Of course, it was all because I'd met Garry. I was aware of the irony: that falling for him seemed to have made me more noticeable and, possibly, more attractive to other men. This came in handy as I still had another 20 dates to go, but at the same time I didn't want to do anything that was going to threaten my relationship with Garry.

I'll be honest, I really didn't understand how he was managing to cope: it must have been a nightmare for him. If the tables were turned and he told me he was dating 20 women, I can tell you now, I would have completely lost it. Maybe it was because he'd known all along that this was what I was doing or maybe he was just choosing not to think about it? Whatever the reason, I wanted to help by making it as painless for him as possible. I tried to get the balance right between telling him what I was doing (whether going swimming with Cath or securing a date in Melbourne) but being sensitive to his feelings and not telling him in a way that would hurt or distress him. It was important I didn't keep things from him: honesty was one of the few straight lines we had in this hall of mirrors situation. But I didn't want to make him jealous either, a strong but ultimately useless bond that would foster nothing good. I wanted him to choose to be close because he liked me, not because I was driving him mad and he was scared of losing me.

So I got on with my job.

I dated Robert (or Irritating Robert as I was soon to think of him), one of the website dating people who'd been the most persistent. Every couple of weeks or so for the last three months it had been:

Hello Jen, Rob here again!!!! So where are you now?!! Still travelling or are you back in old Blighty? Any chance you might have time for a little drinky?!! Rob xx

The abundance of punctuation was unnerving, but it was the excessive use of animated *smilies* that had me on red alert – reading an email peppered with flashing grins, waves, winks and blinks was like sitting in front of a short-circuiting traffic light.

Whether I saw myself as the Patron Saint of Single Souls, dispensing *mercy dates* amongst the *relationship needy*, finally giving in to Robert turned out to be a bad idea. **Robert (Date #61)** asked me to dinner at the Dorchester. Not my kind of place but I went, only to find he'd invited me to his office Summer Ball and told everyone I was his girlfriend.

Robert worked at the head office of a national couriering company and the party was like going to the wedding of someone you've never met (including, in my case, your date): a room full of people talking animatedly about things you didn't understand and couldn't contribute to.

It was a long night, made longer by the sit-down meal where I accidentally bonded with *the loud, drunk wife* who then tried to give me a head massage during the awards ceremony. There was also a Brotherhood of Man tribute band (though, who knows, maybe it was the real thing). Robert led me onto the dance floor and proceeded to throw some moves reminiscent of the scene in *Diamonds are Forever* where the man has a scorpion dropped down the back of his shirt. Not that I did much better. Accepting that resistance was useless, I gave it some Travolta. Assuming the position, hand on one hip, I energetically flung the other hand out, rapping the old man dancing next to me very hard on the back of the head with my knuckles.

My final sight of Robert, as I mouthed I was *going to the loo* and fled the building, was him doing the funky chicken with *the loud, drunk wife.* I vowed no matter how much the Numbers God needed appeasing in the future, I was never doing a mercy date ever again.

And then Garry rang to say he'd booked his flight to London.

I had a million emotions, all of them good. In the time I'd been back, I'd realised how much I loved London. I wanted Garry to see the city, but also to see me in my home town. He was the reason I felt good about being here – when you're happy and in love, London is a wonderful place. In fact my new found All-purpose Flirty wasn't just for the people I beamed at walking down the street, I was flirting with the city too. And from the red of the double-decker buses, the white of the Brick Lane bagels and the boys in blue on the beat, the city was flirting right back. Eros had shot his arrow from Piccadilly Circus, the London Eye was giving me a big, cheeky wink.

God, I needed to stop being so cheerful: any minute now I was going to break into song and the entire street would join in, dancing like a scene out of Mary Poppins, singing: '*It's a jolly holiday with Garry.*'

And it would be good to have a break from having a long-distance relationship: emailing, Instant Messaging and chatting on the phone was an important part of both of our days, but it was also frustrating at times. Not just that we weren't face to face, but because of the logistics of being an ocean apart. The time difference meant there was always one of us sitting up until 2 a.m. or getting up at 6 a.m.

I loved our marathon conversation today. I feel
bad, though, that it is on the wrong side of the
clock for you. Next marathon, we can do it on the
wrong side of the clock for me. (gotta keep
things fair!)

We rarely talked for less than two hours (after the terrible shock
of the first phone bill we'd renegotiated phone plans to get the
cheapest international rates), so we were both constantly
exhausted from broken sleep patterns and harassed that we were
always late for work or meeting friends in the evening.

One good thing, though: the stress and excitement of the
situation meant that the weight was finally falling off me. I
might have become clinically insane by the time Garry got
here, but at least I'd look good in a pair of shorts.

11 p.m. at Heathrow airport and I was sitting in a grim, smoky
café waiting to meet Garry.

Not that I was particularly aware of my surroundings: I had
so much adrenaline racing around my body, I was concerned I
might actually start astral-planing. I was drinking herbal tea to
try and calm my nerves, but that and the nerves were making
me want to pee constantly. Every time I popped to the loo, I'd
worry I was going to miss him coming out, and then I'd catch
sight of myself in the mirror, see how anxious I looked and get
nervous all over again.

But the moment he walked through the gate, all nerves
vanished instantaneously. I suddenly didn't feel awkward or
nervous about seeing him at all, just really, really glad he was
here.

Looking amazing (he'd had a long flight and looked great; I'd had a short drive and looked crap – where was the justice in that?), he cut through the barrier, finding the shortest possible route to my side. Walking up with a huge smile on his face, he said, 'Hey, Baby,' dumped his bags on the ground, reached out and pulled me into a close embrace.

I buried my face in his neck and silently hugged him right back. I was just so happy to see him, I couldn't say a word, I couldn't even kiss him. I just stood wrapped in his embrace, pulling my fingers through his hair, trying to absorb the fact that after the last few weeks of emailing and phoning and waiting, he was actually here in London.

We must have looked like the poster ad for *Lovers Reunited at the Airport*, but I didn't care. I felt only relief. Like arriving back from a school trip late at night and sleepily spotting your parents waiting to collect you, a sense of *all is right in the world* washed over me.

It was now my turn to play tour guide and I really enjoyed it. We explored the huge Buddhist temple by Wimbledon common; watched the herds of deer roaming wild in Richmond Park; wandered wide-eyed around the cornucopia of Harrods' food hall and annoyed everyone as we sang '*I don't want to go to Chelsea*', jumping on and off buses in Chelsea and along the King's Road.

I explained the mystery of roundabouts, Marmite, Teletext, the *Telegraph* crossword, clotted cream and night buses. Unable to find a pub serving food after 2 p.m., I tried (and failed) to make a case for English licensing laws. I also tried to explain why Garry couldn't find anywhere serving decent cocktails. That British people drink beer to be sociable, wine to be sophisticated and cocktails to be insensible. Cocktail names did seem to indicate the drinker's intent: Americans were moderate, elegant drinkers, and they had the *Manhattan* and the *Cosmopolitan*. As night follows day, so the Brits had the *Slippery Nipple* and *Sex on the Beach*.

Garry loved my flat and by being there made me realise how much I'd missed living with someone, cooking together and listening to music in the kitchen or content to do our own thing in separate rooms.

There was an ongoing fuss about coffee. Garry had brought his favourite coffee, *Peet's*, with him but my coffee maker broke on the second day. As Garry tinkered with it, I confessed that I'd bought it at a jumble sale 13 years ago for 50p.

'There was a reason it was being sold cheap,' he said dismissively.

'Oh, you mean there was a chance it would stop working a decade later?' I replied smugly.

In the spirit of Access All Areas, Garry was meeting my parents. I was nervous because I knew Garry would be nervous; I thought maybe my parents would be a little nervous too. As the pregnant woman eats for two, the woman introducing her boyfriend to her parents eats anxiously for four. I bought my body-weight in ciabatta from the Italian bakery round the corner and we set off.

But as invariably happens in these situations, from the moment my parents opened the front door and slightly awkward introductions were made, everyone immediately hit it off. Garry was charming and funny, and my parents clearly liked him straight away. My dad had spent quite a bit of time working in the States and since my mother has long followed international politics, they were both full of questions about Garry's life, American domestic policy, the NBA and 'Do you know that bar in Vegas . . . ?'

Relieved of the role of community liaison officer, I was free to advance steadily up Mount Ciabatta, washing it down with cup after cup of strong, black coffee. After half an hour, bloated with excess wheat but caffeinated to the hilt, I could barely sit still. I bounced up and down, contributing nothing but constantly interrupting the conversation: *'Does anyone want more coffee . . . that's in today's paper, isn't it, let me see if I can find it . . . was that someone at the door . . . did you see that bird in the tree . . . oh, that's in my bag, Garry, I'll get it . . .'*

In the end I went upstairs to my old room and lay on the bed reading the 1972 *Jackie* Christmas annual until I was calm enough to return to the group and enjoy the rest of the morning.

Hugging and kissing my parents goodbye, we drove on to Cambridge. It was a perfect autumn afternoon; both of us were impressed and slightly awed as the city unveiled itself from the shroud of chilled mist that swathed the buildings and streets.

We peeped into the beautiful fifteenth-century inner courts of Trinity College and Queens' College. We walked hand in hand along the paths of damp autumn leaves that lined the banks of the river Cam, watching the boaters elegantly punt their way along the chill, still water.

We drove home via my sister Toz's and spent a boisterous evening with her and the kids. Zack, Tabs and Michael were adorable as ever and raced around showing off their toys, clambering over Garry trying to tickle him. We set off for home at 10 p.m., leaving poor Toz to put three overexcited children to bed.

Collapsing on the sofa with a glass of wine at the end of our long day, Garry looked very thoughtful. 'You know, it meant a lot seeing you with your family today,' he told me seriously.

'Why's that?' I quipped. 'Are you starting to realise anything involving parents turns me into a nervous wreck?'

He laughed. 'No,' he said gently. 'It's that seeing you with your family makes me realise how much they love you.'

I smiled shyly: 'Yeah, they think I'm okay,' I said, trying to make light of it.

But Garry refused to be distracted. 'It's made me realise,' he continued, 'that when you come and stay with me in America, how important it is that I make you feel just as loved and special.' He put down his glass and sat close so he could kiss me: 'I really love you, Jen.'

When I come to stay with him in America . . . ? I looked at the china cats next to the chimney as if checking to see if they'd heard it too. If they had, they didn't let on, just stared back sphinx-like, keeping a dignified silence, their feelings firmly under control.

You can learn a lot from cats. I wasn't going to cry this time: I could easily have done so but I'd decided it was time to find a better way of showing my happiness. So I kissed him back instead and we went to bed.

Apart from the time passing too quickly, Garry's visit was completely perfect. Things took a bit of a downturn, though, the day before he left.

I had to chair a one-day conference in the city. It wasn't how either of us wanted to spend our last full day together, but there was no way around it. So we'd agreed: Garry was going to wander around sightseeing, then he'd come and join me and the speakers for drinks at the end of the day. Paula, Posh PR Emma and Jo would be there too and were all very excited about meeting him.

It was a miserably cold, wet day but the conference was well attended, and after the wonderful but busy and intense week together it felt almost relaxing now to have a straightforward day of work.

Mid-morning, I was up on stage going over some points for the delegates before the coffee break, when someone walked in at the back of the hall.

It was Kelly.

It was nearly a year since we'd seen each other, and that had only been brief, dropping off some of the things he'd left at my flat at his office. The shock of seeing him now felt just that, like a harsh jolt of electricity slamming into my body. He looked over in my direction but was too far away for me to know if he could see me staring incredulously back. He took off his jacket and leant against the wall.

I'd forgotten what a presence he had; I hate to use the word *smouldering* but unfortunately I have no choice.

All credit to me, I have to say, I kept talking as if the man who'd broken my heart hadn't just walked into the room. Instead, I reminded the delegates that the coffee break lasted only 15 minutes and please remember that phones had to be switched off as soon as they came back into the auditorium.

Experts at precisely how many calls they could make and

how many chocolate biscuits they could get through in the 15 minutes allotted to them, 300 people looked at their watches then stampeded out of the hall in unison. Only two remained.

I stepped down from the stage and walked over to the end of the aisle from where Kelly was now casually watching me.

'Hi,' he said in a friendly, relaxed way as I walked up. 'Seminar going okay?'

'*It was until you turned up*,' I felt like retorting, but I didn't. I just nodded and said: 'Hello, Kelly, how are you?'

He was fine apparently: work was going well; he'd just got back from a job in Algeria and was off to China at the end of the month. I watched him as he talked. I watched the way his mouth moved, the way he tugged at his dark curls to process a thought, the way his head tilted slightly as he listened. It was all very familiar. And that it was so familiar triggered an almost forgotten sensation inside me. Over our five years together, we'd gradually grown into a certain *shape*. I could feel my part of our shape forming now: the *girlfriend shape*. But even as it developed, and even as we talked, and even as I looked at the handsome face and strong body of the man I had loved so much, a far more powerful feeling grew alongside it: one of impatience. Growing together and learning each other's ways and worlds had been for nothing – Kelly had never wanted a serious girlfriend. And I had never wanted to seriously admit that.

I now knew that to be the truth. I recognised the role I'd played in my own deception. But I'd known that for a while, I'd done the work and was a long way past that insight. I wasn't angry any more, I just wasn't interested.

Another bond between us flexed, stretched, then shattered into a million pieces.

I stood up: 'So, it's lovely to see you again, Kelly,' I said, really meaning it. 'I'd better get on with all this but thanks for dropping by. I'll see you around.'

In my head, I stood in the centre of a Coliseum, Kelly's broken body crumpled on the ground before me. My bloodied arms held aloft, I acknowledged the cheers of the crowds and saluted as they threw flowers and bags of Kettle Chips at my feet in exaltation. My female friends poured into the arena, stamping their feet and clapping their hands, chanting: '*Jen-ny, Jen-ny . . .*'

But the body got back up.

'I'll see you tonight,' Kelly said. 'Jo's asked me to the drinks.'

Crowds stopped cheering and an eerie silence filled the arena. Bags of Kettle Chips rolled like tumbleweed across the dusty ground.

'Ummm, Kelly, well, that's nice,' I replied weakly, my thoughts freefalling in shock. '. . . But you don't have to come to the drinks . . .'

'I know I don't,' he shrugged. 'But I'll be in town anyway, so why not?'

This was very, very, very awkward. 'Kelly . . .' I said tentatively, groping for the right way to phrase this. 'You know I'm seeing someone?'

He nodded and shrugged again, as if to say: what of it?

'Well, he's over from America at the moment and is coming along to the drinks tonight.'

'Yeah, I heard something about that,' Kelly replied nonchalantly. 'Well,' he said, picking up his jacket and fixing me with a lazy grin, 'I don't mind if he doesn't.' And, kissing my cheek and gently squeezing my shoulder, Kelly turned and walked out the hall.

I watched him go in amazement. *If he doesn't mind . . .* what about if *I* sodding mind? Had Kelly done this on purpose? Did he know Garry was in town and was checking him out? Was this some kind of macho guy thing? And how would Garry feel about meeting a load of my friends *and* Kelly?

All around me, delegates were flooding back into the hall, chancing one last hurried phone call through a mouthful of biscuit crumbs. They took one look at my expression and turned off their phones guiltily, mouthing their apologies.

Was this going to be okay? Was Garry going to be okay? Was *I* going to be okay? One thing I was sure about, Jo was *not* going to be okay. In my head, I was back in the Coliseum, Jo peering anxiously out from behind the rump of a nervous-looking lion. The crowd held their breath as I grimly crunched over flowers and Kettle Chips towards her, hands on hips.

The rest of the day passed quickly. And juggling a busy seminar packed with high-maintenance speakers, I actually managed to forget about pretty much everything but the task in hand. For once I didn't mind work monopolising my attention.

After the final speaker had delivered her presentation, I gave a summary of, then conclusion about, the day's key points, thanked everyone for coming, and with that we were finished. As I stood in front of the stage with the organiser, fielding individual questions from the delegates, I saw Garry walk in at the back of the hall. Although I was happy to see him, I also felt quite anxious: I really had no idea how he was going to react to the news that Kelly was here. Garry came down to join us – windswept but very upbeat after a day spent exploring –

and I introduced him to some of the speakers. Twenty minutes later we all managed to escape to the pub.

The whole time we were walking through the driving rain to the bar, I tried to get Garry on his own so I could tell him about Kelly. Whatever his reaction was going to be, for both our sakes I wanted to give him the chance to have it now, rather than in a room with my friends, colleagues and ex. But it was impossible for us to break away from the group, and as we walked into the smoky bar I could see Kelly over on the far side of the room talking to Posh PR Emma.

Paula (who had set up the date with Seattle Jason) was right by the door, and as soon as she saw me she broke off from her conversation to come over and give me a big hug. She hadn't met Garry yet and on being introduced to him gave him a warm hug too. She clearly wanted to make him feel welcome, but the whole time she was hugging Garry she was also looking at me and frantically wiggling her eyebrows and gesturing with her head in the direction of Kelly.

'*I know, I know,*' I mouthed helplessly. '*Bloody Jo invited him.*'

Paula rolled her eyes and we both looked over at the bar to where Jo was standing, rifling through her handbag for her purse whilst shouting exasperatedly into her mobile: '. . . but Ryan, you promised you'd be here . . .'

The bar was crowded, but as Paula (one of life's wonderful people) engaged Garry in an animated conversation, I fought my way across the bar to Posh PR Emma (Kelly had moved on and was now lost in the crowd). I pushed past a ton of people I vaguely knew, but all of whom seemed to know me. As I '*Excuse me please . . . can I just squeeze through here . . . ?*'-ed my way around them, I was relentlessly quizzed: 'Jennifer did you know Kelly's here . . .?', 'Is it true you met your Soul Mate on your 80 Dates trip . . . ?', 'Has your Soul Mate really come over from America to see you . . . ?', 'Ohmigod, are Garry and Kelly both here **now**?'

The chatter seemed to grow from a mutter to a rumble, until it swelled into what felt like a football chant reverberating around the terraces. Any moment I expected to see people waving scarves and blowing on their hands to keep them warm, singing to the tune of 'Blue is the Colour': *'Garry's her boyfriend, Kelly is her ex, they're here together, and Jennifer is stressed . . .'*

I fought my way through the inquisition and finally made it to where Emma was standing: 'Ohmigod, Jennifer, did you know . . . ?' I held up my hand to stop Emma saying any more. She squeezed my arm sympathetically and signalled the barman to serve us. 'I just couldn't believe it when I saw him,' she said, shards of incredulity splintering from her cut-glass accent.

'Ummm, me neither,' I said grimly. We both turned in synchronised disapproval to glare at Jo, who was now deep in conversation with Kelly about ten feet away. Kelly's body-language said 'get me away from this mad woman' but I had no intention of rescuing him.

Emma frowned and gave a little huff of irritation: 'You know, darling, this nonsense of hers over Ryan really has been going on far too long. That Jo is making a mess of her life doesn't give her the right to make a mess of yours too.'

I smiled at Emma fondly and gave her a hug: 'I got Garry . . .' I whispered in her ear, and we both looked over to Garry, chatting easily with the organiser and a couple of the delegates. '. . . my life has never been less messy.' She smiled, happy for me.

Jo and Kelly had spotted us and started making their way

over. But in the crush, Jo ran into another friend and fell into conversation. Emma's phone started ringing (PRs are never off phone duty) and she took it outside to talk. Kelly arrived on his own and stood next to me at the bar.

'Can I buy you a drink?' he asked. I shook my head politely and pointed to the wine Emma had just bought me. 'You're looking well,' he said.

I smiled graciously. 'You too.' It was true: he never looked anything less than amazing. I was tempted to ask about his girlfriend but decided against it.

'It didn't work out with that woman I was seeing,' he said, as if reading my mind. I nodded neutrally. I wasn't going there: I didn't want to have any opinion about his love life, or any other part of his life. He was in my past and that's where I wanted him to stay.

But before I consigned him to Another Country, there was one last thing I needed to do: introduce him to Garry. I felt awkward about it but for some reason compelled to, not for Kelly's sake, but for Garry's. I didn't know what the etiquette was, but if he found out (or indeed already knew) Kelly was here and I hadn't introduced him, he might read something into it. I left Kelly talking to other people and fought my way back to Garry. 'Kelly's here,' I told him quietly, linking my arm through his. 'Do you want to meet him?'

Garry looked a little surprised and an expression I couldn't read flickered across his face. He shrugged (it really was my day for shrugging men). 'Sure,' he said. 'Why not?'

I could think of any number of reasons *why not*, my friends and peers having front row seats at the premiere of *When Garry met Kelly* being one of them. I raised my eyebrows: 'Are you sure?' and he nodded.

I had such a bad feeling about this.

On my way back to find Kelly, I bumped into Jo. I gave her a look but didn't say a word.

She burst into tears: 'I know, I know,' she blubbed. 'Ems has already told me what a despicable person I am. I didn't mean it,' she cried miserably. 'I bumped into him and he told me he'd split up with whatshername and I wasn't thinking and I just . . .' She faltered, looking at me wretchedly, then, 'Sorry, Jennifer,' she whispered plaintively, looking down at the floor.

What could I do? I gave her a hug: 'You are such a twit,' I told her exasperatedly as she continued mumbling apologies. 'Go and introduce yourself to Garry, your punishment is to be there when I introduce him to Kelly!' She looked horrified and I gently shoved her in Garry's direction.

Back at the bar, Kelly was talking to Paula. I asked him if he wanted to meet Garry and we pushed back through the crowd to Jo, now animatedly talking with Garry. It was the moment of truth and I could tell people were watching.

But when we got there, something completely unexpected happened: Garry ignored us. Jo chatted and laughed and fluttered her eyelashes. Garry smiled, asked her questions and generally paid her a ton of attention that kept Jo – delighted to sparkle for a change rather than be miserable about Ryan – spinning like a top.

Kelly and I stood waiting for them to stop talking and acknowledge us, but Garry kept talking and Jo kept spinning. After waiting like idiots for a couple of very long minutes, Kelly turned to me with one eyebrow raised. 'It seems your man is busy,' he said, the sarcasm clear in his voice. 'I'll be at the bar if you fancy a drink.' And with that he walked off.

I was mortified and furious, furious, furious.

I instinctively looked over at Emma and Paula who were looking back with expressions of disbelief. This wasn't right. What the hell was Jo doing inviting Kelly here, and then chatting Garry up in front of us both? And why was Garry chatting up Jo? And doing it in front of the man who'd broken my heart being unfaithful?

And all this on Garry's and my last night.

Suddenly it was all too much. I grabbed my coat and marched over to where Emma and Paula were standing: 'Sorry, but I have to go.' On the way out, I stopped by Garry and said: 'I'm going home, I'll see you later.' And without stopping to see his reaction, I stormed out.

Outside, the weather was cold, wet and miserable. It fitted my mood perfectly as I whirled down Upper Regent Street towards the tube. I hadn't got far before I heard someone running up behind me and then grab my shoulder. It was Garry.

'What the hell are you doing?' he shouted in exasperation.

'What the hell am *I* doing?' I shouted back. '*I'm* going home so you can stay and ignore my ex and flirt with my friend,' I exploded.

'What are you talking about?' Garry retorted, his coat flapping in the wind that blew wildly all around us. 'I wasn't flirting with your friend, I was trying not to get in a fight.'

Not get in a fight? Whatever was he going on about? 'Garry, I'm tired and I can't be bothered to talk about this: you have a key, stay or go, the choice is yours, but I'm going home.'

And now, although at the entrance to the tube, I marched straight past it: I needed to walk off my anger.

Garry next to me, we walked together in silence. It was the

Misery Walking Tour of London. We tramped furiously down Oxford Street; angrily around Piccadilly Circus; heatedly down Haymarket; bitterly past the National Gallery and speechlessly around Trafalgar Square; irately along Whitehall; unhappily past Downing Street and miserably over Westminster Bridge to Waterloo.

About halfway over the bridge, I'd walked off enough of my rage to be able to listen when Garry tried to talk to me. We descended the steps onto the promenade along the South Bank and sheltered under a tree as the rain grimly lashed the marble lions stoically waiting it out.

I knew I was punishing Garry for something that ultimately Kelly had done, but at the same time, I didn't understand why Garry had ignored us and got so wrapped up in Jo.

'Jen, I'm sorry if I hurt your feelings or embarrassed you in front of your friends,' Garry said. 'But seriously . . . Kelly? What did you think I was going to do?'

I looked at him in surprise. 'What do you mean?' I asked in spite of myself. Garry suddenly looked as angry as I'd felt moments earlier: 'All I know about this jerk-off is that he cheated on you and treated you really badly. I love you and I think you're the most beautiful, kind, loving and giving person I've ever met. He totally fucked you over and you think what . . . ? That I'm going to stand around and make small talk with him? How did you think that was going to go?'

Now it was my turn to look amazed. I hadn't even considered that.

But Garry, who had just been forced to march across London in the pouring rain, was not happy and had not finished. 'And as for your friend Jo . . .' he continued heatedly, '. . . she said some guy called Ryan had just walked in and could

I look like I was having a good time talking with her to make him jealous.' He shook his head as he talked: 'I thought it was weird, but she's your friend and you'd been over at the bar for ages talking to that jerk . . .' Garry looked at me exasperatedly. 'It's our last goddamn night: I had dinner reservations and was trying to get you out of there, but I didn't want to take you away from your friends . . .' He spread his hands in a gesture of frustration and looked out across the river, clearly trying to control his temper.

I listened quietly as Garry talked. When he finished, I scrunched my face up in a half smile, half frown. 'Really?' I asked. Garry didn't answer, he just looked off into the rain with an impenetrable expression.

Oooops.

Ryan *had* walked in. I'd seen him but hadn't paid any attention to him. And it was exactly the kind of stunt Jo would pull – their relationship thrived on drama and make-up sex.

I sighed. I didn't want to be a doormat again but what Garry said made sense. I'd dropped him into the middle of a really difficult situation; finding a clear path through tonight's social minefield would have been virtually impossible. But he'd tried anyway.

It seemed I wasn't the only one blasting off on an inter-galactic leap of faith.

I shuffled closer to Garry on the wet bench and tried to work my hands into his, which were clamped down hard on his wet legs. 'I'm so sorry, Garry,' I told him penitently. 'I can only imagine what tonight must have been like for you. I really, really appreciate you sticking it out.'

Garry continued to stare out at the water for a few more

moments, then, breathing out slowly, let me slide my hands under his. We looked at each other and both smiled wryly.

And so the moment passed. It was too late and we were both too cold and wet to stay out any longer so we went home and curled up in front of the fire with a pizza, happy to watch TV rather than talk any more. But in amongst the pizza and sitcoms, there was a strange feeling of closeness, having resolved and survived such a bizarre, emotional evening together.

By the next morning, our first row was not so much forgotten as one more thing we'd shared and experienced. Garry had an early afternoon flight back to America. Although seeing each other soon in Tokyo made it slightly easier to say goodbye, I was still in such a daze afterwards I had to text him from the car park to ask if he remembered where I'd parked the car.

So Garry went back to America and I finalised the Australasian trip. We quickly fell back into our emailing, Instant Messaging and two-hour-phone-call pattern. But this time as well as being able to ask about Garry's friends I'd met in Seattle, Garry asked how my family was; what Paula was doing . . . if Jo and Ryan were still up to their old tricks?

And three days after Garry left, a huge box arrived from Amazon. Mystified, I opened it and laughed out loud as I pulled out a brand-new coffee grinder, coffee maker and a note from Garry:

'*Coffee in the house!*'

I was thrilled and very touched, so putting some beans on to grind, I went into my little office to email him a thank you. But in my befuddlement, I hadn't put the lid on properly and as I typed the coffee beans rattled against the blades and fresh grounds whizzed out the top of the machine, spraying every surface in the kitchen.

Coffee in the house indeed.

CHAPTER THIRTEEN

Tokyo, Japan

And now, final dates lined up, accompanying logistics locked in, I was ready in all senses to embark on the concluding leg of my journey. One Soul Mate and 19 dates in nine cities and six countries, spread across Japan, Indochina and Australasia.

It was the final stage of a long journey and, mission partially accomplished, I was setting off on my Date Odyssey facing a completely new set of challenges and experiences.

I'd needed to go to the Date Wranglers one last time to ask for their help rounding up the remaining dates. I was slightly nervous about approaching them since I suspected they might be ambiguous about helping me. Not with my decision to complete the journey. All big travellers themselves, the Date Wranglers would feel the same way I did: that to end it now would be like Jason and his Argonauts heroically battling through to Colchis, then, on finding the Golden Fleece, checking it as hand luggage and flying home with British Airways from Tbsili.

No, what I expected to be the sticking point was me still needing their single friends to make up the rest of my dates. I braced myself for a reaction of: '*Well, great, Jennifer, you've met* The One *and I'm happy for you, but what about my friend? He's still out there looking. Why would he get his hopes up and go to the trouble of dating a woman who's not even available?*'

In fact, worse than unavailable: newly and – almost certainly annoyingly – in love.

But, as it turned out, I couldn't have been more wrong. The Date Wranglers were actually even more into my journey than before.

This was partially due to the fact that they'd been emailing regular progress reports to the Date *Wranglees*, including the fact that I had now met The One. And as a result, rather than being put off meeting me, Wranglees now *really* wanted to meet me. It seemed they saw a date with me as the chance to learn the mysterious secrets of Soul Matery, presumably so they could use this hard-won knowledge to track down Soul Mates of their own.

I also got the impression they believed once I turned up for their date, I'd take one look at them and realise I'd got it terribly wrong: Garry wasn't my Soul Mate after all, *they* were.

If you don't apologise for having met 'your man', I won't apologise for trying to change your mind when you get here . . . Daniel, emailing from Kuala Lumpur

And, in a strange way, I think the Date Wranglers encouraged this kind of thinking. I'd picked up little undercurrents of displeasure in their ranks – they seemed a bit peaked that after all their matchmaking efforts I'd found Mr Right almost by myself.

It's not that the DWs didn't want me to meet The One –
they did – but they wanted just as much to *be* the one who
found The One for me. They loved a challenge, and appeared
determined to have one last shot at winning the Date Wrangler
crown. Like supermarkets tailoring special offers to your
buying patterns, the DWs seemed to be operating on a '*If you
liked that . . . you might also be interested in these . . . ?*' policy.
There was the journalist in China; the environmentalist in
Kuala Lumpur; the Chief of Sydney Harbour Police in
Australia; even a *mystery date* in New Zealand:

```
I've been working on it for a while but he's been
out of the country. Clues: handsome (Julia says a
knockout), single, well off, very exciting
profession (but dangerous), interesting, good
company, works with a famous film producer . . .
etc, etc. Chris, emailing from Marlborough
```

But that was fine, I wasn't worried: I loved Garry and felt
confident in our developing relationship. That's not to say I
wasn't expecting the journey to throw all sorts of unexpected
surprises at me. I was, but I was sure whatever it was wouldn't
be in the hands of the Date Wranglers, it would be in the hands
of Fate.

But although Fate may shape your life, she doesn't book the
airline tickets or arrange the visas.

As ever, the task of tying all the unconnected strands of the
journey together had been an exercise in logistical gymnastics.
I was meeting Garry in Tokyo, but wanted to go via India as I
had the chance of a great date in Calcutta.

As a member of the Laughter Club of India, I
believe in the curative power of joy. We meet
each week to laugh health and happiness into our
lives . . . Bhaskar, emailing from Calcutta

After Tokyo, I was flying to Beijing where I hoped to make a
little detour on to Shanghai:

Jennifer, remember me? Tom. I emailed in March
from Hong Kong after the article in the *China
Daily*. I am now living in Shanghai and – as
expected – my Long Distance Relationship didn't
survive the journey. I'd love to show you around
if you make it over this way. All the best, Tom

And although it was still mind-bogglingly stressful trying to
pull it all together, I felt incredibly energised and enthusiastic
about both the travelling and the dates. Out from under the
God, am I ever going to meet anyone? yoke, I was free to do what
I did best: travel the world having adventures, dating and
meeting lots of interesting, entertaining people along the way.

But there were limits to what could be achieved in the time
I had left and trying to work Bhaskar and Tom into a trip that
already jumped from Tokyo to Beijing, Bangkok, Kuala
Lumpur, Perth and ever onwards, was – despite my best
efforts – impossible. Reluctantly I crossed their names off my
dance card.

But that was fine – there were so many things I was already
looking forward to and, best of all, it would be summer again.
I was flying to Tokyo, hitting the southern hemisphere, just as
the weather had gone to hell in a hand basket here in London.

• • •

The Seattle Super Sonics basketball team was in Tokyo playing a couple of pre-season games against the LA Clippers. Although not quite as big as baseball, basketball is a very popular sport in Japan and the games were long sold out.

It was all new to me: basketball and Japan. So as the shuttle bus inched for two hours through traffic, solid from the airport to the Four Seasons in Chinzan-so, my eyes scoured the people, buildings and streets outside, taking in as much information as possible. The elevated expressways were built, what felt like mere inches from the housing complexes and office blocks that sprouted up from every inch of ground. You could virtually read the computer screens in front of row after row of office workers – a unisex uniform of black hair, white shirts and black jackets hanging from the backs of every chair. The offices were full even though it was close to 9 p.m. With working hours notoriously long in Japan, I wondered how the staff unwound in the small window between one working day ending and the next beginning. I hoped for their sake it wasn't by hanging out in the café-pub we passed, neon sign advertising *Dancing and Fruit*.

Although flying in separately from London and Seattle respectively, Garry and I arrived at the hotel within moments of each other. It felt a little odd to be in a hotel, but we picked right up from where we'd left off in London.

Rather than succumb to jet lag, we joined Garry's co-workers JR, Jon, Doug, Bob and Bobby (all of whom I remembered fondly from Seattle) for a night out with JR's Japanese friend, Toshi. We piled into two cabs and fought to get the best views out the windows as we inched through Tokyo by night.

Mini-skirted teenagers chatted in private huddles as they waited to cross the road. Their bodies flickered with light from the billboard video screens and neon signs suspended from every building around, giggling mouths hidden modestly behind cupped hands and long fringes. A couple of feet away tired-looking businessmen – shoulders drooping; suits crumpled; briefcases held limply in their slack hands – stared off into space, seemingly aware of nothing but the red crosswalk light that stood between them and the remains of their evening. Behind them all, in brightly lit alleyways, streams of people disappeared into bars that seemed too small to contain the numbers pouring in.

In Tokyo, it seemed *packed* was the norm, whether in the office, traffic or bar.

We arrived at our destination, a teeny noodle place in Shibuya. The waitress led us three short paces from the door to the bar and gestured that we should sit on the stools squeezed in front of it. Heads bent low over their steaming bowls, all around us locals scooped soba noodles into their mouths, chopsticks swooping rapidly and efficiently from bowl to mouth in a movement that was both graceful and (to our Western eyes at least) a bit greedy. Jet-lagged, disorientated and bigger than all the other diners there, our knees and elbows clumsily clashed and prodded as we swivelled around on our stools and gulped down every movement and moment being served up around us.

The next morning Garry and I had a couple of hours to explore a little of Bunkyo-ku – the ward or district the hotel was in – before he headed off with the rest of the broadcast crew to the arena where the games (basketball has *games* not *matches*, apparently) would be played, two days from now.

After Garry left, I lost no time heading back out into the city on my own: my traveller's instincts were tugging – like a dog on a lead – to be free to explore. The first thing I liked to do in a strange city was to find my bearings: I didn't feel comfortable until I knew where I was in relation to everything else. Also, I wanted to know as soon as possible what was out there to see and do. Tomorrow there was the date with Will the journalist; three days from now I had a date with Kylie's friend Rob, a Brit working out here for one of the big airlines.

So today I wanted to explore Bunkyo-ku.

I peeked into rice cracker bakeries, watching old ladies deftly wrap long, pungent strips of seaweed around little bricks of puffed rice, or lay hand-lacquered wafers on yards and yards of bamboo mats to dry. I braved the deafening racket of the Pachinko Parlours, where businessmen sat for the duration of their lunch break compulsively feeding ball-bearings into slot machines: a dexterous and addictive mix of hard concentration and soft porn.

After a long day, Garry and I arrived back at the hotel again at the same time. Too jet-lagged and weary to do much, we lay in the hotel's spacious steam room and caught up on each other's day. Garry had never seen me with my Road Head on and was eager to hear my stories of the world around the hotel as he'd been working in the arena for twelve hours. Swathed in towels and steamed near insensible, we lay in the sauna and sweated companionably together.

And the next morning, like an old married couple, we had breakfast, kissed each other goodbye and went off in separate directions to work: Garry to continue setting up for the broadcasts at the arena, me to date Will the journalist.

• • •

Although I'd walked as far as the subway station at Edogawabashi, I hadn't yet travelled on the subway.

The first cut may be the deepest, but the first hurdle for solo independent travellers in a new country – whatever it may be – is always the highest. Until you have a sense of how routine things operate, a city remains frustratingly inaccessible. Today was no exception. All the ticket machines were in Japanese and although countless locals were kind enough to stop and ask *'Can I help you?'*, since it turned out that that was the full extent of their English, I remained stuck on square one.

In the end I just randomly bought a ticket. Through the barrier, I stood in front of the huge wall-mounted subway map to work out which lines would take me to Shibuya-Ku. Although the colour-coded lines meant I could easily figure out where I had to go, it was going to be a fiddly journey and I spent a few minutes looking for the shortest route. A student stopped and asked: *'Can I help you?'*

Thinking it was another well-meant but ultimately pointless offer, I gave the briefest answer, only to be surprised and delighted when she replied: 'Ah, Shibuya-Ku is on my way. Come with me and we will travel together.'

I didn't discover her name but the young Japanese woman was a fascinating guide and we chatted all the way to my destination. She worked hard: in her fifth year of studying to be a doctor, she was also working in a bar to pay her tuition fees. I asked if that was how she had learnt such good English?

'No,' she replied earnestly. 'I spent last summer studying in New York.'

'Oh,' I said curiously. 'On a medical programme?'

'No,' she answered gravely. 'I was training to be a cheer-leader.'

As my eyebrows shot up in surprise, she gave a little moue of alarm, instinctively covering her mouth as she did so. 'Here is your stop,' she said, bowing her head urgently as she gestured towards the closing door. 'I hope you have a good stay here in Tokyo.'

I thanked her and jumped off the train, joining the crowd heading for the exit onto the street.

I was in Harajuku ward and was meeting **Will (Date #62)** here, at the entrance to Yoyogi Park. It was next to the square where the Japanese teen fashionistas bussed in from the surrounding towns to show off their *look* (running the entire sub-cultural gamut from Ninja nurses to Goths and skate punks). Although curious about the phenomenon, we weren't meeting here for that reason: Will wanted to show me the Meiji Jingu shrine.

Will was very much the boy next door, tall with floppy, light brown hair, he looked a little warm in his thick blue cords and long-sleeved shirt. But he was good company, chatty and obviously pleased to see someone from home. As soon as he'd spotted me, he'd rushed over, given me an awkward hug, then bombarded me with questions about album releases, Premiership results and the progress of the repairs to the Central Line on the London Underground.

When moving overseas, there is a transition point at which the enthusiasm and excitement of being somewhere new has worn off but the routine sense of comfort and familiarity with your new home has yet to kick in. The result is homesickness, and Will was clearly at that point. I tried to answer all his questions as we walked along the peaceful, tree-lined path to the Meiji Jingu shrine.

The building was a faithful reconstruction of the prized

Shinto shrine built here with dedication and reverence in 1920 then destroyed by incendiary bombs during WWII. Simple but imposing, monks in deep green robes and tall black head-dresses sat in the shrine's inner courtyard. Although perfectly still, their eyes sternly followed the white-robed acolytes humbly sweeping the ground between them and the altar.

Although Will wasn't my type, he was a nice man and it was a charming date. Quite literally, actually – we were both fascinated and tickled to see the stalls outside the shrine selling charms and offerings. They were extremely specific and covered everything from health and happiness to passing your driving test, having a good visit to the dentist and getting a university scholarship. As a little offering to Fate, I bought one of the many charms dedicated to meeting your Soul Mate and was intrigued to see they were far more expensive than all of the others. It would seem that even in the more spiritual world, falling in love was big business.

I was already asleep when Garry got back from the arena that night, but at breakfast the next morning we had a chance to catch up. 'How did it all go yesterday?' Garry asked in a tone that seemed – to me at least – to indicate concern for my well-being rather than anxiety over my fidelity. 'Was everything okay?'

I told him all about it: how frustrating the underground had been; how I'd been saved from aimless wanderings by a cheerleading doctor; how interesting the shrine had been and how Will was like a million people I knew from home.

Without dwelling too much on the date, we talked on, about Garry's day and the progress they were making over at the arena.

'You know,' he said, grabbing a bottle of water and dropping it into his bag, 'it looks like we'll have all of tomorrow off. What have you got planned? If you like we can go exploring?' A smile blossomed on my face, then just as quickly it froze and died.

Tomorrow I had a date with Rob.

The thing was, after this week I didn't know when I'd see Garry again. If he had a day free, I wanted to spend it with him. But at the same time, I was here to date and committed to doing it thoroughly and to the best of my ability.

And of course there were Rob's feelings to consider too. Even though we hadn't had much contact, I still felt a great sense of responsibility towards him. I couldn't drop a date because I'd got a better offer from my boyfriend (not for the first time I wondered if *anyone* knew what the rules were in this situation). But if I said all of this to Garry, I knew his response would be: '*Baby, you've gotta go on the date: it's what you're here to do.*' And that would be our only day gone.

Oh, this was tricky. What to do?

Garry gave me a ticket so I could go to the basketball game that night, then he left for the arena and I for our room.

In the lobby, I jumped into one of the lifts just as the doors were closing. As I tumbled in, I belatedly realised that the lift was already full of people. And not just *any* people: it didn't take me long to recognise that I had inadvertently crashed in and was now *going up* with the Seattle Super Sonics basketball team.

Although I'd seen some of *the wives* around the spa, it was the first time I'd actually seen any of the players. And they were really quite a sight, like long ladders of muscle, propped up against the lift's interior. I wasn't sure what the protocol was, so I didn't introduce myself, just stood quietly as they discussed their training session. It was surreal being stuck in a lift with a group of seven-foot athletes. I looked up instinctively as they conversed in the air a foot above my head and it was like gazing up into the muscular branches of a forest of bench-pressing oak trees. And when they did complicated handshakes and talked in completely incomprehensible slang, I felt myself getting smaller and smaller.

'We're not in Essex any more, Toto.' I observed to myself sagely.

Up in our room, I sat distractedly on the toilet and wondered what I should do. I didn't actually need to go to the toilet, but it had a thermostatically controlled, five-setting heated seat and after all the walking around yesterday the hot seat on my aching thigh muscles was bliss.

These bathrooms were the Rolls Royces of the peeing world. If the hotel had charged for each of the facilities the toilet offered, like, say, the minibar or the pay-per-view TV, they would have made a fortune. In addition to the *hot seat*, it sported two bidet-esque water jets, both with fully adjustable water pressure and temperature settings. There was also a hot air fan (for drying), an air extractor, an air freshener and a panel with built-in sound effects including that of a toilet flushing and waves crashing on a shore (both presumably to cover the sound of what you'd shortly be needing the air freshener for).

But unfortunately all the fluffing, flushing and freshening didn't seem to be helping today, so I decided to call Rob and take it from there. He was in a meeting when I rang, so I left a message on his voicemail explaining my situation.

The phone rang virtually the second I hung up. Snatching up the receiver, I found not Rob but Garry on the end of the line. 'Hey,' he said busily, 'just wanted to check you're okay to get out to the arena tonight.'

'Ummm, yes, there's a bus going from here,' I told him a little distractedly.

'Cool,' he replied, 'and if you're up for it, we'll go out with the boys after the game tonight: I'm definitely not working tomorrow so we'll be able to stay up late tonight and sleep in tomorrow.'

Okay, now I really had to sort this out.

As I put the phone back in the cradle, the voicemail light started flashing. I punched in the code: Rob had called. Could I either ring him back in the next few minutes or email him as he was in meetings the rest of the afternoon. 'I've been thinking about the date tomorrow,' he continued in the message. 'There's an incredible fish market called Tsukiji-shijo, it handles the seafood sales to most of the restaurants in the country. It's an early start but absolutely worth it: I thought we could meet at, say 5.15 a.m. then have a sushi breakfast afterwards? Let me know if that suits.'

What was it with men, that the dates always seemed to include boats or raw fish?

But more to the point, I'd just managed to arrange a very late night out drinking, immediately followed by a very early morning eating raw fish. It would be full-on no question, but that was my fault for not coming clean with Garry.

But there was one more twist. 'Oh, and as for Garry . . .' Rob continued in a winding up the message voice, '. . . why not just bring him along too?'

I looked at the phone in amazement.

Bring Garry on our date? How would that work? Was Rob serious? Did he really think that was a good idea?

I shook my head and blinked hard as if trying to dislodge something blocking my logic circuits. No, it was still there. I sat in front of my laptop for about half an hour trying to compose my response. I had no idea if Garry would want to come along or not. He was certainly a huge fan of Japanese food: a fish market and sushi breakfast was definitely his thing (in fact far more so than mine, probably). But would he agree? I sighed heavily as I typed:

```
Rob, you are an amazing man! Thank you for being
so kind and understanding. I'll find out if Garry
can make it tomorrow. Either way, I'll be coming
so can you please let me know where I should go?
I'm really looking forward to meeting you. Take
care, Jennifer x
```

I then went to the hotel gym and ran on the treadmill like a woman possessed for the rest of the afternoon.

Just before I left for the game, I checked my emails and Rob had got back to me with the details of our rendezvous:

```
Let's make it 5.15 a.m. at Shintomi-cho station
(Yurakucho line), on the platform as you get off
the train.
```

Well, so far so good. And with that, I picked up my coat and my ticket: after a day of jumping through hoops, I was glad to now have the distraction of watching a group of men shooting them instead.

When I arrived at the game, I didn't see Garry or any of the crew as they were in the broadcast truck behind the arena. But both JR and Bobby waved to me during the break from their camera positions courtside.

I loved watching the game: it was easy to follow and the enthusiasm of the crowd was infectious. I was lucky – my seat was next to Mimi and Missy, wives of the team doctors, friendly and funny women who had been going to the games together for years. They knew all the rules and all the players and they entertainingly explained everything that happened on court.

The Sonics won, and later, back at the hotel, I joined Garry and the crew for drinks. The broadcast had gone well and everyone was boisterous and upbeat, chatting animatedly and drinking steadily.

Suddenly it was well after 3 a.m. and I was quite tipsy. Garry put his arm around me: 'Ready for bed?' he asked. I'd had a lovely evening and I couldn't wait to see the next game, plus the guys were all so much fun to be with.

But I still hadn't got around to telling Garry about the date that was, in fact, happening two hours from now.

Back in our room, standing in front of the bathroom mirror brushing our teeth, I knew I had no choice but to bite the (minty) bullet. 'Garry . . .' I started.

'Ummm?' he replied sleepily through a mouthful of tooth-paste.

'Garry . . .' I said, spitting out the toothpaste and going for it. 'I know I should have told you earlier . . .' Garry continued to brush his teeth, but raised one eyebrow quizzically. 'You see, the thing is . . .' I continued, '. . . I actually had a date lined up for later today, but when you said you'd be free, I really wanted to spend the day with you.'

Garry had stopped brushing his teeth. I looked at the clock on the wall: 3.45 a.m. I had to meet Rob in an hour and a half.

I spat it out. 'So I rang Rob – he's my Date – and he's invited me to look around a fish market and go for a sushi breakfast afterwards . . .' Words tumbled out of my mouth; Garry frowned in concentration: '. . . and he said why don't you come too?'

There was a brief delay as Garry made sense of the sentences I'd just rattled out. He smiled unexpectedly, then laughed. 'That's really funny,' he said, apparently genuinely amused at the prospect of coming on a date with me . . . and my Date. 'There's never a dull moment with you, is there?'

I smiled weakly: if Garry was okay about this I didn't want to change that by saying the wrong thing.

'Sure, I'd love to come,' he said with a broad grin. 'In fact, it sounds like fun. But let's go to bed now, huh, I'm pooped.'

Ahh, I'd forgotten one vital piece of information. I looked up at the clock again: 4 a.m. 'Right,' I said with a *the show must go on* smile. 'That's good, I'm so pleased you want to come. But here's the thing . . . we have to meet him in an hour and fifteen minutes . . .'

Garry's smile gently fell from his face like a balloon deflating after a party. 'An hour and fifteen minutes . . . ?' he repeated incredulously. I grimaced and rolled my eyes, spreading my hands feebly as if suggesting *who would have thought it?*

He looked at me carefully, as if trying to decide whether to waste any more of the very small amount of time we had left asking why I was only telling him this now, then deciding against it. 'Okay,' he said. 'Half an hour's sleep, then we'll get a cab.' I nodded meekly and we went to bed.

A little over an hour and twenty minutes later, I was running down the steps of Shintomi-cho station, ten minutes late for meeting **Rob (Date #63)**. He'd said in his email we'd have no problem spotting each other and he was right: in a sea of Japanese, we were the only Westerners. We towered over them, just like the basketball players had towered over me in the elevator yesterday.

A little shorter than me, with close-cropped brown hair and pale skin, I immediately had a good feeling about Rob. He looked relaxed and cheerful, not at all worried about the tandem date.

He looked up, smiled and started walking over, as he saw me fighting my way down the stairs that the crowds of disembarking commuters were all surging up. We met at the bottom of the steps and gave each other a big hug. 'Is Garry not with you?' Rob asked. I shook my head. Rob frowned.

'No, no, sorry,' I protested. 'He's upstairs, waiting for us outside, trying to come to terms with how little sleep he's had.'

So Rob and I went upstairs, slightly awkward introductions were made, then the three of us set off together to walk to Tsukiji-shijo market, for my date with Rob.

All was fine: we chatted generally about Tokyo and what we thought of it. Rob had just got back from Beijing and I said I was going there in two days; Garry talked about his love of Japanese cuisine and the places he'd eaten at.

We arrived at Tsukiji-shijo market and spent a couple of hours making our way through the crowds. I'd been to a lot of food markets in Asia and they were invariably the *Apocalypse Now* of the culinary world. Tsukiji-shijo was no exception. Twelve million people came here every day to buy over 4000 tons of seafood: it was an incredibly busy place with porters racing around, trolleys piled high with dripping boxes and wilting fins. The vast warehouses were dark and noisy; we waded through blood and melting ice as all around us ban saws screamed through huge tuna carcasses and octopuses lay on their sides, one dark eye sadly following us from shallow plastic trays as we walked by.

The conversation got a bit bogged down: I'd ask Rob a question, as per my dating MO, but Rob, being polite, would address his reply to Garry as well as me and then they'd end up disappearing into a big chat together. I wanted to make good on my plans to date Rob, but, slightly hungover and surviving on one hour's sleep, it was too complicated. I walked a few paces ahead and left Garry and Rob to their own devices, sensing that before I could get anywhere with Rob, the guys needed to suss each other out.

And, without my input, they did this in no time at all. Thankfully Rob then suggested coffee and food.

We found a tiny sushi bar – about 8 ft by 4 – in the outside part of the market (fresh air, thank god) and crowded in around the counter. Rob spoke excellent Japanese – he was one of those people who spoke any language you could think of – and Garry was delighted to be able to quiz the sushi chef with Rob acting as interpreter. Just as we'd finished ordering the food, Garry fell into conversation with two Canadian women and I could finally get on with the date.

We talked about living overseas and the chance it gave you to re-invent yourself. We also talked about Japanese culture, the subculture of the Burning Man festival and, of course, love and how sometimes it's easier just to work harder and forget all about it.

Three hours later, we stood on the steps of Rob's office, saying goodbye with real affection. It had been a unique and special morning. But just as Garry and I turned to go, Rob called us back. 'Come with me,' he said in an almost guilty whisper. 'There's something I think you should see.'

Taking us into the building, through the lobby and into the lift, 45 floors later we stood in front of a vast panoramic window surveying the Tokyo cityscape.

It was a clear, sunny morning and both Garry and I gasped in awe as we looked out across Tokyo: built-up and bustling as far as the eye could see. But, looking more closely, we realised that that wasn't quite true. Beyond the landmark Tokyo Tower, Fuji TV buildings and a jumble of greater and lesser structures, rising up from the horizon, marking the limit of the city's relentless urban ambition, Mount Fuji loomed majestically over the city, its roots seemingly in another world.

I looked out across the cityscape to the mountain and was struck powerfully, not for the first time, by what an incredible experience this all was. Time and again, the dates had given me a perspective that was unexpected and poignant. As I looked over to Garry shaking hands with Rob and thanking him once again, I knew today was no exception.

The next three days passed quickly, but in between the basketball games, where Mimi and Missy once again schooled me on play and players, we crammed in as much as we could.

We walked through the serene gardens of the Imperial Palace and watched a delicate geisha girl in traditional dress walk in tiny steps over a wooden bridge, hand cupped to her mouth as she talked into her mobile phone. Late at night we ate at one of the small, anarchic yakitori stalls under the arches of the Yamanote subway line. Then, going into the station, we watched in amazement as scores of businessmen dropped dead drunk onto the floor. They collapsed on top of each other and gathered in drunken piles, like an impromptu flea market, on the entrance steps.

It was wonderful to be able to share this time and I was thrilled to see Garry curious and energised by the surroundings. One of the main reasons why Kelly and I had stayed together for so long was our compatibility as travelling companions. It wouldn't have been the end of the world if Garry hadn't been enthusiastic about travelling, but that he enjoyed it so much was great: like showing him my life in London, this was another important part of who I was.

Because although it sometimes exasperated me, made me tired, meant I missed my friends and liposucked all the money out of my bank account leaving it svelte and lean, I loved travelling. My mother had travelled solo through Europe in the Fifties (unheard of then); my father had worked in China and Russia when they were closed to most of the world.

For people of my parents' generation, travel was a hard-won opportunity. My generation just assumed we would do it, we saw it almost as a right. But I cherished it anyway. It might make no sense to some but it spoke to me and I couldn't be without it.

It was the reason I'd met Garry. And – as I prepared to go to China, Garry back to the States – now it was the reason we had to say goodbye again.

'So, let's see how we get on, but maybe there'll be time after New Zealand for me to pop in and see you in Seattle?' I told him, a brave stab at nonchalance as we stood in front of my packed bags in our hotel room.

I had a round-the-world ticket and was flying east all the way. The grand finale of my International Tour of Shame was in New Zealand, so I'd fly over the US on the way back to the UK. But time was tight: I was godmother to Toz's son Michael and needed to get back for the christening.

'And you'll email me when you get to Beijing?' Garry re-iterated.

I was staying with Hector and Ang and didn't really know how easy it was going to be to phone or email from there. Also, two days ago they'd had a baby daughter, Grace (or Haixin, her Chinese name), and I was anxious not to get in the way of their parental learning curve.

Suddenly it all seemed very tentative. Every other time we'd said goodbye, we'd known when we were going to see each other again. This time we didn't and I felt unsettled and a little scared by that.

Walking down to reception together, Garry carried my bags out to the shuttle bus as I hugged and kissed all the Seattle guys goodbye. Then Garry reappeared in the doorway and we held each other close one last time.

'Thank you for inviting me out here,' I told him.

'Thank you for inviting me on a date with your Date,' he replied with a cheeky smile.

For some reason that made me tearful. 'I'm saying goodbye

now,' I told him firmly, 'or you're going to have to put up with me crying again, and, for once, I'd really like not to.'

Garry smiled and walked me to the bus, his arm tight around my waist. We kissed goodbye and kissed goodbye, then I boarded the bus and found my seat.

'*Call me from Beijing,*' he mouthed as he stood on the pavement below my window. '*You want to hear me sing?*' I mouthed back teasingly. He smiled, then took a step back as the bus started up noisily. Looking back up at me, Garry pressed his fingers to his lips. Then the bus pulled away and he was gone.

CHAPTER FOURTEEN

Indochina – Beijing, China

Hector was an old friend of mine. I'd known him originally through work: he was news editor on one of the papers and used to interview me whenever a travel story came up. He'd travelled a lot himself and he was a huge music fan, too. We quickly became close and stayed that way ever since.

Another thing we had in common was a suspicion that hard work had taken over our lives and that travel had the power to put things back into perspective. In some respects, Hector had achieved by chance what I was trying for via my fiddly geo-social engineering. He'd left Britain for a job at *China Daily* in Beijing and met a gorgeous Chinese woman, Ang, virtually the day he'd arrived. They'd dated, fallen in love and now they were married.

In the early days, as the romance had developed, Hector had emailed pictures of them both to us back at home. He was clearly besotted with her and you could see them growing closer and closer with each new photo. Instinctively I felt protective of him: when you see a good friend wholeheartedly fall for someone, there's always a part of you that's anxious on their behalf. You hope it really is as good as it looks and something isn't about to happen that will make it end badly.

But as soon as I met Ang at their wedding, any worries I had vanished completely: she was great and they were perfect for each other, total Soul Mates. Ang had a witty yet shrewd attitude that I particularly liked and respected. Whenever I emailed Hector as a Date Wrangler, I always asked for Ang's opinion and advice too.

And they had both more than lived up to their responsibilities as Date Wranglers: I was arriving in Beijing, ready to go to work.

After the balmy sunshine and techno-opulence of Tokyo, Beijing was a shock to the system. China seemed everything that Japan wasn't. It was freezing cold and snowing, cars were full of dents and rust. They rattled down pot-holed streets at night with headlights switched off, bicycles pelting past them in their hundreds, equally unilluminated. Crossing the road was a perilous affair: it took the courage and faith of a fire-walker. Everything seemed chaotic. Tokyo had been busy too, but there had been a sense of order and serene dignity to the place. Beijing seemed poorer, dirtier and louder by far.

It was brilliant.

I flew into Beijing quite late, so after a meal at a local café, Hector and I spent the remains of the evening at their small apartment on Huixin Dongjie, in the northeast of the city. Like most of the expat journalists, Hector's accommodation was provided by the newspaper he worked for. He lived in an apartment block on a compound, the offices and canteen just a few steps away across the forecourt.

It was good to see him. The two of us sat and caught up on everything: the new baby, Garry, work, friends, Teenage Fanclub . . . As we chatted, Hector noticed I was cold. He apologised and got up to fetch me another sweater. 'The good thing about living in a communist China is that it's cheap,' he explained mildly. 'The bad thing is that the government doesn't turn the city's heating on for another three weeks.'

Ang and baby Grace weren't at home. As is common with new mothers, they were both staying at her parents' house about an hour across town. Hector had been staying there as well and I felt bad that he was forced to play host to me rather than be with his family. But first thing the next morning, we went visiting.

Ang's parents lived in a development over in the northwest of the city, although, as Hector and I walked to the subway, it quickly became apparent that the entire city was a development.

China had been a closed economy to the West for years, but winning the bid to host the 2008 Olympics was confirmation that both China and the West wanted that to change. Although 50 years of Communist rule had kept China isolated from the financial and social growth the West has experienced, China was grabbing it now with both hands. International money was pouring into the country and rural Chinese were moving in their millions into the cities (354 million over the next 25 years, according to the experts), where work, opportunities and a better standard of living would, theoretically, be found.

But there was no infrastructure to support them, not enough housing, roads, shops, restaurants, schools or utilities. There wasn't enough to support the 2008 Olympics, come to that, so China was working at fever pitch trying to get it built in time.

Consequently, Beijing was a building site: deep ruts of dried, frozen mud ran through the city like tram lines. The noise of jackhammers and cement mixers, like industrial elevator music, was persistent, irritating and intrusive. On the way to the station, Hector and I constantly shielded our eyes against swirling eddies of dust and grit kicked up by the drilling and digging going on all around us. On construction sites, men dressed in nothing more protective than slippers and suit jackets hacked at the frozen earth with spades.

Ang's mother spoke no English but managed to make me feel very welcome anyway. She retreated to the kitchen to prepare a big meal for us; she'd never met a western woman before and was shy but extremely curious. When I saw her again later in the week, she got Ang to ask if – since they were '*so long*' – my eyelashes were real? I put her fingers to my lashes and let her gently tug them, which caused no end of giggling. Despite being kept up all night by the baby, Ang was obviously pleased to have company. Grace was cute as a button and we cooed over her.

It was funny hearing how much of each other's language and phrases they'd adopted in everyday conversation. Hector's English (Scottish) was now peppered with Mandarin; Ang's English was excellent, and even more authentic now she was using an increasing amount of slang. The baby had a cold that was giving her some difficulty breathing. It was clearly a worry and Hector had been to the chemist. He gave Ang the drops he'd bought. 'Grace's congestion is caused by snotters,' he said gravely.

'Ah yes,' Ang said, peering up Grace's nose. 'I see snotters too.'

Ang's favourite word seemed to be *dodgy* (in the sense that the subject was suspect or unreliable). She pronounced it *dodtchy* and it always made me smile. Suddenly missing Garry with a sharp pang, I thought how our language had started cross-pollinating too. He loved the British *cheers* but, like Ang, also seemed to enjoy saying that things were *dahgee*.

Promising we would meet up the next day, I managed to persuade Hec that I'd be fine on my own and he should stay here with Ang. I'd be perfectly happy spending the rest of the day exploring.

It was easy to find my way back to the station, which was just as well as no one would have spoken English had I needed directions. This was a Chinese residential area and not a place tourists would ever come to. There were no other westerners around and everyone stared at me quite openly. People had done the same in Japan, especially as I was so tall. On more than one occasion, someone had reached over and touched my face or arm, wanting to know if my skin felt the same as theirs. It wasn't frightening or hostile. Clearly, foreigners were still a relative oddity here and everyone was just curious.

I was curious too.

I poked around shops and food markets; walked thoughtfully around Tiananmen Square, watching clouds of ornate kites skate across the air in front of the Mao Mausoleum; explored the Underground City, where volunteers had built a secret city under Beijing in the 1960s, scared of a Soviet invasion.

It was dark by the time I took the cold, dusty walk from the underground station back to Hector's flat. Street traders sold potatoes and apples from huge mounds laid out on cloths on the irregular pavements; a woman sat before a sewing machine in the middle of the street, a pile of repairs and alterations folded neatly in a plastic sack by her feet. In the doorway of a DVD shop, the owner was engrossed in an American workout programme blaring out of one of the TVs. As he watched the perfectly toned, heavily made up, lightly dressed Californians stretch and jump in time with the music, he jumped and gyrated along with them. Completely absorbed in what he was doing, as he kicked his leg out, one of his slippers shot off his foot and lay unnoticed in the road, only to be run over a few seconds later by a stream of bicycles. His body may have been in Beijing, but his pounding heart and mind were pure Beverly Hills.

I popped into another of the countless CD and DVD stalls that lined the road and browsed through copies of pirated films yet to be released in the cinema. As I flicked through the racks, I half-listened to the old woman behind the counter talk to a young man I guessed to be her grandson, busy taking cases from cardboard boxes and arranging them on the shelves.

The cadence of their conversation seemed to jab and twang sharply, rising and falling atonally like a Japanese lute. I've often noticed how the singsong sound of certain Asian accents could make a perfectly ordinary conversation sound like an argument. And as I thought this again now, there was a loud crash. To my astonishment, the old lady came careening out from behind the counter, brandishing a long stick like a samurai sword over her head. Her face brick-red with rage, bellowing and swinging wildly, she proceeded to chase her grandson around the small shop, flailing as she ran.

But she couldn't catch him. And as grandmother and grandson ran around the shop shouting angrily, with each dodge the stick whizzed past the agile grandson and smashed instead into the racks of DVDs. They went flying off the shelves, skidding across the floor and scattering their contents under boxes and life-size cardboard cut-outs of Jackie Chan. There were three Chinese men in the shop along with me and we all stood frozen in disbelief as the scene unfolded around us. But as an airborne DVD caught one of the men painfully in the neck, exchanging a quick look of *No DVD is cheap enough to be worth this*, we all made a beeline for the door and dashed out into the safety of the street. I walked briskly away without looking back, the sound of people shouting and DVD cases splintering clearly audible all the way down the street.

Happily, both my mobile phone and email worked in China, so as I walked, I rang Garry and told him what had just happened.

'What's all that noise?' Garry shouted a few seconds into the conversation.

'That's China!' I shouted back, as all around me the sound of drilling, driving, sewing and shouting filled the air.

We talked on the phone all the way back to the apartment, then – fearing my phone bill – spent another hour Instant Messaging after that. I had so much to tell him, there was so much going on. I really wished he was here; I missed him terribly. He would have loved this.

The next morning Hector and I met early and ambled along the painted corridors and temples around the vast Kunming Lake in the grounds of the Summer Palace, before heading back to Huixin Dongjie. We were having lunch with a group of Hector's fellow journalists at The Great Wall of China, a landmark restaurant just down the road from his flat.

The restaurant was fancy, friendly and insanely cheap. Hector's friends – Siobhan, Marta and Paul – were already seated when we arrived, so introductions were made as the waitress passed the menus around. These were huge: over 30 pages of dishes, each with accompanying photo and description in Chinese and English.

We randomly ordered so we could talk. All his friends loved living here, though it could clearly be quite challenging. Marta had broken her hand that morning when a bike had pedalled straight into her on the road. We talked about running to de-stress: Siobhan got up at 5 a.m. to run on an outdoor track. But there was no lighting; she had to shine a torch in front of her as she ran so she wouldn't fall down the potholes.

Paul was an early thirties Australian. He was tall and handsome, also quiet and a little shy. I chatted with him, asking how long he'd been here, where he'd worked before, where he'd lived in Australia . . . These were actually highlights from my *don't worry it'll all be fine* warm-up date questions, and as if reading my mind, Hector leant across the table and said: 'Jen, you do know that it's Paul you're dating tomorrow?'

God, was it? Why hadn't he told me sooner? I was appalled.

Okay, I'm exaggerating. I was actually very pleased: he was sweet and I already felt so comfortable and curious that I knew he'd be a good date. But I'd been asking him *the date questions* already. What would I talk to him about tomorrow?

'Paul, I'm really sorry,' I told him, in a tone that almost certainly sounded like a guard telling passengers they couldn't board the train even though it was standing at the station with the doors wide open. 'Do you mind if we don't talk until tomorrow? I don't want to peak too soon.'

Hector rolled his eyes and sighed. Paul was too much of a

gentleman to show any of the misgivings he now had about dating me: he merely smiled and nodded.

As it turned out, though, everyone talked non-stop, including Paul and me. It was an entertaining and companionable meal – Chinese food is sociable and made for sharing, quite the opposite to Japanese food which is either in *meal for one* bento boxes or means bending low over bowls of *no eye contact* ramen noodles – and the food was extraordinary. Dish after sumptuous dish arrived: salted fish in black-bean sauce; shredded potato with chilli; aubergine in sour sauce. It was piquant with attention-grabbing flavours and textures. I was amazed at how much I loved it.

I think of myself as being pretty open-minded, but there are two things I've always been sure of: I get really seasick and I hate Chinese food.

Clearly, this journey was playing havoc with my sense of self.

After lunch, Hec and I embarked on a series of cross-town buses – the subway might be fast and easy, but it was the buses that gave you a true sense of what a city was like – to go and meet Les.

It was funny, virtually every date I'd been on, I'd dressed up and gone off on my own like the modern woman I was. But Hector seemed to be acting as an old-fashioned chaperone: arranging dates with people he knew and coming along with me for the introduction. Hector had always been considerate and courteous; I smiled to myself wondering if in the back of his mind he was steeling himself for the day he'd meet his daughter's beaux.

Les (Date #64) was an expat journalist who had worked in

London's journalistic hub, Fleet Street, during its notorious heydays. We met him in a fiddly tea shop in the Foreign Embassy district near Silk Alley (and Starbucks).

Meeting Les – although not obvious date material – was a wonderful encounter. He was a 71-year-old Brit and a larger-than-life character. He'd spent the last 20-odd years stacking up adventures throughout Africa and Asia, writing for and running a variety of newspapers and magazines.

At the height of his career in Fleet Street he'd lost his leg through illness, but he refused to allow this to compromise the quality of his life. His old colleagues in London had had trouble making the same adjustment, however, so rather than accept their pity and the loss of his career, he'd moved to Asia. As he said: 'In Britain people can kill you with kindness: in Asia, they may seem a harder people but at least they don't write a man off who wants to work. They don't look at a man with one leg and see a cripple.'

It was yet another reminder of how travel revitalises you and allows you to, if not be reincarnated, then to focus in on the parts of your life you value and don't want to lose. It was enormously entertaining and refreshing listening to Les. And I did a lot of listening. In some respects, he actually reminded me of my maternal grandfather, who had run away to sea when he was 14 and kept us all rapt with the stories of his adventures on the high seas.

That night, Hec went back to see Ang, and I sat on the computer trying to work out where I was going to stay in Bangkok. I was flying there the day after tomorrow and everywhere seemed to be full. I was just about to get a bit stressed about it and moaned on Instant Message to Garry, when he suggested:

Sounds like you're super busy, just tell me where you want to stay and I'll sort it out for you.

For some reason his offer made me stop short. I'd been setting up stuff for months now and my standard operating procedure was: leave it too late, make a fuss about it, get stressed, then – somewhere in the middle of boring everyone rigid about how demanding everything was – get over it and make the booking.

That Garry had taken my complaints seriously, to the point where he actually wanted to do something to help, was incredibly kind. But to have my boyfriend help with the logistics of dating a score of other men felt just a bit weird. Plus, I was committed to the journey and *sucking up* the logistics was part of that. I just had to tough it out and stop being such a baby.

Nonetheless, I was touched and IM-ed Garry back my appreciation:

Thx that's kind of you. I'm fine, though: I'm just being a drama queen, please ignore me.

I slept badly that night: I dreamt that Garry, Paul, one-legged Les and I were all wandering around Bangkok trying to find somewhere to stay. Hotel after hotel turned us away: they all had rooms but when we came to book we could never agree on the number of rooms we needed and it'd end up with us shouting at each other and the manager kicking us out into the street.

When I woke at dawn I felt rattled and bedraggled from the

unsettled night. As I lay there feeling uncomfortable and out of sorts, my stomach made a strange noise, like water gurgling down a sink. I looked at it perplexed: what was that all about? Thirty seconds later in the bathroom, as I threw up what felt like every meal I'd eaten since 1986, I realised I must have picked up a traveller's tummy bug. Damn, on the day of my hot date with Paul too.

Some time later, crawling from the toilet to the sink, I ran the cold tap and splashed freezing water onto my burning face. Steadying myself against the edge, I slowly pulled myself upright. Catching sight of my reflection in the mirror, I let out a long groan: my hair was lank and stringy, like a dog left out in the rain. And under my right eye was a mosquito bite the size of a pebble big enough to skim clear across the English Channel.

My stomach heaved. It was officially a disaster.

I crawled back to bed and fell into a deep sleep, getting up just once more to be violently sick. But by the time I finally woke at 11 a.m. and was well enough to sit at the kitchen table gingerly sipping bottled water, my temperature was back to normal and whatever had made me so ill seemed to be out my system (in every sense).

As I stared dully out of the window, I was jerked out of my numbness by the shrill ringing of my mobile phone. I fumbled for it in my bag.

'Hello?' I answered scratchily.

'Jennifer, hi,' a man's voice replied. 'You sound terrible, are you okay?'

'I'm fine, thanks, just a little groggy. Who is this?' I didn't mean to be rude but there was nothing like a tummy bug to dull your social skills.

He laughed. 'Sorry, it's Will . . .'

Will . . . ? Will who? I wondered silently.

'. . . your date,' he added, picking up on my hesitation.

My date. My date? I'd dated 64 people and more than one of them had been called Will.

'. . . from Tokyo, four days ago . . .' Will finished, his voice trailing off, clearly hurt.

Oh, that Will.

'Will, hi, I'm sorry,' I apologised quickly. 'I just had a bit of a bad night and I'm not quite awake yet. How are you? How's Tokyo?'

'Well, that's why I'm ringing,' he replied, sounding more cheerful. 'I'm over in Beijing covering the economic conference and I wondered if you'd like to meet up? I don't know anyone here and I thought we could go exploring together.'

He knew I was in Beijing staying with friends near *China Daily*'s building, but it was still a surprise to hear from him. I tried not to show it – I'd been rude enough already. And besides, he was a nice guy. If there had been time, I probably would have met up with him again. 'Will, that's really sweet of you and I really hate to say this, but I don't think I'm going to have time. I'm out tonight and I'm flying to Bangkok tomorrow.'

I heard nothing but silence from his end of the phone. I waited, still no response. I thought maybe the connection had been lost (he was after all ringing on a British mobile in China to another British mobile in China). 'Hello, Will, are you there?' I asked.

'Yes,' he said quietly. 'I am.'

My instincts were immediately primed and on full alert. Why was he being so intense? He answered that question in his next sentence: 'Jennifer, when we had our date in Tokyo, I was worried that I possibly didn't make a good impression.'

'Oh Will,' I replied without hesitation. 'You were lovely: it was really good to meet you. Why would you think that?'

He was silent for a moment, then said dejectedly: 'Oh, you know, I just really enjoyed meeting you: it was so good to meet someone I could really talk to.'

'And I enjoyed talking to you too, Will,' I replied, trying to reassure him, but at the same time thinking how unexpected it was to be having this conversation. I knew he liked me when we met, and we had got on well, but I hadn't picked up any indication he was really keen on me.

'Well, that's how I felt,' Will said firmly. 'And I don't want to make you feel uncomfortable, but I just thought if we could have another date . . . I'd be more prepared and we'd really hit it off this time.'

Another date?

'Will,' I said, trying to sound reasonable rather than panicky. 'I promise you made a really good impression: I really enjoyed our afternoon together. Honestly, you don't have to worry about going to all that trouble. And anyway . . .' I said kindly but firmly '. . . I hate to say this but I'm going to be flat-out right up to the time I fly.'

'I've just been in at *China Daily*. I'm in the café across the road,' Will blurted out. 'You could come and have a coffee with me. It wouldn't take long.'

I shut my eyes and opened my mouth to let out a long, silent shriek.

Living overseas can be an intensely lonely experience, so I didn't take what Will was saying as a sign he was necessarily a scary stalker. But the fact was I looked and felt like crap, I still had a lot to do and I really wasn't in the mood for a Date Addendum.

Will must have sensed my reluctance to meet. 'Please, Jennifer,' he asked sadly. 'Let me have another date. I just want the chance to prove to you that I can be fun.'

I wanted to shout: '*It's not fun I flipping need: it's more sleep and some quality time with www.hotels.com.*' But I didn't. I felt sorry for him. And the fact was, he'd gone out of his way to meet me when I needed to see him, it was only fair I did the same now he needed some company.

So I went across the road and had a coke (my stomach rebelled at the thought of anything else) with **Will (Date #65)**.

And he was exactly the same as he was before: chatty boy-next-door, full of talk of London and the life he'd be having over there if he wasn't over here. After an hour talking about politics and our favourite bars, I looked at my watch. 'I am so sorry, Will,' I told him gently. 'I really have to go.'

He smiled happily. 'Please don't apologise, Jennifer,' he told me cheerfully, clearly restored by having a chat. 'I really appreciate you coming to meet me: it was good being able to talk like this.'

As I nodded amiably, my heart went out to him. He hadn't wanted the chance to prove he was The One, he'd just wanted to talk to someone from home. And because we had a lot in common and could talk easily, I helped him believe he wasn't sad and anxious but happy, with friends, opinions and good times ahead. Will was clearly desperately homesick and struggling with the sense of isolation he felt over here.

But he was right: I was glad I'd met him; no one deserved to be lonely and on their own in a foreign country.

Hector was back at the flat, getting it ready for Ang and Grace's arrival tomorrow. He smiled as I walked in the door. 'Hello, Dater Girl, how's your day going? Or, more to the point, how're your Dates going? Got them under control?' I rolled my eyes and told him it was most assuredly *they* who had me under control. But I didn't want to think about it, so instead I helped him carry furniture into the spare bedroom.

Paul said he'd ring before he picked me up for our date, so relying on having a good half hour to get ready (29 minutes of which would be spent putting concealer on the bite under my eye), I lost track of time helping Hector get the flat straight. I also (finally) feigned left and dodged right around the obstacle of my indecision and booked a hotel in Bangkok.

But Paul lived in the compound too. I'd forgotten how living somewhere akin to a student hall of residence can blur the social boundaries and create a sense of informality between residents.

So, instead of calling, Paul just turned up. He knocked on the door and let himself in, looking far more dressed up – black trousers and shirt, with nicely gelled hair – than he had done yesterday at lunch.

I was unprepared for his arrival in every sense, no make-up and wearing an old pair of jeans. As I scurried around the flat frantically getting changed, Hector teased Paul about wearing aftershave. The two of them sat down at the kitchen table and chatted over a beer while I got ready.

Hector's flat was small and although I could disappear into

the bedroom to change, I also needed to go to the bathroom. Only a glass door separated the small kitchen from the small bathroom, and the kitchen table was about two feet away from it.

I hate it when people can hear me pee. Even more so when I'm about to go on a date with one of them. But I had to go, so, avoiding eye contact as I passed in front of the table, I went into the bathroom and pulled the glass door shut behind me.

From my vantage point on the toilet, I could see Hector's and Paul's outlines through the frosted glass and I could clearly hear every single word of their conversation about football.

I couldn't go.

Five minutes passed. I could make out the sleeve being pulled back on a shadowy arm, as Paul checked his watch to see what the time was. We were obviously running late. I still couldn't go.

In the end I did what I am certain all women do in these situations: I dropped some paper down the toilet and peed really slowly and very quietly. It took forever and was excruciatingly painful, like an instant case of cystitis.

I'm sorry if that seems like too much information but you don't get a second chance to make a first impression: I didn't want Paul to spend our entire date thinking about . . .

Okay, I'll move on.

Paul (Date #66) and I finally left the flat and caught a taxi to a Chinese foot-massage place five minutes away. I was absolutely delighted: I really love having reflexology (the belief that each part of your foot is linked to a part of your body, so massaging your feet can relieve anything from an upset tummy to tension in your shoulders). Paul had chosen a perfect date (and there wasn't a boat or raw fish in sight).

When we arrived at the centre, there was a moment of slight confusion as Paul tried to explain to the manager what type of treatment we wanted. ('My Chinese isn't that good,' he confessed with a self-deprecating grimace.) But the situation was resolved by using Travellers' Semaphore (basically a lot of pointing and nodding). We were then led down a white corridor to a small unadorned room, two large wing-backed chairs in the middle, a low table between them, two footstools in front. Up on the wall, a television belted out a Chinese soap opera at a deafening level. The place felt less curative, more geriatric: I wondered if we'd come to a local retirement home by mistake.

But then a Chinese man and woman in their twenties walked into the room. Each was holding a footbath and a jug full of scaldingly hot water. They gestured we should remove our shoes and socks and immerse our feet in the baths they had laid at our feet.

That neither of our reflexologists spoke English didn't stop them from gamely trying to engage us in conversation. They gave up after a few minutes, though, and settled on chatting animatedly with each other instead. They clearly enjoyed each other's company: crouching over our feet washing them vigorously, they talked and teased each other non-stop. It was almost as if they were on a date too.

'So I hear you have some dating questions for me?' Paul teased good-naturedly.

I gave a rueful smile and blushed slightly: 'It's survival of the fittest out there in the dating world,' I told him in mock seriousness. 'A girl's gotta be prepared.'

He laughed. Graciously accepting the two beers the manager had just popped in to offer us (just a thought, Western Masseurs: less Enya, more alcohol), Paul opened both cans and handed one to me. I smiled and raised it in a toast: 'Here's to Hector, Ang and Grace,' I declared.

'Hector, Ang and Grace,' Paul echoed and laughed.

We clunked cans and drank. Then, leaning back in our chairs, we put the cans down on the low table between us and relaxed as the young man and woman expertly worked our feet.

And of course we chatted. Paul was lovely and as he told me about growing up in Perth and we talked about the places we both knew there, I wondered how he could still be single. He was really sweet, good-looking and gentle, entertaining company. I thought of Garry and felt a bit guilty that I was enjoying myself so much.

Apart from the occasional moment of excruciating pain where the masseur probed a tender part of my foot ('*I bet that's the bit linked to my tummy,*' I thought each time), we were so engrossed in conversation that I almost forgot there was someone working on my feet.

Until suddenly I was jolted back into reality by the sound of my masseur gasping in shock. His fingers were pressing painfully into the sole of my right foot. I froze in horror: I knew exactly what he'd found and I cursed myself for not having thought about this sooner.

There was a huge, horrible verruca on my right foot and the masseur had clearly just spotted it. To my humiliation, he was pointing flamboyantly, trying to bring it to my – and in the process everyone else's – attention.

Okay, I had a terrible verruca. He knew it and I knew it: for god's sake, couldn't we just leave it at that?

I felt my cheeks grow scarlet with embarrassment. My masseur didn't speak English so thankfully wasn't able to come out and say what the problem was. And, mercifully, although Paul did speak a little Chinese, he'd obviously been off the week the class had covered *diseased feet*, and his vocabulary didn't extend to the word for *verruca*. So as my masseur gesticulated urgently, and as Paul's masseur scolded my masseur furiously, and as I sat there red-faced and mortified, Paul was the only one who had no idea what was going on.

I badly wanted to keep it that way.

'Is your foot okay?' he asked in his Australian drawl, clearly concerned for my well-being.

'Ummm, yes,' I replied brittly. 'It's . . . errr . . . a blister from running. I did a bit of training with the NBA in Tokyo.' (Well, I'd chatted with the Sonic's assistant coach in the gym, that was like training, wasn't it?) I was desperately trying to sound ladylike and dignified. I was also trying to ignore the completely appalled expression on the face of my masseur, who continued to point animatedly at the sole of my foot.

'Mate, must be a pretty bad one,' Paul observed in a mixture of sympathy and awe.

The pantomime continued.

At the end of my leg, my masseur had given up pointing and was now miming a vigorous chopping motion with his hands instead. The girl working on Paul's feet rolled her eyes and hissed at him angrily. I think she'd picked up on my fervent and increasingly desperate wish that he would please, for the love of god, shut up about my foot.

But he wouldn't. He continued to energetically act out the chopping motion.

I guessed however bad the verruca, it was unlikely my masseur was recommending amputation as the most appropriate course of action. I wondered if perhaps he was advising some light pumicing. I would have agreed to pretty much anything at this point, so like a secretive bidder at an auction, I gave my masseur a discreet but definite nod to proceed with whatever he had in mind. The man immediately jumped to his feet and dashed out the door.

In the face of such sustained drama, all pretence that everything was fine was abandoned at this point. Conversation stopped dead as Paul, his masseur and I sat silently watching the space in which the man would soon reappear. Thirty seconds later, he did. He burst theatrically through the door, dropped to his knees and with much ceremony took a long roll of black cloth from under his arm. Laying the cloth reverentially on my footstool, my masseur unfurled it slowly. And as he did, one by one, 15 deadly silver scalpels came terrifyingly into view.

That would explain the chopping motion then.

There was a collective intake of breath. '*Jeez*,' Paul breathed out, openly horrified as we watched the light fall and die on the cold edges of the pitiless steel. 'I hope he knows what he's doing.'

I know this sounds ridiculous but I was genuinely in a quandary at this point. Of course I didn't want the masseur to hack out my instep, but at the same time this was excruciatingly embarrassing and had gone on for what felt like forever. I wanted to go back to the happy chatting of ten minutes ago; I wanted us all to forget about why my hideous feet had become the uneasy focal point for the entire room. If my masseur's plans kept him quiet and happy, let him get on with it; I was willing to take my chances with the consequences.

Paul's masseur had lost patience by now and resumed her work on his feet. But both Paul and I watched mutely as my masseur trailed his fingers gently over the handles of his scalpels. They came to rest on a knife whose broad blade resembled a flat chisel. Untying the ribbons that secured it to the pack, my masseur carefully plucked it from the cloth and oiled the blade lovingly. Lifting it high, then pausing for a moment to admire its wicked edge, he plunged it down dramatically on the sole of my foot, again and again and again.

I let out a gasp and braced myself for the terrible pain, but, surprisingly, there was no sensation at all. I felt nothing. The knife was so sharp it sliced effortlessly and painlessly through the skin (or the whole thing was a cruel joke and he wasn't chopping at all).

Mortification turned into irritation. I was meant to be on a date; this had now taken up more than enough time. I turned to Paul and, stuttering in an unstable, high-pitched voice, demanded: 'So Paul, why did you decide to move to China?'

And incredibly, the dating questions worked their magic.

As I asked and Paul answered, gradually we forgot about the stupid drama that had distracted us and instead focused on the task at hand. Our date. We chatted about loves we'd had and lost; places we'd visited; how work can absorb and make you feel good about yourself. We lost ourselves in conversation, talking easily and comfortably. All was as it should be once more.

Until, from outside the cocoon of our conversation, a sound jolted us back into our surroundings: we were having our feet massaged and the man working on mine was clearing his throat, trying to get my attention. Paul and I stopped mid-chatter and I instinctively reached forward as my masseur held something out for me to take. He dropped it into the palm of my hand and I retracted my arm so I could inspect it more closely. Paul looked over curiously.

As I unclenched my fingers, Paul and I looked in. Nestling in the centre of my palm was the large, yellowing, blood-encrusted lump that up until very recently had been my verruca. Like something out of *Reservoir Dogs*, the masseur had cut it off and given it to me. Paul and I both looked at it open-mouthed. We turned to each other, our eyes wide and blank in surprise. We looked back: I was still holding a verruca.

It's easy to know in hindsight what the correct response to a given situation should be. And, looking back, I can see clearly mine was *not* the correct response. But it was a very difficult situation; I didn't know what to do. I have to admit, I panicked.

I put the verruca in my pocket.

Looking up, I could see this was the wrong thing: even the man who'd been unsqueamish enough to cut it off was now regarding me with an open look of horror and disgust.

The date ended pretty much there and then. Paul was good enough to last through the end of the massage and the taxi back to Hector's. He didn't stay long once we got there, though.

'Did the date go okay?' Hector asked curiously as soon as Paul had left. I watched him dropping into a chair, exhausted from a frantic evening of getting the flat ready for Ang, the baby and his new life.

'Hector, do you have anything stronger than beer to drink?' I asked him in a tone that suggested it possibly hadn't gone well at all.

Hector and I sat up all night drinking. I stayed long enough the next morning to see Ang and Grace arrive home. Then, hugging and kissing everyone, wishing them luck and thanking them for their help and hospitality, I caught a taxi to the airport.

I was ready to move on.

CHAPTER FIFTEEN

Australasia

As I flew out of Beijing, I curled up in my seat thinking about the date with Paul. Every now and again a primal whimper escaped, as I replayed the action lowlights of the evening again and again in my head.

It had all been going so well too.

But even as I beat myself up with the shame of it all, I wondered if – apart from the embarrassment, the humiliation, the *can't-get-out-of-here-fast-enough* goodbye and the subsequent all-night drinking with Hector – it would have ended any differently? I mean I had liked Paul, and I'd really enjoyed meeting him, but he wasn't The One, there wasn't the instant attraction and solid sense of connection I'd felt on meeting Garry.

I felt relieved, since it meant that I hadn't really messed up anything with Paul after all, but also a little disingenuous. Was I going on the remaining dates just to check that no one else matched up to Garry? Was this like shopping for a new style of clothes, but in this case it was suitors I was trying on for size?

I hoped not: it was cold and cynical and not fair on the dates or Garry. But at the same time, how could it be any other way? And, perhaps more importantly, if in a twist of Fate, I actually did meet someone who measured up to Garry . . . what then?

Bangkok, Thailand

I felt a little troubled as I flew southeast from Beijing across the Chinese mainland and down over northern Vietnam, Laos and into Thailand. But I've never had a bad time in Bangkok, and during the drive from the airport to the city, the excitement of being there chased away any lingering anxiety.

The hotel turned out to be perfect: La Résidence was a boutique property near Silom. It was cool, quiet and easy walking distance from Chong Nonsi Skytrain station, Bangkok's life-saving monorail that allowed you to bypass the city's notoriously gridlocked traffic and pollution.

The weather was over a hundred degrees and insanely humid: I felt like I was being poached in my own perspiration every time I stepped out the hotel. But Bangkok was not a place to stay in your room and watch MTV. With the gilded curlicue and ornate carvings of the Grand Palace; Wat Phra Kaew and the Emerald Buddha; the 7000-stall Consumeropolis that is Chatuchak market, selling everything from snakes to milkshakes, you didn't have to go far to find something amazing.

In fact, Thailand in general was an incredibly easy, friendly, forgiving country to travel around. Asia 101: wobble up the first-time-traveller learning curve here and you'll find it much easier than say India or Cambodia.

But it would be a mistake to stereotype Thailand as a living museum of tradition and culture, as special as they were.

Bangkok in particular was an educated, affluent city with sophisticated urban tastes.

This was clear the moment I walked into the entrance lobby of the Conrad Hotel for my next date. Endless marble columns rose up from oceans of gleaming marble floors, tiny, beautiful women floated across the surface in sparkly, diaphanous outfits, like jewelled dragonflies. I was meeting my date in the Diplomat Bar at 9.30 p.m. and, depending on how it went, I would take him along or go on my own to meet my friend Joe at the ultra-hip Club 87 at 11 p.m.

Andrew (Date #67) was a friend of my Australian friend Lorna (the one who'd set me up with her *he ain't heavy metal, he's my brother William* in Stockholm). I hadn't had any previous contact with Andrew because – and this shocked me almost more than the incident with Paul, Lorna's brother, Garry meeting Kelly and every other crazy thing that had happened on this trip – he wasn't on email.

Imagine.

Andrew was a wine importer and was clearly nice, but a little bland for my tastes. Or, to be more specific, there was no chemistry: he just wasn't my type. He made a bit of a fuss about ordering the right wine and then spent a long time telling me how if it was more *this* and less *that*, it would have been superb. He had very fine blond hair which he fiddled with constantly. He'd sweep his fringe across to the right, smooth it into place, then once it was perfectly neat he'd push it back off his face and start all over again. It was mesmerising: like watching clothes in a tumble drier go round and round and round.

I didn't take him to see Joe, and as it turned out I didn't get to see Joe myself: popping into the toilet on the way down to the club, I managed to *misfaucet* (like Japan, Thai toilets favoured water over paper and had little extendable hoses for that purpose). A combination of high water-pressure and poor coordination meant that at the vital moment, a jet of water shot up from between my legs, soaking the front of my skirt and drenching my fabulous Rodeo Drive boots. The look on the faces of the beautiful women around the mirror (who'd probably never peed in their lives) as I emerged, confirmed my worst suspicions regarding how bad it looked and I decided to call it a night.

I stopped for a drink in a laid-back bar round the corner from my hotel on the way back, wanting to take a moment to review how everything was going before I went to bed. It was time to face something I'd been trying to ignore but couldn't any longer. I was developing a bit of an attitude problem regarding the journey – my attention was beginning to wander and I was in the grip of Date Doubt.

'You've come so far,' I told myself sternly. 'You have to focus. Your job is to stay in the Date Zone: the reason for what you're doing will become clear when the time is right.'

In truth, I was struggling to see where all this was leading. I mean, I loved dating and I wanted to give the Dates my very best. But acting as a counsellor to Will, then the drama with Paul, then the so-so date with Andrew just now, made it hard to see what purpose these dates served in the larger scheme of things. And the less I was absorbed by the Dates, the more I missed Garry (which of course made me wonder anew why I was still dating). I wished he was here with me now.

But, I told myself severely, Garry *wasn't* here now. I was, though, and so were my Dates. I needed to keep to the course, navigating from date to Date, as planned and plotted by the Date Wranglers and me.

I had to take another leap of faith: to believe there was an important discovery still to be made on my quest, and that the course I was on would lead me to it. I had to trust in that now, as I had when I'd been 'looking' for Garry.

Giving myself a talking to must have worked, because the next date was brilliant.

My friend Katia lived in Bangkok, but bad timing meant she was in London when I was there: 'I don't know how you expect to find a date in Asia if you won't date anyone shorter than six foot. Tall Asian men aren't exactly the norm here you know,' she'd remonstrated earlier that month. But Katia was one of the Date Wranglers who seemed to think that the belief I'd met my Soul Mate needed to be tested:

I have an absolute corker for you though. I've set you up with my friend Toi. He's a model. Half Thai, half Italian and wholly gorgeous. Date him at your peril . . . then tell me how it goes. Kat xxxx emailing from Bangkok

This, of course, reeked of The One Who Could Have Been, but that was fine: as Katia had rightly observed, my height requirement had made Asian dates thin (and short) on the ground. And **Toi (Date #68)** turned out to be the perfect cure for my severe case of Date Doubt.

There was no doubt that he was a model. Tall and slim, with high cheekbones and beautiful soft brown eyes, he was as striking as he was elegant. People stared as he passed by. Not that any of this was the reason he was the perfect cure (in fact

– good-looking and confident – he should have been the perfect nightmare), he was just lovely. Full of energy and enthusiasm, Toi was completely unaffected. He was also really into music and we twittered on about the Asian and European music scene for ages. He was also fascinated by my journey and couldn't seem to hear enough about it.

Toi took me to a traditional Thai festival for our date.

Loi Krathong took place during the first full moon in November. Across Thailand people gathered at rivers and floated boats made from banana palms as an offering to the river goddess. It was a huge occasion, and in Bangkok thousands of Thais came to the banks of the Chao Phraya river by the Shangri La hotel, all looking for the best spot to launch their krathongs from.

In Bangkok, krathong-making was a thriving cottage industry since people buy rather than make their own. The stall-holders that lined the street were doing brisk trade in what looked like colourful cakes, but were in fact huge lotus flowers. Their green outer petals were folded neatly back, creating a frame of little green triangles around the flower's centre which was then studded with marigolds, orchids, candles and incense sticks. I exclaimed they seemed far too beautiful to float. 'Ahhh, but we float them for love and what is more beautiful than that?' Toi replied.

I laughed, thinking how Toi's head may have been Thai, but his heart was pure Italian.

There must have been five thousand people on the street around us, pushing their way down to join the thousands already on the riverbank. We stepped out of the crush to buy krathongs of our own.

'You see,' Toi explained. 'Krathongs are an offering to the river goddess, but they also tell the future of your love.'

I stopped trying to choose from the stall's array of krathongs, each more beautiful and delicate than the next, and listened more closely. But Toi shooed my attention back to the stall, clearly intending I should listen as I chose.

'When single people place their krathong on the water, it represents the baggage of old relationships. It floats away leaving them free to find someone new.' Toi sounded very serious as he described the ritual. 'And then when you've met someone new, you come back the next year and place your krathong in the water as an offering of thanks, and to ensure a happy future together.'

I inspected the krathongs even more closely on hearing this: I wanted to say the best possible 'thank you' for finding Garry.

I looked up to tell Toi this, but then suddenly thought maybe he didn't know about Garry. I wondered if he'd mind that I'd already met someone. I could tell he liked me, but, now I came to think about it, the vibe I was picking up from him was one of preoccupation rather than of interest. I watched him as he talked and wondered what could be the reason.

'When you meet someone, you should bring them here,' he continued, 'and you both launch your krathongs into the water. How far they float downstream together tells you how long you can expect the relationship to last.'

It was a beautiful story and one that felt extremely pertinent to me. But I was now also intrigued by Toi. Maybe because I knew of his Italian connection, there was something about his tone that reminded me of sorrowful Solimano in Verona, weighed down by the thought of playing Romeo in perpetuity.

But the stall-holder had no time for our poetry-of-the-soul moment: she was in the business of selling krathongs and so far we were all talk, no action. Growing impatient with my

distracted dithering, she grabbed the nearest krathong, shoved
it into my startled grasp and held her hand out to be paid.

I was too shocked to be polite. I shoved it right back at her
in indignation: I was picking the krathong that was both the
thanks for meeting Garry and the down payment on our future
together. Was she mad? One wrong krathong and that was my
love life sold down the river, gone forever, thank you very
much.

But fair enough, it was time to make up our minds.

Toi and I picked out – to our eyes anyway – the nicest
krathongs and once again joined the dense crowd of families,
couples, teenagers and pickpockets squeezing over the bridge
to the water's edge.

There was such a crush we could hardly move, so as we
inched along, we chatted about my journey and how much
travelling Toi got to do as a model.

Impetuously, I suddenly asked: 'Toi, is everything okay?' We
couldn't move much because of the crush, but even so, Toi
jerked around involuntarily at my question.

'Why do you ask?' he demanded, not angrily, more
intrigued: as if I could see something he couldn't.

'I don't know,' I shrugged neutrally. 'It was just a thought.'

I've learnt two things on this trip. One, my dates always
seem to be at a crossroads and therefore think (probably
rightly) that I am too. Two, they agree to date me because, in
my role as *pair of ears today, gone tomorrow*, they want to talk
to someone outside their circle about the cause of their
crossroads.

Toi sighed, turned to face me and assumed an expression of
'*you asked, so . . .*' (Mentally I ticked all the aforementioned
boxes.)

Apparently he wanted time-out from modelling. He'd gone into it because it was easy: he'd been spotted by a scout when he was 20 and had worked regularly ever since. 'But you know, Jennifer,' he said without a trace of irony, 'I keep thinking to myself, "Is how I look all I amount to? Am I really just a face and a pair of shoulders?"'

It would have been easy to tease Toi but I didn't: my conversation with International Correspondent Will in Beijing was fresh in my mind and I didn't doubt that glamorous jobs could be lonely.

We were over the bridge by now, but Toi and I walked slowly, resisting the surge of the crowd that pressed all around us. He seemed disorientated by his confession and I was waiting to see if he had anything to add. But he remained quiet and troubled.

'So what are you going to do about it?' I asked. He looked up and studied my face. I thought instinctively how beautiful he was: if people had said that his whole life, I could see how it could get on your nerves after a while.

'What do you mean, what am I going to do about it?' he asked slowly, suggesting he knew exactly what he wanted to do, but was too scared to come out and say it.

Suddenly, a chill hit my stomach: I had the most awful premonition. 'Oh no,' I thought, 'he's going to tell me he wants to be a priest and give up this life of vanity.' I forced myself not to roll my eyes, imagining all those poor women looking at this exquisite man's face and having to confess to impure thoughts every time they clapped eyes on him. Every day there'd be queues around the confessional box, like the first day of the Selfridges' sale.

Toi took a deep breath. So did I. 'I want to be . . .' he started.

I was still holding my deep breath. '. . . a foreign-aid worker in Africa.'

My breath shot out like I'd been given the Heimlich manoeuvre. 'Great idea, do it,' I shouted, almost before he'd finished the sentence.

Toi raised one perfectly shaped eyebrow, like a rainbow made of black silken threads. 'Really? Wow. Jennifer, I wasn't expecting such encouragement. You really think it's a good idea?'

Actually, now that the shock of thinking Toi was going to be a priest had passed, I did think it was a good idea. I mean, why not: why shouldn't he follow his heart and do some good? We talked about various schemes I knew; the type of experience and training he'd need; the reality of life in a refugee camp. Toi borrowed my notebook and wrote down all my suggestions. He listened carefully to what I said and asked a lot of questions; he'd obviously been thinking about this for some time.

All around us people pushed and squeezed, carrying krathongs carefully in front of them, or in some cases over their heads out of the way of the crowds.

As we joined the throng, Toi whispered in my ear: 'I really want to thank you for taking me seriously, Jennifer. It means so much to be able to see a way forward.'

I smiled and squeezed his arm. 'You're very welcome, Toi: if this trip has taught me one thing it's that, however freaky it feels, sometimes you've just got to take a leap of faith.'

'Like you meeting Garry?' Toi stated. He knew all along.

'Yes,' I nodded firmly. 'Exactly like me meeting Garry.'

And maybe more than that besides? I thought to myself, realising that the Date Doubt I'd experienced earlier was – like

Will and Toi – a feeling of isolation: a sense of momentum without connection. Talking with Toi had helped me feel connected again.

And with that we both went down to the moonlit river. Standing on the bank, we lit the candles and joss sticks in our krathongs, and, reaching down into the dark, placed them carefully in the water.

I didn't ask Toi whether he was letting go of old baggage or wishing for new. Instead I watched my krathong gently bob on the water's inky surface. It was soon joined by another krathong, then another, then ten more, then fifty. They were all swept into the current and glided like swans into the centre of the river and gradually out of sight. They were joining the thousands of wishes and dreams, launched in hope and carried by Fate, into the current under the moonlit sky that night.

At times, the dates appeared to me like pieces of a jigsaw: helping me build a picture that, although tantalising me with glimpses, would remain obscured from me until I had completed the whole puzzle.

Toi was **Date #68**, and there were 12 more pieces of the jigsaw to find.

Daniel (Date #69), Mr 'I'll make you change your mind about Garry when you get here' in Kuala Lumpur, turned out to be a non-event: he had been forced to go to Bali on business and wasn't able to take me on the elaborate date he had planned. He insisted we meet at the airport for coffee, though, and after a long time spent to-ing and fro-ing with airline schedules (I was off to Perth afterwards), we managed it. Daniel was stressed and apologetic. 'Jennifer,' he said wretchedly, 'I had it all planned. I was going to take you sailing.'

'Of course you were,' I thought to myself with a little smile (boats and fish, boats and fish – the man may vary, but the date remains the same), as I nodded sympathetically.

Perth, Australia

I'd flown into Perth when I'd come out to Australia in the Eighties for my three-month visit that turned into six years with Philip. I'd spent my first year here and although I'd been back to Australia at least once a year since I left (Lonely Planet's head office was in Melbourne), I hadn't spent much time in Perth and I couldn't wait to see my old and very dear friend Jude who I also knew from my puppet-theatre days.

I was also dating one of the puppeteers I'd vaguely known from that time. It was years since I'd seen **Toby (Date #70)** and I was looking forward to catching up. But the date ended up making me rather uncomfortable. I'd met Toby roughly the same time I'd met Philip. He was convinced that I'd made a mistake marrying Philip and spent the whole date quizzing me as to why our marriage had broken up.

When Jude came to pick me up from the Esplanade Hotel that night, I was still irritated and slightly perplexed by his behaviour. 'I mean, honestly Jude, Philip and I got divorced over ten years ago,' I told her exasperatedly, as we sat on the sea wall watching the sun disappearing into the Indian Ocean in a blaze of red, orange and purple, 'but Toby was going over it all like it was just yesterday. And what the hell does it matter to him anyway?'

But I was too happy to see Jude, and the night was too beautiful to waste getting agitated. We talked about more recent relationships: one that Jude had just ended and the one I had just found. And Jude listened carefully as I talked about the reasons behind my journey and the adventures I'd had since leaving Britain. 'Had you ever really thought about who you wanted to be with before this?' she asked thoughtfully. I admitted I hadn't: thinking about who you wanted either seemed too calculating or just impossible to achieve.

Wistfully, Jude said she hadn't either and she really wished she had.

'But Jude,' I said with some feeling, 'even if I had've given it some thought back then, it wouldn't have made any difference: I would have assumed the man I wanted didn't exist, or if he did, I wasn't pretty, smart or lucky enough to get him. That's why I needed to go on this adventure: I needed to feel good about myself before I could meet the right man. Also, to realise the right man wasn't someone so different to me he'd be out of my reach and I might as well settle for less.'

But, for now though, the man of my dreams really was out of my reach: Garry was touring the States with the Sonics, and as both his and my time differences constantly shifted, trying to catch up with each other was proving harder and harder. And I was forced to admit that although now back in tune with my journey, I still missed him horribly.

7 a.m. the next morning found me on the edge of my bed nursing a scalding cup of black coffee and an evil hangover. The coffee was too hot to drink but the pain of holding the cup

was forcing me to focus my attention on that rather than on how desperately I wanted to go back to bed.

And I couldn't go back to bed: I had a date with a surfer at 8 a.m.

Surfing Western Australia was a school based about 45 minutes north of Fremantle. They gave lessons to members of the public, but since surfing was on the school curriculum, they taught students as well. (Can you imagine being taught surfing at school? When I was a student, we thought we were lucky if we got to hold the school guinea pig.) Jude knew someone, who knew someone, who had a friend who taught there. He'd agreed to date me as long as it was a surf date.

Steve (Date #71) was an ex-champion and looked incredible. With a rock-hard body, he had short, sun-bleached hair, luminous periwinkle-blue eyes and a rugged, handsome face, etched deep with lines from a lifetime spent in the sun. He looked uncannily like a young Samuel Beckett, so much so that I dubbed him *Salty Beckett* (but not to his face).

I struggled into a full-body wetsuit (imagine putting on washing-up gloves that've got water in them, on your entire body, with a hangover) and after the rudiments of surfing had been explained and demonstrated, we plunged into the ocean.

I quickly discovered that I loved surfing. As the waves crashed over me and the board – tied to my ankle – dragged me back into the surf and ground me into the sand, I felt invigorated and energised (and discovered a new beauty treatment cum water sport: Extreme Exfoliating). With Steve's patient encouragement I finally sussed out how to snatch my feet out from underneath me and spring from a lying position to standing upright on the board riding the wave to the shore. I was completely euphoric.

And then utterly exhausted.

We collapsed onto the sand afterwards and chatted. Steve talked about his life surfing and how although it had knocked out his teeth, wrecked his knees and destroyed his shoulder, it made him feel alive and he couldn't live without it. As he talked, my sinuses endlessly and uncontrollably emptied the gallons of salt water I'd sucked up through my nose. It wasn't a good look but no amount of sniffing would keep the water from coming out.

At that moment, one of the young girls having a lesson walked past, three of her girlfriends crowding in concern around her. She had possibly the worst nosebleed I'd ever seen in my life: blood streamed from between her fingers as she held them protectively around her face. Steve watched carefully as they all disappeared inside the office.

'Board to the face,' he observed sagely.

I had a suspicion I was far too vain to be a surfer chick.

Melbourne, Australia

From Perth I went on to Melbourne to stay with my closest Australian friends Linda and Dale, and their children Grace and Patrick. It was wonderful to see them all. Dale brought Patrick and drove me down to Phillip Island, 75 miles southeast of Melbourne, where I was dating one of the Penguin Rangers.

Phillip Island was home to a colony of wild blue or Fairy Penguins. Each night at sunset the penguins, around 4500 of them, waddled in from the sea and scurried for the safety of their burrows. Over dinner, **Jarvis (Date #72)** told me that as a ranger, amongst other things, his job was to gather on look-out posts along the beach and count the penguins as they came in each night. I thought he was joking, but after dinner we went and counted penguins.

Dale and Patrick joined us and we all stood in the observatory tower, watching the penguins emerge from the fog-shrouded sea. They were tiny, vulnerable things and there was something incredibly heroic about the way they waddled drunkenly from the cold sea, then, suddenly alert to danger, scuttled in terrified huddles from clump of grass to clump of grass, peeping little *the coast is clear* messages to the ones still sheltering one clump back.

Jarvis was actually extremely cute and we had a wonderful evening. He clearly loved his job and was devoted to the penguins, though I wasn't sure how he or any of the rangers would have time for 4500 penguins and a woman (unless the woman was a ranger, of course).

I felt really lucky to be able to have this time with Linda. She was my best friend in Australia; we'd both lived in Brisbane and had managed to see each other regularly and stay close even when I'd moved back to England and she'd moved down to Melbourne. It had been good to see Jude, too.

At the same time, though, I was starting to feel pulled in all different directions. In Australia I was seeing friends who'd known me when I was married. Logging on to my computer, my friends at Lonely Planet's Melbourne office had heard I was around:

```
Don't you dare leave town without coming to see
me: so much has happened since you've left I'm
dying to talk to you about and I reeeeaally miss
you. Lisa xxxxx
```

Plus friends in London had (not unreasonably) lost track of my
travels and assumed I was at home:

Not sure where you are, Jen, but James and Ian
and everyone else are going over to play table
football at Exmouth Market tonight. We're meeting
at 7 p.m., do you think you'll drive or take the
tube? See you there, Love Glam Tan xxxxx

There were also the rest of the dates:

Hi Jen, I'm really glad you'll be arriving in
Queenstown a day late: I've got something very
special lined up and it gives me more time to
take care of details! Sorry to be personal but
can you please tell me how much you weigh? Love
David, emailing from New Zealand

Talking to some people about my long divorced ex-husband, to
others about what was going on at a company I didn't work for
any more and to another set arranging a social life in a country
I'd just left or was yet to arrive into was a real juggling act.
Every group felt or assumed I was *around* and available because
technology made it so easy for them to get hold of me.

I could never have contemplated organising this journey
without modern technology, from emailing the Soul Mate Job
Description around and recruiting ranks of Date Wranglers to
setting up the Dates themselves and carrying all their details
and emails with me on my laptop. It also made researching
dates possible as well as booking flights and hotels, and of
course doing all this when on the road via email, mobile phone

calls and text. Modern technology had made this journey possible. ·

But technology is just a tool. And one which didn't seem to be working for me and Garry at the moment. Although we communicated constantly – texting, emailing and leaving messages on each other's home and mobile phones – all the technology in the world didn't seem able to connect us.

We wanted to be together. Trying to find a brief space to share in each other's ever-changing time zones and schedules was a constant battle. All we seemed able to share was our frustration.

I'm really missing you Jen

Garry said simply in a text.

And I knew it to be true.

It was late when I read the text. I was packed and ready to fly to Sydney early the next morning, but I lay awake for a long time after I got the message. For the first time I felt really scared. What if Garry forgot me? What if he forgot what I was like and why we were so good together. Forgot why it was worth putting up with this. Forgot why he'd agreed to be boyfriend to a girl living in England and currently travelling across Australia dating other men.

What was I doing to him? And to us. I had no answer, only a sense of dread.

Sydney, Australia

I was happy to arrive in Sydney. As ever I hoped the change of scene would, if not improve the situation with Garry, at least distract me from it. Not that we really had a *situation*, more an intangible and unsettling sense of being dislocated and drifting. It was hard to put my finger on it and – now that the demands of my long journey were starting to take their toll – I couldn't work out if it was just me being over-tired, the inevitable powering down that couples default to when apart, or something more serious altogether.

I didn't know, so I got back to what I did know: dating.

Early the next morning I dated **Terry (Date #73)**, Commander of the Sydney Harbour Police. Terry was a charismatic, fascinating man, who was clearly loved and respected at the station. ('Morning Boss,' everyone chimed as we walked from his office to the quay.) He asked one of his men to take us in a patrol boat from the police headquarters over to Balmoral, a slight delay as they tried to hide a dead body they'd fished out of the water moments before I arrived.

It was exhilarating to motor through the harbour (at least I'd been *expecting* a boat on this date). The sun gleamed on the water that sprayed out from behind us as we cut through the water past the Opera House and the Harbour Bridge.

Disembarking in Balmoral, we walked across the beach and into the ultra-chic Bathers' Pavilion for brunch.

It was great to walk anywhere with Terry: he looked fabulous in uniform and people touched their caps or just smiled. He was lovely to talk with, a really nice man. He'd carried out close protection for all the big politicians that visited (he'd been out with Prince Harry just the day before) and had me wide-eyed and rapt at his stories. Divorced, he talked about how being a policeman was very hard on relationships. We agreed, inevitably, that sometimes it's easier just to stick to your work.

Terry and his sergeant dropped me at the Rushcutters Bay

Yacht Club, which was a short walk from my hotel in Darlinghurst. Waving them off, I switched on my phone and a message popped up from my next date, Nathan.

Nathan (Date #74) taught Bikram yoga: the Indian discipline of yoga in a room heated to 100 degrees (the idea being that it relaxes your muscles, releasing trapped toxins and allowing you to efficiently sweat them out). I'd been put in touch with Nathan through my friend Kate at the Australian Tourist Commission in Sydney.

Our date was tonight, but in his message Nathan suggested I come to his class that afternoon, then we could go straight on to our date afterwards.

Unfortunately, I'd had my phone switched off. Date Protocol: I felt it was bad form to take a phone call from your next date whilst the current one was still in progress – and now it was already afternoon. I stuck out my arm and hailed a cab downtown.

I arrived at the Bikram centre with five minutes to spare. As I dashed up the steps, I caught sight of a completely gorgeous man disappearing into a room, steam already condensing madly on the windows. He was followed by group of star-struck women (and a couple of men). If that was Nathan I could see why the class was so popular . . . and why the classroom was hot and steamy (I'm always happy to embrace my *inner shallow*).

But I'd been in such a rush I hadn't given any thought to what I was going to wear. The bra I had on was okay, but no way was anyone going to see me *going lotus* wearing a thong.

I went careening over to the woman sitting at the reception

(so far yoga was proving anything but relaxing) to see if they had a spare pair of shorts I could borrow. No, but 'Go to Gowers on the corner,' she told me shortly, looking with disapproval at her watch, 'they're real cheap and you'll pick up some shorts for nothing. Once the class has started, you can't go in, though, so quick, go, go,' she shooed.

I raced across the street to Gowers but all I could find cheap was a nasty pair of men's grey Y-fronts. I held the packet at arm's length and examined it speculatively. Nathan was gorgeous and these Y-fronts were ugly, ugly, ugly. But I'd never wear them again and they were only $9, so sod it, I was in a hurry. I shoved some cash at the sales clerk and dashed back to the centre. In the changing rooms I ripped the knickers out the packaging, and, without stopping to inspect them, shoved them on, pulled my top off, grabbed my bags and bolted for the yoga room.

I got to the doors just as they were locking them. There wasn't time to introduce myself so I quickly walked into the class, past mats full of limbering ladies to a free spot at the front of the class and sat down.

Nathan stood before us, lithe and muscled to the point of being edible. As he walked us through the first positions, I attempted to bend my upper body down over my extended thighs. As I strained downwards, I caught sight of my pants for the first time. The thick grey flannel was so stiff that the 'Y' flap at the front was poking straight out in a disturbingly suggestive manner. Embarrassed and trying not to draw attention to it, I quickly reached down and pushed the flap back into place.

But it was having none of it and sprang straight out again, veering purposefully like the rudder on a sailboat.

It was horrible. I tried another tack: leaning into my stretch,

I surreptitiously attempted to pin the protruding piece of material flat with my elbow. But it was impossible to concentrate on both this and the yoga, and the front of the pants sprang straight out again, wagging from side to side, like the tail of a dog happy to see you.

The room was as hot as a furnace by now, and soon the pants were thoroughly soaked in my sweat, turning the dark grey flannel an even darker grey – apart from the flap at the front, which, since it wasn't in contact with my body, remained free from sweat and light grey, sticking out in lewd shamelessness.

After what seemed like an eternity, the class ended. And – all credit to me – I was brave enough to stay behind and introduce myself to Nathan. But as I hadn't thought to bring a towel for the shower or any clean clothes, our date ended up too *yin and yang* for comfort: he was serene and self-aware, I was sweaty and self-conscious. I stayed for one drink then went back to the hotel, lay on the bed and watched *When Harry Met Sally* on TV, using biscotti as spoons to eat a tub of ice-cream.

CHAPTER SIXTEEN

New Zealand – Auckland

New Zealand was the last leg of my journey and involved a complicated itinerary of dates dotted around the two islands. It was very much an all-singing, all-dancing grand finale – one last blaze of dating glory – rather than the gentle coast to the finishing line that would have been more sensible to aim for.

I was dating Frank in Auckland, then flying into Blenheim for Chris's mystery date, and two more flights, a four-hour train journey and a two-and-a-half-hour bus journey would put me into Middlemarch, where I was dating their Bachelor of the Year ('He's as good at changing nappies as he is at changing tyres,' one of the female judges had observed approvingly). Then it was a three-hour bus journey into Queenstown to date *speak your weight* David.

And I was waiting to hear back from Justin, another Queenstown date who was currently leading a rafting trip somewhere around Wanaka but had promised to *take you to Paradise and back when you get here*. (According to my guidebook, Paradise was a trail.) Whatever time I could meet Justin would decide when I'd fly back into Auckland, meet Nick, my

80th and final date, and from there catch the plane back to London.

I really hoped there'd be time to visit Garry on the way back to London.

We hadn't managed to speak for three days now. After months of staying up till 3 a.m. or waking up at 6 a.m. for a common chink of time across the time zones and the phone satellites, we were both exhausted. It was a struggle to find energy to put into our schedule and conversations, as well as keeping up with the demands of the lives we led separately.

I trusted Garry (which felt good: I was glad Kelly hadn't destroyed my ability to believe in faithfulness) and I'm pretty sure he trusted me. Neither of us lacked the desire or commitment to make this work, but we'd been apart longer than we'd ever been together and logistics didn't seem to be favouring us.

Dammit, I was going to call him. I looked at my watch, did some mental gymnastics – 2 a.m. his time, the poor love would have just arrived in Texas – and dialled his number. I heard the connections leap across the satellites before getting through to . . . his voicemail. I drooped disappointedly, but tried not to let it come across in my voice: 'Hello, love, this is your wandering girlfriend. I've just got to Auckland. I'm staying at the Hilton, you've got the number – give me a call and tell me what the weather's doing in Texas when you've got a moment. I miss you.'

Doing a double take at my watch, I realised I was running late for my next date. I threw open my case and rummaged around, desperately trying to find anything I could wear that was clean and presentable.

• • •

• • •

Frank (Date #75) was actually Posh PR Emma's The One Who Could Have Been from when they'd both lived in Sydney. He and I had missed meeting up there as he was over here on business. But our stay in Auckland overlapped by one night, so we'd arranged to meet in the hotel bar for a drink.

The bar had extraordinary views across Freeman's Bay and ultimately the South Pacific, and we admired them now as we chatted. We talked about mutual friends; how *Yes, Emma worked too hard* and *Yes, how she absolutely deserved a decent boyfriend*. We also talked about my dating. Since he was obviously interested in Posh PR Emma rather than me, I talked about the situation with Garry. I confided that I was worried that although we were both working hard at including each other in what we were doing, we still seemed so far apart.

Frank looked sympathetic: 'Jen, your schedule sounds exhausting and from what you've said about Garry, he's working and travelling like crazy too. You just have to accept that that's the way it's going to be for a while: it's very demanding travelling for work, inevitably relationships suffer.'

Frank was head of PR for an upmarket hotel chain. Posh PR Emma had told me he'd got divorced a couple of years ago because he spent so much time on the road. I nodded in agreement, Frank obviously knew what he was talking about.

But even so . . . 'That's true, Frank, but I am trying: I'm still putting energy into our relationship,' I countered a little defensively.

Frank looked at me over the top of his martini glass: 'Right, Jennifer,' he said with one raised eyebrow. 'You're putting energy into your relationship with Garry. So how is it you're in a bar, in Auckland, out on a date with me?'

He did have a point.

And I don't want to sound like I'm changing the subject here (okay, maybe a little) but he obviously had a thing for Posh PR Emma, and I wondered if I should put aside my dating for a moment and do a little freelance Date Wrangling instead? He talked about her constantly, wanting to know everything going on in her life at the moment. ('Work, Frank,' I told him honestly. 'She's in a relationship with her job, like everyone we know.') I was glad I didn't fancy Frank, but I really liked him, and I think he would have been perfect for Ems. They seemed less like a case of Could Have Been and more one of Still Might Be.

Blenheim, New Zealand

New Zealand is made up of two islands, one above the other. Imaginatively, the top one is called the North Island and the bottom one the South Island. Auckland is two thirds of the way up the North Island and I was flying down to Blenheim, which is at the top of the South Island. (Got that? I shall be asking questions later.)

The area I was flying into is called Marlborough, New Zealand's famous wine region, where some of the world's best sauvignon blanc and pinot noir come from. I love Marlborough's Cloudy Bay wine, so when I'd been thinking about where in the world I might find my Soul Mate, coming here had seemed a good idea. Who I would meet here was now down to Chris and his much-hyped *single, well-off, interesting, good company* Date.

Chris was a friend of my friend Susie, who did PR for the

New Zealand Tourist Board in London. Chris and his wife Julia ran the Hotel D'Urville, a charismatic property made from a converted bank in the middle of Blenheim and my home for the next two days.

Chris met me straight off the 12-seater plane at Blenheim's tiny airport and wasted no time planting a big wet kiss on my cheek and enveloping me in a huge hug. With his curly hair, ruddy face and thick-knit sweater, he looked just like a Cornish fisherman. But Chris was sharp as tack and very much in demand: he wheeled and dealed via his constantly ringing phone as we drove to the hotel, stopping at a couple of notable wineries on the way.

The town itself wasn't impressive. A wide high-street of half-empty shops, Blenheim reminded me of depressed Outback farming towns in Australia or the American Midwest. The hotel was fabulous, though: gourmet cuisine and luxurious, themed rooms. I was very happy at the thought of spending some time here. In fact, I'll be honest, I was happy at the thought of getting through whatever Chris had cooked up date-wise and whiling away the rest of my stay by lying in the huge free-standing iron bath in my room, applying a face mask, painting my toenails and soaking the knots out of my muscles.

So, over dinner that night, as Julia buzzed around the busy restaurant checking all the diners were happy, Chris joked with me about finally meeting my Date tomorrow morning.

I'd long since learnt not to react to his teasing but I did think it was funny that he was displaying all the classic signs of what I now recognised as a Control Dater. This was someone who liked to hold all the cards, enjoying the sense of power over you. Chris did it nicely, but it was still there. And he was a second-generation Date Wrangler, he wasn't even a Date.

While he talked on, a wave of tiredness suddenly washed over me. I'd dated 75 men. There were just five more to go.

The journey had been incredible and I felt lucky to have had all these experiences, but at the same time it felt like I had been doing nothing but dating forever. Seventy-five dates – that's how many applications of mascara? How many '*oh you must be*'s? How many life stories confided over drinks and dinners? As I said, there are far worse things in life, but the fact of the matter was that going on this many dates had slowly turned into aversion therapy. I never wanted to go on another First Date as long as I lived. If things didn't work out with Garry, I swear, I would go back to London, get 102 cats and never leave the house again.

Trying (and failing) one last time over breakfast the next morning to get a rise out of me, Chris then drove us out to Marlborough Air Club, a private airstrip and hangar on the edge of town. *It would seem the date has something to do with planes*, I thought to myself limply.

We got out the car and walked towards a tiny hut with a sign over the door identifying it as the reception. A man in pilot's uniform was leaving as I approached and he stood politely to one side, holding the door open so I could go in. But I wasn't at my most alert and I remained outside so he could come out. We stood gazing at each other, waiting for the other to make a move. Chris pushed past us both. 'Come on, kids,' he said mischievously. 'That's no way to greet your Date.'

Chris was having fun, that much was clear.

As he marched off into a large aircraft hangar, the man and I looked awkwardly at each other. So this was the mystery

Date. He looked nice: about 6 ft 2, broad shoulders, slightly wavy brown hair and an easy smile. He must have been about my age, with the air of someone sure of himself, but in a capable rather than an arrogant way. There was also something boyish about him, his green eyes crinkled playfully as he smiled, as if we were already sharing a joke. He was smiling now. 'You must excuse Chris,' he said with an American accent and a resigned yet affectionate expression that led me to believe he was Chris's friend. 'He means well! My name's Gene by the way. I'm a pilot; I think I'm also your Date?' Gene smiled reassuringly at me. 'It's good to meet you.' And with that he held out his hand.

I put out mine and we shook. 'My name's Jennifer,' I said smiling back at him. 'I think I'm your Date too, but I'm afraid that's all I know at this point.' We both laughed.

As it turned out, Chris had kept both **Gene (Date #76)** and me completely in the dark about each other, so rather than intriguing and exciting, meeting Gene was just a blank. That would have been fine – I had immediately warmed to Gene and we could easily have filled in the spaces by talking to each other now – but Chris had other plans and shouted for us to come over.

He was out on the runway, next to a small vintage plane (a Provost, in case you care). He held out a flying suit (nothing glamorous – shapeless green overalls) for me to wear whilst tapping his watch theatrically. 'Come on, Young Lovers,' he teased, making my toes curl with the inappropriateness of the remark, 'it's time for you lovebirds to fly away.'

Obediently, Gene and I clambered into the plane. Checking I was strapped in securely, Gene then systematically checked the gauges on the panel in front of us, fired up the engines, and off we went, taxiing bumpily down the short runway. I held my breath as the little plane picked up speed then rose unsteadily into the air, like an old man stiffly getting up from his armchair at bedtime. Slowly climbing up through the clouds, we levelled off after a couple of minutes and headed out across the patchwork fields and valleys of Marlborough.

Gene and I still hadn't said more than ten words to each other and I felt quite self-conscious to be in such intimate proximity – wedged close to each other in the cockpit, sharing this incredible view – without really knowing more than his name.

But it was a spectacular sight. I craned my neck to look around at the mountains, vineyards and fast-flowing rivers we were flying above. 'I was rafting down that river on the weekend,' Gene shouted into his headset microphone over the thundering of the engines. He looked really happy when he said it and I immediately wanted to know more: what had the day on the water been like; how often did he do it; could I do it in the short time I had left here; what else did he do in his free time . . . ? But when I tried to answer by shouting back into my microphone, it kept breaking up and Gene couldn't hear me.

So I gave up trying to talk. Sitting back in my seat and looking down into the coves and islands of Marlborough Sounds and the shimmering waters of Cloudy Bay, it was wonderful not to speak: I felt like I had been talking forever. I could now speak First Date so fluently I was in danger of suffering from the first ever recorded case of RSI (Repetitive Speech Injury).

But even as I enjoyed the breathing space and chance to soak up the views, I felt the first tell-tale signs of travel sickness suddenly grip me. The smell of the hot engines and the way the small plane banked and bobbed in the air was making my mouth grow dry and my stomach crawl (oh, the irony: not a boat in sight and here I was having my first bout of motion sickness in a long time). Gene must have picked up on the change in my demeanour, and I was extremely grateful that he decided this was a good time to gently and smoothly take the plane back to base.

We touched back down on the runway. And as soon as the engines had been turned off and we could hear each other talk, I congratulated Gene on his flying and thanked him for giving me the chance to enjoy the magnificent scenery from the air. I then scrambled out of the plane as fast as I could and savoured the relief of being back on the still, flat earth once more.

Chris was waiting excitedly for us on the tarmac. 'Wasn't that knock-out?' he said with a huge, excited grin. 'Wasn't it exciting? Did you think you were going to crash?' he demanded, hopping from foot to foot in glee.

I felt more than a little irritated: why would I want to go on a date where I thought I was going to die? (Though god knows, I thought grimly, remembering the date with the verruca . . . the grey Y-fronts . . . moaning Lars in Christiania, there'd been more than one where I'd wanted to kill myself.)

I wanted to take Chris aside and tell him: 'Look, that was a boy's date not a girl's. Girls don't care about going up in planes where it's too loud to talk and all the flipping around makes you want to throw up.' Instead I nodded graciously and told Chris it was wonderful.

It was a shame about Gene, though: from what I could tell he seemed funny, charming and definitely the type of person I would enjoy getting to know. But I was saying this based purely on instinct, we hadn't been allowed to fall into a conversation that would have strayed and wandered naturally, opening random windows of our personalities and experiences to each other. If Chris had involved us a little more, or himself a little less, I'm sure we would have got on well, but we'd both held back, waiting patiently for an opportunity to talk that had never presented itself.

'Great,' Chris said, rubbing his hands happily. 'So let's move on to the next part. We're running late.'

Late? *Next Part?*

The date wasn't over.

Gene and I exchanged weary and wary glances as we were bundled into Chris's car and driven halfway up a mountain to the Tohu winery, a local Maori-owned vineyard run according to tribal values.

Parking in a small gravel drive, Chris led Gene and me into a tiny hut that looked out across a dramatic glacial valley. The wind ushered puffy white clouds in and out of the glare of the sun, which alternately shot long shadows and blazed white light across the rocks and hillocks. Chris gestured for us to take a seat at a table facing the view. He brought the head of the winery in to meet us. We all chatted for a while, then were joined by the Wine Master and her assistant for a tasting. After a little while, Chris's chef arrived with his assistant to cook us a gourmet lunch in the corner of the hut whilst Chris stayed to keep an eye on things. There was standing-room only by the time the eight Maori singers squeezed in with their guitars and pom-poms to serenade Gene and me as we self-consciously ate.

I'm sure the intention was that the meal, eaten overlooking this beautiful valley, would be romantic. But the room was so crowded and Gene and I were under such intense scrutiny, it felt more like we were day-release prisoners from a maximum security penitentiary, expected to escape at any moment.

Gene was an attractive, interesting man, but after five hours in his company, I knew nothing whatsoever about him.

Finally, the busiest date in the world came to an end.

Gene and I shuffled past the singers, the owners, the Wine Master, the chef and half a dozen other people assembled in the hut, thanking them for their efforts, like the Queen backstage after a performance of *Cats*. Shell-shocked, we climbed into the rear of the car and Chris took off down the track, retracing our route along the roads that twisted back through the vine-strewn countryside to Blenheim.

In the back of the car, finally out from under the tyrannous dating yoke, Gene and I both became giggly and rebellious. We teased Chris for being controlling and bossy. Chris, now off-duty and able to relax, rolled his eyes at us in the rear-view mirror and joined in the fun.

The whole atmosphere changed and we started enjoying ourselves. And Gene and I, now able to act like adults, chatted easily, getting on with each other every bit as well as I'd suspected we would.

Chris dropped me back at the hotel and we all bade our farewells. I felt fond of them and a little sad it was only now that we were able to enjoy each other's company.

Early the next morning I arrived at the airport feeling groggy but with my travelling head firmly on. This was going to be a long day of planes, trains and minibuses. I could hardly believe my eyes when I saw Gene sitting over by the window of the teeny departure lounge reading a newspaper. I went straight over and tapped him on the shoulder: 'Hey, what are you doing here?'

Apparently he'd been on the 6 a.m. to Wellington but there'd been a problem with the plane. ('I bet someone turned their cell phone on and messed up the plane's navigation system,' he joked dryly.) 'And now I'm wait-listed on your flight,' he told me as he rose to his feet, asking politely if I would care to sit down and join him.

So for the first time since we'd met, and despite all the hours we'd already spent in each other's company, Gene and I were on our own. Unsupervised. We joked how scandalously improper it was: it was as well we were flying in an hour, otherwise we'd be run out of town.

Gene was relaxed and funny. He had a wry sense of humour and made me laugh as he told me all that had been going through his mind the day before. 'Chris said you were four-foot tall and weighed twenty stone,' he said. 'It's just as well flying suits are one size only; I'd spent a sleepless night wondering how you were going to fit into the one I'd brought for you, not to mention the cockpit of the plane?'

I laughed and explained that Chris had made a point of giving away nothing whatsoever about him and how I'd hoped we could have talked over lunch but had just felt too scrutinised. Gene agreed. He'd bumped into Chris's chef later that night, who'd apologised for crashing our date.

Gene suddenly got to his feet: 'Allow me to introduce myself,' he said with mock formality. 'My name is Gene and it's my pleasure to meet you. You are . . . ?'

I laughed and got to my feet too. 'It's a pleasure to meet you too, Gene,' I said with a little curtsy. 'My name is Jennifer and

I have travelled far, through the Land of Many Dates. Please tell me how it is that you came to be upon this fair isle.'

And sitting back down, we settled into our chairs and talked. Gene was in his late thirties, divorced and a pilot from New York. He lived in Blenheim for about six months of the year, designing flying sequences for the blockbuster films everyone seemed to be shooting in New Zealand these days. The rest of the time he travelled around the world restoring and flying planes, catching up with friends and hanging out.

It was ridiculously glamorous but the way he described it was more self-deprecating and down to earth. 'Besides,' he said, 'flying is not to everyone's liking as I think you demonstrated yesterday?'

I grinned ruefully remembering the motion sickness. I explained to Gene that – although I had appreciated it – I thought the plane had been a bit of a *guy date*.

Gene agreed: 'If it had been down to me, I would have taken you to a gorgeous old lodge I know on that lake we flew over, the other side of Nelson. I would have brought some great wine and made you lunch by the water.'

Mmmmm, I agreed that sounded far more appealing.

We talked about travel and relationships, jobs and friends.

'You know,' Gene said suddenly looking at me very seriously. 'I wish I'd organised the date yesterday.'

'Yes, I do too,' I agreed wistfully, instantly feeling a twinge of guilt about Garry.

I hadn't actually told Gene about Garry. Yesterday, I'd barely had the chance to tell him my name; going into details about the minutiae of my love life would have felt completely incongruous.

But then I heard the boarding call for my flight. Although it seemed like only five minutes, Gene and I had been sitting there deep in conversation for over an hour. Gene got up and went to confirm at the check-in desk that he had a seat as well, but he returned minutes later with a grim expression.

Sitting back down next to me, 'The flight's full,' he told me flatly.

'Oh no,' I said dismayed, instinctively putting my hand on his arm. Gene took my hand in his and looked equally distraught. It was as if after all the false starts, we'd finally begun our date, only to have it stop just as it was getting going.

But even in the middle of all this, I thought of Garry, and felt I had to tell Gene.

'You know I've met my Soul Mate, don't you?' I told him gently.

Gene looked away for a moment, then, moving closer and making eye contact again, said gruffly: 'Well, I heard you were spoken for.'

'He's an American too,' I said, as if by way of consolation.

Gene looked very serious. 'How do you know when you've met your Soul Mate?' he asked, watching my reaction very closely.

'You just know,' I replied evenly.

It's a trite, annoying answer and it's what people always say, but it's true. You do just know. Like a key fitting in a lock: it feels right and natural, you don't have to force it.

'This is an announcement for Miss Jennifer Cox. If Miss Jennifer Cox is in the airport, can she please make her way as quickly as possible to gate number one, where flight 2454 to Wellington is boarded and ready to depart.'

'Gene,' I said, startled out of the intensity of our

conversation, realising I hadn't even heard them give the final call, 'I'm going to miss my plane, I have to go.'

I felt like a WWII forces' sweetheart; I knew that once I got on that plane I was never going to see Gene again. And in that moment, the reality of it seemed both intense and tragic, with an underlying sense of loss and sadness.

It was also confusing: I could hardly wait to be with Garry but at the same time, and out of nowhere, something was happening with Gene. I felt I had to say something.

'Gene, apart from Garry, you're the only man on my entire journey that I've really connected with,' I told him truthfully. 'I know this has all been very strange,' I continued, 'but I want you to know I'm really glad I met you.'

We rose to our feet together, looking into each other's eyes the entire time. 'I'll be in touch,' Gene said, pulling me towards him and holding me tightly. 'You can count on it,' he whispered. Then he kissed me.

He kissed me on the cheek. Which was probably just as well: the tension between us was so electric by now that if he'd kissed me on the lips, the release of pressure would probably have taken out the coffee shop, if not the entire air-traffic-control's navigation system for a week.

But even in the eye of the storm, I thought of Garry. I pulled back and looked into Gene's eyes. I felt torn: knowing nothing could happen but at the same time sensing something already was. And liking it.

I gently broke away from the embrace. I had to go. Now.

I didn't even say goodbye to Gene. Picking up my bags, half walking, half sprinting, I stumbled away from him and out of the building across the tarmac to the tiny aircraft waiting on the runway.

I felt light-headed, like I was in a film where every moment and action was charged with purpose and significance. As I handed my pass to the '*so there you are*' attendant, I paused at the bottom of the aircraft steps and looked back across the runway to the airport building. Gene was standing where I'd left him, meeting my gaze head on.

We stared at each other, steadily and unflinchingly, neither of us looking away even for a second. Then we smiled. It was an intimate and private smile, acknowledging the deep, still waters we had both dipped our toes into, and on whose bank Gene still stood, holding a towel out for me to join him.

I blew him a kiss and boarded the plane.

As we taxied down the runway, I felt thrilled and excited at the intense and romantic scene that had just unfolded. And at the unexpectedness of it too. Yesterday I was thanking my stars that my dating days were nearly at an end; today a handsome pilot had waved me off from a tiny airstrip in a remote part of New Zealand.

It seemed the only two who had a handle on the big picture of my Dating Odyssey were Fate and Chris. Dammit.

So I flew to Wellington, made my connection and flew on to Dunedin where I was going to pick up the Taieri Gorge steam train. This would take me as far as Pukerangi, from where I would travel a further two hours by bus to Middlemarch. I was dating Bachelor of the Year there tomorrow but having dinner with one of the judges at the Kissing Gate Café tonight.

But I was having trouble focusing. When I'd woken up

this morning, I'd prepared myself mentally for a very long day of scenic travelling. What I wasn't ready for (and frankly didn't know that I could have been if I'd tried) was a Date I'd pretty much written off, reappearing and making the remaining *straightforward* days of my trip suddenly seem anything but.

I just had to tell someone before I burst.

Across the road from the railway station was an Internet café. Although I'd pretty much disbanded the Date Wranglers now (my trip was on the home straight and foolishly I'd imagined I wouldn't be needing them any more), they were still my friends and there would be just enough time before I boarded the train to get an *ohmigod* message off to one of them. Whether to The Sonar Sisters, Lizzy and Grainne, my real sisters Mandy and Toz, or Belinda, Charlotte, Cath or even Jo, I needed to talk to someone about what had taken place in the airport this morning.

I found a free terminal and as AOL flashed through its paces, I suddenly really hoped there'd be an email from Garry.

There wasn't.

But there was one from Gene.

I sat and stared at the screen. Which should I do: get advice from one of my girlfriends or open Gene's email and get in deeper?

I dithered for a second.

Then I opened Gene's email.

And it was light and fun. An uncomplicated and un-demanding message, saying how much he'd enjoyed meeting me and embarking on our slightly surreal adventures together.

Also how – like me – he wished we'd had more time to get to know each other:

I had a whole bunch of questions for you, he wrote. And proceeded to ask me 20 fun, silly questions, like Does every cloud have a silver lining? I smiled as I read them: his tone was just right – conversational but with a hint of confidences.

But scrolling down to the bottom of the message, the last question was very different to all the others:

20. When can I see you again? he'd asked.
Wondering, Gene

I pressed my fingers to my lips as I read the question, as if trying to suppress any emotion that might show on my face. Gene was raising the stakes with question 20. I read and reread it: what was the best way to handle this? Reading Gene's email was one thing; replying, and replying to *that question*, was quite another. There'd been a real sense of *connection* at the airport this morning, both spontaneous and unexpected. But to reply to his email was different, it would nurture an intimacy – currently bud-like and innocent – that would inevitably develop and grow. And however much I tried to pretend to the contrary, it would be the start of something between us.

I couldn't help being flattered, though, especially since the memory of our morning in the airport was still so fresh and real. In the end I opted to reply, but in a way that was light-hearted – friendly but not flirty – and I chose to ignore question 20 for now. As I finished typing, I hovered over the keyboard for an instant. Was this a good idea? Should I just delete it and not reply to him at all? But stealing a quick glance at my watch and realising I was running late, I impulsively hit *send*, then, grabbing my bags, ran for the train.

The Taieri Gorge is rightly known as one of the world's classic train journeys. Sixty km of track was painstakingly and gruellingly laid across the beautiful and remote centre of the Otago Peninsula at the end of the 1800s. It connected out-of-the-way towns like Cromwell and Alexandra to the coast, allowing trade in and out of the otherwise isolated communities living there.

The cargo the train now transported across the region – like steam trains everywhere – was tourists. Over the summer months the wooden carriages were full of Japanese and European visitors *oohhhing* and *ahhhing* at the dramatic gorges that dipped beneath the rails, falling steeply away to end in fast-flowing rivers lined by spiky clumps of yellow gorse and broom.

Today was no exception.

I love steam trains: my paternal grandfather worked on the Great Western Railway and as kids we spent many happy afternoons either travelling up front on the trains with him or going with my parents on lines like the Bluebell in Sussex or the Lappa Valley in Cornwall. The Taieri Gorge train transported me back to my childhood, the plumes of acrid smoke streaming back to us from the engine's funnel, the soprano whistle echoing urgently through long, dark tunnels.

The whole journey had a homely feel to it: the staff all seemed to be old steam enthusiasts, volunteering out of their love for the trains. The guard gave an on-off commentary over the train's PA system, an introductory '*Righteo Folks*' alerting us to each upcoming point of interest. He had a butter mint in his mouth and as he described each new feature, the mint clicked comfortably against his teeth, keeping time with his words like a spun-sugar metronome.

But as much as I was enjoying the journey, I was increasingly preoccupied by a creeping sense of wrongdoing. The heady excitement of this morning's encounter with Gene and subsequent email exchange had dissipated slightly and I was now able to think more calmly about what had happened and put it into a larger context.

Or, to be more specific, a *Garry Context*.

I'd been attracted to Gene, no question, but why? I adored Garry and – although missing him and going through a bit of a weird spell at the moment – I genuinely didn't want to be with anyone else. So why had Gene made such an impression?

I could blame it on being tired or feeling neglected or even *survivor bonding*, the way hostages unite to get through their ordeal. But where there may have been elements of truth in all these explanations, they weren't the real reason. The real reason was less noble and more basic, and it was that Gene – like Garry – was completely my type, so I'd been attracted to him and we'd clicked, instantly and powerfully.

A while ago, back in Europe before I'd met Garry and I was struggling to maintain faith in my quest, I speculated on what my Soul Mate odds might be: one in how many dates before I met Mr Right? Then I'd met Garry and had learnt - using the Soul Mate Formula – my Soul Mate odds were 1 in 55. Well, perhaps I should have asked what the odds of meeting *two* of my Soul Mates were, because sticking to the same formula, I'd inadvertently come up with the answer: 2 in 76.

Because I believed that Gene, Date #76, was my Soul Mate #2.

As the train puffed up hills, and grazing sheep, balancing unnecessarily on rocks, watched us pass with startled but lazy expressions, I tried to put aside my feelings of guilt to understand the chain of events that had led to them.

But no matter how much I tried to rationalise and explain away what had happened, I couldn't argue with how I felt. Gene, Date #76, was a man about whom my Soul Mate Job Description could have been written. And what did that mean? I'm no good at maths – and do feel free to shout out the answer if you know it – but surely there must be some kind of Soul Mate Formula here, which, I figured roughly, would mean if I kept on dating, I would meet Soul Mate #3 by around Date #100.

Apart from all else that was going on, this was actually an incredibly reassuring and exciting discovery in itself: that with the right attitude and effort, meeting your Soul Mate was a demonstrable and calculable proposition. And the longer you applied the formula, the shorter your Soul Mates odds became.

But my Attraction Fraction calculations were suddenly interrupted by a tugging on my sleeve. 'You're for Pukerangi, aren't you, miss?' the guard was asking me urgently. He sounded slightly concerned, as well he might: I'd been staring out the window wrestling with my thoughts for four hours and hadn't even noticed the train pull into Pukerangi Station. This was my stop and I had a connection to make.

Hurriedly thanking the guard, I scrambled to my feet, grabbed my bags, and in my dazed state almost fell off the train as I rushed to make the Middlemarch bus before it left without me. I found the bus, a small ten-seater minivan, easily: it was the only vehicle in the exposed, windswept car park.

Lloyd the driver noted my panic as I bustled up. 'No need to worry, miss,' he said calmly. 'Just you and two others getting on. We're not going anywhere without you.'

I smiled my thanks and, realising I must be radiating a slightly manic air, attempted to get aboard in a manner that denoted both composure and dignity. But as I found a seat and dumped my bags down on the floor, I realised in my hurry to get off the train I'd left my laptop behind. My laptop, with my files, photos, emails and itineraries – my *life* – on it. *Count your bags on, count your bags off* is the first lesson any traveller learns.

Furious with myself for being so distracted and disorganised, I hurtled off the bus past Lloyd and sprinted across the gravel towards the train, which was slowly shunting out of the station. Shouting up at the driver, I asked if he could stop so I could jump on and retrieve my computer.

I scrambled on and off the train, then, laptop safely back in my possession, I meekly returned to the bus. Lloyd had the measure of me after that little display and there was no point in trying to persuade him otherwise.

All four of us – plus bags – safely aboard, Lloyd then drove the bus out of the station car park. And as we started our journey out across the scrubland plains and stoic, weather-beaten granite of Otago's barren interior, once again I became lost in my thoughts.

So, if I'd uncovered the Soul Mate Formula, and my Dating Odyssey – leading me first to Garry, now Gene – had been such a resounding success, why was it that I felt so confused?

The question was rhetorical, really: I already knew the answer. I was Garry's girlfriend and I shouldn't be accepting romantic overtures from anyone else. Garry trusted me. He was my Soul Mate for chrissakes: I'd literally travelled the world to find him. And so what if Gene was my Soul Mate too, I didn't need any more Soul Mates – it wasn't like I was looking to collect a set of them. I just wanted one, and Garry *was* that one. But by responding to Gene's email I ran the risk of starting something I couldn't finish with Gene and having Garry finish with me altogether.

With a flash, I suddenly realised that this was why Fate had wanted me to keep travelling, to force me to realise that the journey was about more than just finding my Soul Mate. That was just the first – and in a crazy way, the easiest – stage of my adventure.

Fate had shown me conclusively that the Soul Mate Formula worked: the right effort and attitude could and would lead to Mr Right. But unless I wanted to keep on meeting Mr Rights forever, I also had to have faith that I'd met The One, stop applying the Formula and move on to the *next* stage of my journey *with him*.

And the truth was, deep down, putting my heart on the line and running the risk of being hurt again felt like a gamble for this *gotta catch a plane* girl. Safer just to keep travelling.

But the journey I'd undertaken hadn't only led to my Soul Mate, it had also led to people wise about relationships and with faith in love. Having met them, I now had the tools to help me through the scary minefield of actually *being* in a relationship – if I could find the courage to use them.

Or I could just carry on hedging my bets and travel forever.

Well, as Chester, the professional gambler in Vegas, had told me: 'Think about how much you have to lose . . . set your limit and when you reach it, get up and walk away.' I'd reached my limit now, and I had too much to lose. I'd bet all the way up to Date #76 and I didn't want to play any more. Garry was The One and I didn't want to hurt him, I didn't want to deceive him and I didn't want to lose him.

It was time to fold. It was time to close my Date Wranglers' Little Black Books. The challenge wasn't playing the Soul Mate Odds from country to country, date to date any more, it was taking that leap of faith and placing all my chips on Date # 55.

I'd really liked Gene, and in other circumstances, who knows . . . ? But I knew one thing for sure now: the answer to '*When can I see you again?*' question 20 would be a tactful but unequivocal *never*. I was hanging up my dating shoes and calling it a day.

I love New Zealand and – even in the midst of my dilemma – was enjoying Lloyd driving us along the deserted roads that crossed the bleak plains and skirted the desolate foothills of the dramatic Taieri Ridge. But I'd just made the decision to end my dating tour, this was a huge deal and I wanted to get the hell out of here as soon as possible. I contemplated my date escape route.

Middlemarch is a lick of a town – a petrol station and a general store – in the middle of nowhere. But I knew a bus went from Middlemarch to Queenstown. I had no idea how often it went, but if I could catch it I'd be able to fly from Queenstown on to either Auckland or Wellington, and from there out of the country and away.

I walked down to the front of the bus and sat on the seat behind Lloyd. 'Excuse me, but do you know how often buses go from Middlemarch to Queenstown?' I asked him.

'Just once a day at 5 p.m.,' Lloyd replied in a mildly alarmed way, as if I'd just asked where in Middlemarch I'd be able to buy a Ferrari after 10 p.m.

'Oh, it's okay,' I reassured him, 'I'm booked onto it tomorrow, I just wondered if there was more than one a day?'

'No,' Lloyd said apologetically, as if personally troubled he couldn't provide a more frequent service. 'I'm afraid that's all there is.'

I thanked him and made my way back to my seat. Glumly staring out of the window, I could see we were the only vehicle on the only road for miles. I watched a cinnamon-coloured colt race exuberantly around the grass, radiating an absolute joy at being a horse and alive on the side of this desolate mountain. I suddenly felt trapped and more tired than I'd ever felt in my life. *Please don't make me have to do any more dating*, I thought earnestly. I had to find a way out. I just had to.

Going back up to the front, I apologised for interrupting Lloyd again: 'But I was just wondering,' I asked him, 'will we make it to Middlemarch in time for the 5 p.m. bus to Queenstown?'

'Madam,' Lloyd replied solemnly, 'we ARE the 5 p.m. bus to Queenstown. We go right the way through.'

I could have kissed him. Lloyd must have sensed this and, seeking the protection of his steering wheel, hunched over it defensively. This wasn't going to make me popular but I sensed an escape plan. 'Lloyd,' I said (he was my getaway driver, I had the right to call him by his first name), 'I might need to do some explaining, but if I wanted to ride all the way to Queenstown with you tonight, would that be okay?'

'Yes, that's fine by me,' he replied gravely.

• • •

So we pulled into Middlemarch.

I'm ashamed to admit that, when the bus came to a stop, I hesitated in my seat. If my mobile had been working I could have just rung and cancelled all the arrangements, but we were miles from any phone reception so I was going to have to do it in person. For a moment I was tempted to just stay on the bus, keep going and sort it all out when I got to Queenstown.

Lloyd had other ideas, though: 'Barry and Lorna run the B&B you're staying at, he runs the garage too. You could go over and tell them you're not stopping but I thought I just saw Barry drive off.'

I felt rightly chastised by Lloyd for thinking of taking the cowardly way out. I got out the bus and walked across the road to the neat bungalow Lloyd had pointed out to me. Two old men were standing talking outside the general store, but they broke off their conversation to watch me cross the road. This was a small village: if Lloyd knew where I was staying, he – and everyone else – probably knew what I was doing here too.

But, whatever. I was more concerned about how I was going to explain to Barry and Lorna why I wasn't staying at their house tonight: – '*I seem to have over-extended myself romantically and need to leave the country as soon as possible.*' I felt so overwhelmed, I barely understood what was going on myself; how I would explain it to Barry and Lorna was anyone's guess. *Or*, I suddenly thought, hope erupting like a volcano in my heart, was I going to be lucky enough to find them out and escape having to make any explanation at all?

As I opened the gate and walked up the path to the front door of the bungalow, an intense feeling of guilt and fear washed over me, like a burglar who could be caught at any moment.

Arriving at the net-curtained front door, through a side window I could make out a neat single bed, covered with a candlewick bedspread, a towel folded tidily on the pillow. My room. 'Please be out. Please be out,' I whispered over and over again as I rang the doorbell.

The seconds ticked by. Please . . . Please . . .

I let a full 30 seconds drag endlessly by before breathlessly thinking, *Right – no question, they're out!* and bolting back down the path and out onto the street, slamming the front gate shut behind me.

Running back across the road to the petrol station, 'Is Barry in?' I asked the young mechanic behind the counter as I hurtled into the office. He stopped wiping a silver spanner with an oily cloth and looked at me suspiciously. 'No. He's at home,' he replied shortly, as if fearing to engage me in conversation.

My heart was beating really fast now. *'Please don't let him be home when I turn around, please don't let Lorna and Barry and the Judge and the Bachelor be sitting in the car outside their house waiting for me,'* a voice gabbled wildly in my head.

'No, he's out,' I replied with more certainty than I felt and without turning around to check.

'Oh,' the mechanic replied dully.

He studied me through half-downcast eyes. He almost certainly knew why I was here. It was as if he was refusing to make eye contact with me for fear I'd leap over the counter, rip the spanner out of his hand and ravish him where he stood.

Well, frankly, if he wanted ravishing, he'd have to take a ticket and wait his turn.

'Can you please give him a message?' I asked politely in my best *'I am respectable, you know'* posh English accent.

'Sure,' the mechanic replied, though clearly he was anything but.

'Please tell him Jennifer came by and she's very sorry but something came up and she's not going to be staying. Please tell him I'm very sorry,' I repeated. 'Tell Lorna, too,' I added guiltily.

'Okay,' he said, making full eye contact for the first time and looking surprised.

'You got that?' I checked. He nodded, looking down again now as if I'd already left.

Suddenly elated, I rushed out the garage and jumped back onto the bus that was waiting on the forecourt, engine running.

'Everything okay?' Lloyd asked as I collapsed into my seat. I nodded, too wired to talk.

'Want to use the rest room before we go?' he enquired. I looked at Lloyd in wide-eyed amazement. Was he insane? I could be dragged off the bus and made to date the Bachelor of the Year at any moment. We didn't have time for me to go to the toilet. We needed to leave this very moment.

I shook my head and the automatic doors whirred shut. And without being pulled over by police sirens blazing, giving me the choice of dating the Bachelor or serving a long stretch in jail for wasting police and everyone else's time – we quietly drove out of Middlemarch. After 15 minutes, we started climbing up into the mountains. And Middlemarch was lost in the distance.

It was over. I couldn't believe it. My journey was over. All those dates; all those adventures; all those people; all those places. It was over. I was going home.

It had been quite a journey: the skaters; the Vikings; the midnight-sun sauna; the festival in the desert; the fires in the mountains; the Elvis impersonators; the surfer; the ravers; the Romeos . . . All those bloody boats.

It had been an emotional journey too: learning to trust my instincts and know that because I'd made rubbish mistakes in the past, didn't mean I was going to make them forever.

And to realise how wonderful my friends were and how lucky I was to know them. I go on about how technology made the journey possible, but, really, it was my friends (and their friends) who had made it all happen. And I'm not just talking about their contacts; accepting my friends' and family's support and realising the value of their advice had been an important lesson in itself.

Just at that moment, from inside my bag, my mobile phone gave a little cheep. Now down from the mountains and driving through lush green valleys where farms were fringed by wide rivers, their water cold and fresh from the mountains, I finally had a signal on my phone. Phew, I was back in the world again.

I took it out of my bag, and there was text from Garry. I knew he'd be packing up after a basketball game, with Jon, Doug, JR, OB and the rest of the crew. *sorry I've been so busy: I want u 2 know how v important u r 2 me* it read.

I gave a wobbly little smile and felt the tears sting in my eyes. I blinked hard and texted him straight back with my news: *dating tour over. thank u 4 being so loving and trusting. am so lucky 2 know u*

u've finished? he texted back immediately.

chosen 2 finish, I replied carefully.

How u feel – exhausted, victorious . . . ? he asked.

Feeling a little ashamed and very emotional, I texted back: *v long story, will tell all when c u. 4 now feel drained but happy. love & miss u. flying to Seattle 2MORROW if okay?*

I had to see Garry. And I wanted to tell him everything that had happened: he deserved to know the truth. But I was going to tell him in person, not over the phone or email or Instant Message or text. In fact, much as I loved technology, I was sick of having a relationship through it. I was going to try and have our relationship face to face from now on.

I had no idea how it would all work. Would I move to America? Would he move to London? Would we commute between the two?

I had no plans. And that was fine: we'd make them together.

Looking out the window at the soft chocolate-coloured mountains topped by the purple clouds at sunset, I felt utterly spent. But I also had a sense of absolute certainty about this. I'd made the right decision. I was sure of it.

Another text popped up: *YES! It's about time u came home.*

I smiled and shut my eyes. That's how it felt to me too: like coming home.

Acknowledgments

This book would not have been possible without the help and encouragement of a huge number of people. For any I now fail to thank, sorry, but you know what a thoughtless cow I can be.

Firstly, I owe a huge debt of thanks to my agent and dear friend Lizzy Kremer from David Higham Associates: such a rock throughout the entire researching and writing process, she made granite look positively flighty. Also to Grainne Fox at Ed Victor Ltd who had an unerring knack of buying me strong cocktails at just the right time. I would like to thank all at Random House for their tireless support, enthusiasm and hard work, in particular my editor Nikola Scott, who did a brilliant job whilst womanly resisting the temptation to shout *Do you know what a deadline is?* Also Susan Sandon for her open door and desktop Mr Right.

My family and friends deserve some kind of an award for not only making their address books available but also their time and patience throughout my obsessive *soul searching*. I lost track of the number of '*no it wasn't you, it was him*' and '*you are KIDDING – if it was me, I would've called the police*' emails, phone calls and cups of coffee/glasses of wine moments that kept me going. In particular I would like to thank: my sisters Madeleine and Rosalind Cox for late-night chats and afternoons at the Sanctuary, and my best friends Belinda Rhodes, Charlotte Hindle and Cath Urquhart for helping me remember boyfriends I'd managed to forget, for my Relationship Résumé. For never mentioning the times when my biscuit eating spiralled out of control, thank you to my special friends: Paula Shutkever, Eddie Mair, Ian Belcher, Hector and Ang MacKenzie, Linda Ferguson, Jude Espie, Sheena MacBain, Eleanor and Adam Garland, Jeannette Hyde, Sarah Long, Sara-Jane Hall, Malgosia Czarniecka, Simon Calder, Jilly Mead and Stevie *Bee* Benbow, Lyn Hughes and Paul Morrison, Tania Cagnoni, Paul and Jude Mansfield, Nigel Tisdall, Steve Bleach, Sue D'Arcy, Rob Ryan, Alison Rice, Dea Birkett, Sally Shalam, Sophie Campbell, also Anna Cherrett.

Not to mention all the people who helped with the *is there a plane that leaves later than 5.30a.m.?* logistics of the trip itself. Fujifilm for the S300 digital camera that captured my dating high and lowlights, Karin Hop at the Netherlands tourist board, Ann-Charlotte and Emelie at the Swedish tourist board as well as Madeleine Meech at Travel PR. Catherine Raynor at VSO, Allesandra Smith at the Italian tourist board, Elena at Il Club di Giulietta, all at Berlin Tourismus Marketing GmbH, Nim Singh at the Canadian Tourist Commission, Jill White and Wendy Burns at Yukon tourism, Erika Brandvik at the Las Vegas CVB, Susie and Anna at Cellet PR, Jenni at First PR, Wendy King and Olaf Kaehlert at the LA CVB, all at Missoula CVB, Kylie Clark at JNTO, Abi and Khun Lilly at the Tourist Authority of Thailand. And in particular a huge thank you to all who helped me with the very end - therefore at the apex of my

Ummm it might be Friday, it might be Wednesday – it's hard to say at this point wavering. In particular Fiona Reese, Viv Kessler and Emma Humphreys at BGB and Associates, Rae White, Jac and Belinda at WATC, Kate Kenward at the ATC in London, Kate Bailey at the ATC in Sydney, Karen Reid at Random House Australia, Susie Tempest at Saltmarsh PR and all at Tourism New Zealand and Air New Zealand.

I am extremely grateful to all my Dates for taking me out and showing me a good time, as well as the Dates who would have taken me out if only things had worked out differently. In particular David O, Per, Beaver and the VSO man working as a yak cheese farmer on the Chinese-Mongolian border.

When I arrived in Seattle at the end of my adventure to write this book, there were some people without whom it would never have felt like home. Bette 'Burien' Allen, Terri Bassett and Ann Anderson, as well as Judy and Gerry Greth, Hank and Rachel, JR, Doug, Jon and OB.

And talking of adventures, I'd not only like to thank Lloyd, my getaway driver, but also thank and apologise to Louise Kiely at Queenstown House B&B in New Zealand. The first person I spoke with following the dramatic final 48 hours of my journey, she made the mistake of innocently asking over breakfast how my visit was going?

At various points I have changed names and muzzed the edges of personalities and events in the telling of my story. I wanted to spare people's blushes but also emerge with my social life vaguely intact.

I would like to thank everyone for helping me with my quest, but none more so than Garry Greth, who took it all in his stride and made his home my home.

A sincere and heartfelt thank you to you all.